SOMETHING
BEAUTIFUL
HAPPENED

Center Point
Large Print

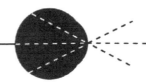

**This Large Print Book carries the
Seal of Approval of N.A.V.H.**

SOMETHING BEAUTIFUL HAPPENED

A Story of Survival and
Courage in the Face of Evil

YVETTE MANESSIS CORPORON

CENTER POINT LARGE PRINT
THORNDIKE, MAINE

This Center Point Large Print edition
is published in the year 2018 by arrangement with
Howard Books, a division of Simon & Schuster, Inc.

The text of this Large Print edition is unabridged.
In other aspects, this book may vary
from the original edition.
Printed in the United States of America
on permanent paper.
Set in 16-point Times New Roman type.

ISBN: 978-1-68324-640-4

Library of Congress Cataloging-in-Publication Data

Names: Corporon, Yvette Manessis, author.
Title: Something beautiful happened : a story of survival and courage
    in the face of evil / Yvette Manessis Corporon.
Description: Large print edition. | Thorndike, Maine :
    Center Point large Print, [2018] | Large print.
Identifiers: LCCN 2017046265 | ISBN 9781683246404
    (hardcover : alk. paper)
Subjects: LCSH: Jews—Greece—Corfu Island. | Holocaust, Jewish
    (1939-1945)— Greece—Corfu Island. | World War, 1939-1945—
    Jews—Rescue—Greece—Corfu Island. | Corporon, Yvette Manessis. |
    Large type books.
Classification: LCC DS135.G72 C673 2018 | DDC 940.53/18092—dc23
LC record available at https://lccn.loc.gov/2017046265

For my children, Christiana and Nico.

For the children of my heart, Reat and Lukas.

And for the children who made
my heart burst when we found them,
Inbar, Sapir, Maayan, Tal and Maiyan.

Live life to the fullest and never give up.
REAT GRIFFIN UNDERWOOD

_____

The light shines in the darkness, and the darkness has not overcome it.
JOHN 1:5

CONTENTS

introduction
They Weren't Really Gone After All   13

PART ONE
chapter one
We Loved Them Like Sisters   19
chapter two
The Jews of Corfu   24
chapter three
You Are Orphans Now   42
chapter four
Pass the Lamb. We Saved the Jews.   53
chapter five
Papa Savvas, the Jewish Tailor of Corfu   59
chapter six
The Nightly Knock at the Door   73
chapter seven
Yia-yia Never Told   83

PART TWO
chapter eight
Searching for Savvas   113
chapter nine
Righteous Among the Nations   122

chapter ten
Whatever You Do, Don't Challenge Him
to a Game of Chess   143
chapter eleven
I Think Our Grandmothers Were Friends   152

PART THREE
chapter twelve
Reat and Bill   161
chapter thirteen
When Words Don't Make Sense   184
chapter fourteen
Tragic Irony   202
chapter fifteen
He Picked the Wrong Family
and the Wrong Community   219
chapter sixteen
He Was Watching Over Them   235

PART FOUR
chapter seventeen
The Ones Who Stood Up   247
chapter eighteen
Heaven Is All Around Us   258

PART FIVE
chapter nineteen
It Was Nothing. It Was Everything.   297
chapter twenty
Piecing Together the Story of Savvas   322

chapter twenty-one
Rosa's Family   339

chapter twenty-two
Modern Miracles   359

chapter twenty-three
Reunion   366

chapter twenty-four
Erikousa's Icarus   378

chapter twenty-five
Finding Savvas   396

chapter twenty-six
Full Circle   403

epilogue   421
afterword
Lessons from New and Cherished Friends   429
acknowledgments   444

introduction

THEY WEREN'T REALLY GONE AFTER ALL

New York
April 13, 2014

It was 1 a.m. when I walked into Nico's room. His back was to me, but he was still awake. I knew he would be. We all were.

Earlier that day we had gotten a call that didn't seem real. It still doesn't, and I imagine it never will. My 14-year-old nephew, Reat, and his grandfather, Bill, were dead.

Bill and Reat had gone to the Jewish Community Campus in Overland Park, Kansas, so Reat could attend a singing audition. They were shot and killed by a white supremacist neo-Nazi as they exited their car. The man who killed them shouted "*Heil Hitler*!" when he was arrested and said he wanted to know what it felt like to kill Jews before he died. He murdered three beautiful people that day, none of whom were Jewish.

I sat on the edge of Nico's bed and reached my hand out to stroke his hair. My sweet nine-year-old boy rolled over to face me, his big brown eyes brimming with tears. And then he spoke, breaking my heart for the second time that day.

"I'm so sad, Mom," Nico said. "I don't understand. When you told me about our family and what they did, you told me the Nazis were gone and that the people were saved. How could this happen?"

Nico was right. I did tell him that the Nazis were gone. And I did tell him that the family was safe. I'd thought they were. But then I was branded a liar that day, our family's history rewritten by a hate-filled man on a mission to kill Jews.

Nico knew the story as well as I did. Again and again I'd told him how during World War II, my Greek grandmother, my yia-yia, was one of a group of islanders who helped hide a Jewish tailor named Savvas and his family from the Nazis. Despite the risk, despite the danger, and despite the fact that they were told that anyone found helping Jews would be killed along with their entire families, not one person on our tiny Greek island gave up the secret of Savvas. Not one. Savvas and his girls were saved and they all survived.

For the past several years, Nico had witnessed my personal journey, my search to find Savvas's family, the girls my yia-yia had risked everything for. After countless dead ends and disappointments, I had finally found them. They were a beautiful family, including five people who are alive today because of what happened on our tiny island 70 years ago. We had celebrated with the descendants of Savvas's family. We celebrated and cried, because they had survived; goodness had prevailed and the Nazis were gone. That was on Thursday, April 10, 2014.

Three days later, on Sunday, April 13, 2014, we cried again, because Bill and Reat were dead and we realized that the Nazis weren't really gone after all.

"I don't understand," Nico asked. "How could this happen?"

How do you accept that tragic irony is a cruelty reserved not merely for Shakespearean plot twists?

How do you admit to your son that monsters exist outside of fairy tales?

How do you explain to a child something you can't understand yourself?

PART ONE

chapter one

WE LOVED THEM LIKE SISTERS

New Rochelle, New York
Spring 1981

Y ou have to roll it out thin; otherwise it will be like biting into bread. And it's not bread. It's phyllo. And thin phyllo makes the best pita."

Yia-yia sprinkled more of the fine white flour onto the kitchen table and then rolled out the dough with the old broom handle that she had brought with her from Greece so many years ago. Despite all the gadgets available to modern cooks in America, Yia-yia insisted her trusty broom handle was the secret to perfect pita every time. This time it was *patatopita*, potato pie, the signature dish of Erikousa, the tiny island where my yia-yia and my father were born and raised.

"You want it thin, thin enough to let the light through, but with no holes." Her black dress was covered in a film of white flour. Even the black head scarf she wore knotted under her chin was spotted with white flecks. But Yia-yia paid no mind to her appearance. Her phyllo was perfect. And that was what mattered.

"See?" Her brown eyes crinkled as she smiled and held up the phyllo for my mother, Kiki, and me to inspect. The afternoon light filtered through the pale beige sheet. Not a single hole. Perfect.

As my mother and yia-yia examined and admired the dough, I stared out the window to the trees in the yard swaying in the summer breeze. I could hear the shrieks and splashing of the neighbors' children swimming next door and the laughter of friends riding their bikes and the unmistakable gritty whir of big wheels riding up and down the street. I wanted nothing more than to join them. Or at least to go to the family room (in my friends' homes it was a den, in ours it was a family room), lie on the matted, green shag carpet, and watch *The Brady Bunch*. Maybe even go to my room and read *Are You There God? It's Me, Margaret*, for the hundredth time. I wanted to be anywhere but there, sitting at that kitchen table watching as my mother and grandmother made food my friends couldn't even pronounce.

It was as if my mother could read my mind.

"Yvette, you do the potatoes." She shoved a plate of cooled boiled potatoes in front of me before placing the sheet of phyllo into a large baking dish.

I did as commanded, crumbling the potatoes into the phyllo-lined pan as Yia-yia added the mixture of feta, milk, dill and rice. Instead of using a spoon, Yia-yia dipped the edge of a small plate into the baking dish, fanning it back and forth, mixing the wet filling.

"Your father loves *patatopita*." Yia-yia smiled at me as she folded the excess phyllo over the edge of the pan and brushed the dough with a beaten egg. "Even during the war, when there was not much to eat sometimes, we knew we could always make pita. He would eat an entire pan of it himself if I let him." She laughed as she sprinkled a little sugar on top, just a touch of sweet to balance out the salt, before signaling to my mother that it was ready. "Only then, of course, we cooked it outside, over an open fire with sticks collected from the woods." She closed her eyes and inhaled, as if she could smell the scent of burning twigs and smoke wafting on the evening breeze.

"It must have been hard for you during the war, with your husband away and the Nazis on the island," my mother said as she placed the pita into the oven.

"Oh it was." Yia-yia shook her head as she waved her hand around and around into the air for emphasis. "It was hard, but thanks be to God and Saint Spyridon, we survived. We had our gardens and the sea, so we could eat. We never starved. We learned to stay away from the Nazis as best we could. And my friend Nini taught me how to sew, so we could make our own clothes when we needed to."

"Nini?" my mother asked.

I stared out the window again.

"I thought I knew everyone from Erikousa. But I don't know Nini. You've never mentioned her before," my mother said.

"Yes, Nini." Yia-yia smiled, repeating her name. "We called her Nini but her name was Nina. She wasn't from Erikousa. She was from Corfu. Nini was a beautiful girl, kind and generous, and a beautiful seamstress. She was my friend, and I loved her like a sister." It was Yia-yia's turn now to gaze out the window. "She was Jewish."

"Jewish?" my mother asked.

Yia-yia had my attention now, at least for a moment. Growing up in the predominantly Jewish town of New Rochelle, New York, I was one of two Greek girls in the entire school. Most of my friends were Jewish. Each week, they all went off to Hebrew school together and I sat miserably alone in Greek school, wishing I could join them. I wanted to be Jewish too.

"Yes, Nini was Jewish," Yia-yia continued as she brushed the flour from her dress with her hands. "Her father, Savvas, was a tailor. He taught all of his girls how to sew. And they taught me. They were my friends," she repeated.

"Oh wow," my mother said, shaking her helmet

22

of dyed blond and permed hair. It was the early '80s after all. My mother had been married to my father for fifteen years and her life was intimately tied up with that of his family, and she had never heard of Nini or Savvas or the Jewish family that was hidden on Erikousa. "I didn't know there were Jews on Corfu. Or in Erikousa."

"Oh yes," Yia-yia replied, waving her hand in the air for emphasis, nodding her head up and down again and again. "There were many Jews on Corfu." She fell silent for a moment. Yia-yia again stared out the window, looking past us, past the trees even, into the distance, where the faint laughter of my friends could still be heard.

And then she spoke again. "But that was before the war."

chapter two

THE JEWS OF CORFU
A Lost Story of the Holocaust

They lived on Corfu for 800 years and were as Greek as my own family, but of course, the Nazis didn't see it that way. What the Nazis did see is that there were 2,000 Jews still alive on the picturesque Ionian island, and the Allies were getting closer. Time was running out.

Shaped like a long, slim sickle, Corfu, which is known in Greek as Kerkyra, lies between Italy and Albania in the Ionian Sea on Greece's northwestern tip. Unlike other Greek islands whose arid earth and whitewashed Cycladic architecture make for stark yet stunning imagery, Corfu is an island covered in flowers and fruit trees. It is a panorama of lush flowers, where olive tree groves blanket the landscape and majestic cypress trees stand sentinel on craggy seaside cliffs watching over the impossibly blue water below.

Throughout the centuries, mortal men and mythical heroes have fallen in love with this magical island. Corfu is widely thought to be the home of the Phaeacians in Homer's *Odyssey*, where Odysseus washes ashore and wakes to the laughter of Princess Nausicaa and her friends.

While serene in her natural beauty, Corfu's history is anything but. Annexed by Greece in 1864, the island and her people suffered through centuries of invasions and invaders. While each regime brought with it its own struggles for the citizens of Corfu, each occupation, from the Venetians to the French to the British, left behind its own unique fingerprint. What resulted is a rich, hybrid legacy of architecture, culture and art.

When Nazi troops occupied Corfu in 1943, they left behind a legacy of loss, devastation and death.

While the countryside and villages of Corfu are awash in the bold, vibrant greens and blues of the earth and sea, in the downtown area of Corfu Town, the entire city seems to glow with a golden, rust-hued light. Corfu's narrow and twisty cobblestone streets, alleyways and courtyards are a jumble of weathered homes, shops and churches. Dozens of bell towers soar above ceramic rooftops. Muted red, beige and russet-toned stucco facades peel and crack with weather and wear. There is something special about the way the Corfu light catches each of these perceived imperfections, transforming them into something lyrical and beautiful.

Tucked away behind the wide cobblestone streets and arched portico of Corfu's grand Liston promenade, with its rows of arches reminiscent of Paris's Rue de Rivoli, and behind the expansive Spianada town square overlooking Garitsa Bay, lies a maze of narrow, twisting alleyways. This labyrinth of tiny streets, courtyards and buildings is still known today as the *Evraiki*, the Jewish quarter, or ghetto. It is here, in this shaded winding section of town, that Corfu's Jewish community lived and worked for hundreds of years. The men were mostly craftsmen, artisans and shopkeepers, selling their wares and eking out a living while their wives tended to the children and kept Jewish traditions alive in their homes, which were located above the street-level shops.

Initially, when the Italians occupied Corfu in April of 1941, life in the Jewish quarter went on fairly close to normal, just as it did for the rest of the island. As the German threat approached, Italian soldiers warned the community of the impending danger. But the Jews of Corfu couldn't fathom that the stories of mass executions and violence could possibly be true. This God-fearing people were unable to imagine that evil could really manifest itself in this way. Despite the warnings, most of Corfu's Jews stayed rooted in their community and in their homes as the Germans approached. This decision would have devastating consequences.

Immediately upon seizing control of the island,

the Nazis enforced strict curfews, and all Jews were required to register with the German command. From April to June, they were counted twice weekly, ordered to appear for a mandatory census, then went back to their lives in the ghetto, where they kept to themselves, practiced their faith and stayed out of the way of German troops.

And then, in June 1944, everything changed.

The signs began to appear in the morning, covering the island before the end of day.

ALL JEWS ARE TO REPORT TO
THE LOWER PLATIA
ON THE MORNING OF JUNE 9

They began to gather as the sun rose over the cobalt waters of Garitsa Bay that warm Friday morning. Men, women, children, babies, the elderly and infirm, all making their way from the Jewish quarter to the lower *platia*, the wide open space between the arches of grand cafés and the old fort. Those who didn't report voluntarily were dragged from their shops or homes at gunpoint. Those who refused, or even hesitated, were shot and killed on the spot.

The Nazis rounded up all the Jews they could find, emptying jails, mental institutions and hospitals. Even pregnant women close to giving birth were dragged out into the square. As Allied bombs rained down on the island, the

Jewish community of Corfu stood together all day under the hot sun with no food or water while German troops and Greek police guarded them at gunpoint. Most had no idea what was happening, assuring their children they would be back home by evening. But the Nazis had other plans. The warnings of the Italian soldiers, once thought to be nightmarish exaggerations, soon proved to be prophetically and tragically true.

Slowly the gravity of the situation began to sink in, the cruelty and motives of the Nazi soldiers becoming clearer with each passing moment.

The Greek Red Cross came and handed out bread and water to those who needed it, but most Greeks stayed away. Even those who wanted to help their Jewish friends quickly realized there was little if anything that they could do. In the eyes of the Nazis, there was no distinction between being a Jew and helping a Jew. Assisting Jews in any way was as serious an offense as it was to have Jewish blood in your veins. In the eyes of the Nazis, both were cause for extermination.

June 9 was a Friday, the Sabbath. But as the sun set over the western hills of Corfu, there was no going home to set the table for Shabbat, light candles, pray or celebrate centuries-old traditions. Instead, the island's Jews all stood together at gunpoint while the sun set on the Sabbath eve—a heartbreaking metaphor for what was to come next for this centuries-old community on the beautiful island of Corfu.

———————

"Your name from now on is Nikos."

"But I am Daniel."

Errikos got down on his knees; they were eye to eye now. His voice was soft but firm. This was not a time to be rash and let his emotions get the best of him. This was also not the time to make little Daniel any more frightened than he already was. Any more than they all were.

"Listen to me." Errikos took Daniel by the hands and pulled him closer. "From now on, your name is Nikos. Do you understand? If the soldiers hear the name Daniel they will know you are Jewish, and they will take you from us. They will take you from your family. This is very important. Do you understand?" He needed to be certain. There was no room for error.

Daniel was just three years old. But even at that tender age, he understood full well what was at stake. Daniel knew this was so much more than just a game. Errikos was his father's friend, a Greek Orthodox Christian. Errikos had heard the rumors of mass Jewish deportations and knew he could not sit idly by. Over the span of several days, spreading his visits out so as not to draw attention, Errikos had come back to the Jewish quarter and helped friends and their families escape. Errikos had brought Daniel and his sister, Roza, to live with his own family in their beautiful seaside village just three miles from Corfu Town.

The plan was for Errikos and his family to hide the children in plain sight. They would tell neighbors and friends that the children were cousins, Orthodox Christians, like them, who were visiting from a nearby village. Errikos would then return a few days later to bring Daniel's mother and baby sister to hide in the villa as well. The time and date had been set in advance. All they had to do was wait a few more days.

Just a few more days.

The villa was the perfect place to hide their Jewish friends. It was large, with plenty of rooms for young children to roam freely, or hide if they needed to. In the center was a large room with a grand iron table topped by a beautiful, smooth slab of marble that was cool to the touch, even on hot Corfu summer afternoons. The kitchen, where Errikos's mother prepared their meals and somehow always managed to whip up special treats for Daniel, like sweet kumquat marmalade, was on one side of the house. On the other side were several bedrooms, storage, and a large and grand dining room. Surrounding the villa all around were lush and gorgeous gardens. Dozens upon dozens of mulberry, olive and fruit trees encircled the property. There, in the gardens, Daniel could roam freely, protected from the midday sun by the shade of those beautiful trees as he counted down the days until he would fall into his mother's arms again.

Daniel was just outside the house, playing near the garden, when he heard someone approaching and turned to look. Young Daniel spotted the man and froze. The soldier was short and stout. He walked toward the house from the gardens. And then he spotted the boy and called to him.

"Nikos!" the soldier shouted and beckoned. "Nikos. Come here."

Daniel and Errikos had practiced this many times. Daniel knew what he needed to do. He knew he needed to respond to the name Nikos and smile and act as if he were just a carefree young boy with nothing to hide. But he couldn't do it. Daniel froze. He didn't want to go anywhere near the man. He was just a little boy, and he was afraid.

Errikos's mother stepped out of the house just then. She walked over to Daniel, bent down and held him close. "Please go to him," she whispered in Daniel's ear as she smoothed his hair, comforting the shaking child. "Please go, because if you don't it will be dangerous and they will kill us all."

Daniel did as he was told. Slowly, he approached the German.

"Nikos." The German smiled and said his name again. And then he took a piece of chocolate from his pocket and handed it to Daniel. He patted the boy on his head, and then went on his way.

He had done it. Mama would be so proud. Daniel couldn't wait to tell her how brave he had been. Just a bit longer and she would be joining them.

Finally, after what felt like an eternity for Daniel, the agreed-upon day and time had come at last. Errikos left early that morning to bring Daniel's mother, Evthimia, and his baby sister to safety. But as he walked to the apartment, as the wide avenues of Corfu gave way to the narrow lanes of the ghetto, Errikos could hear the commotion before he even rounded the corner.

"What's happening?" he asked as he fought his way through the crowd. There were people everywhere.

"They are rounding up Jews," someone answered.

Errikos stopped in his tracks. He knew he could go no farther without putting them all at risk. There would be no way to get Daniel's mother out of the quarter that day. He turned and started toward home, vowing to return in a few days, when it was safer. He knew the entrance to the family's apartment had been boarded up, camouflaged to make it appear abandoned.

Errikos took comfort in that, praying it was enough to fool the Germans and keep Evthimia and the baby hidden for just a few days longer.

As Errikos made his way back home, the Nazis made their way, street by street, down the blocks of the Jewish quarter. With gloved fists they pounded on doors, demanding to be let in, breaking down any that were not immediately opened for them. They were determined to rid the island of every single Jew they could find. Not one would be left behind.

Evthimia cowered with her baby daughter in her apartment above. The soldiers pounded on the boarded-up door, but she stayed quiet and hidden. The Nazis passed her by. She was safe.

As the soldiers made their way down the street, a Greek Christian woman poked her head out the window of her home. "What's going on?" she asked.

"We are looking for Jews," replied the Nazis from farther down the lane.

"Did you find any?"

"No."

"Well, what do you mean? There's one hiding right there, right across the way."

And with that, the Nazis returned to the door of Daniel's family's home. This time they broke through the boarded-up entrance, stormed inside and dragged his mother and baby sister out to the street below.

Daniel would never see his mother or baby sister again.

They, like the nearly 1,800 Corfiot Jews held at gunpoint on the *platia* that day, spent hours waiting in the hot sun, still unsure of what was happening. Many had brought nothing with them that morning, expecting they would be home for lunch. As morning turned to afternoon, hours passed with no food or water. Still, many of Corfu's Jews thought that surely by dinnertime the Germans would have had their fill of whatever this new level of humiliation and degradation was, and they would be allowed to return to their homes.

But like Daniel Soussis's mother and baby sister, most of Corfu's Jews would never go home again.

From the square, they were herded like livestock to the island's old fort built into a craggy peninsula that juts out into the sea. The very fortress built to protect them became their prison. Men and women were separated, forced to give up any valuables and caged in the fort's dank dungeons as the Nazis made their final preparations.

By all accounts and by the laws of reason it never should have happened, but no one has ever accused the Nazis of being reasonable. It was the end of the war, three days after the Allies landed at Normandy. Salvation was so close, but still not close enough. The Gestapo had arrived in Corfu and the German high command advised them against the deportation of Jews, warning that German boats and soldiers would be at risk as the Allies inched closer, continuing to bomb the Ionian Islands. The Nazis' commanding colonel on Corfu cited the Red Cross's presence on the island, strongly suggesting the deportation be postponed. He knew there would be no way to hide the truth from the international organization, that they would bear witness to the Germans' final act on the island, their final solution. But despite this, the Gestapo went ahead, using small, dilapidated boats of questionable seaworthiness to carry out their plan.

The transport began on June 10, 1944. The Jews were taken from the old fort of Corfu and packed onto rotting boats and makeshift rafts, bound for their final destination, Auschwitz-Birkenau.

As they filed out of the old fort, many of the prisoners clamored to climb onto the boats, pushing to be among the first to board, to escape the dungeon. They didn't know there would be no escape at all. As unseaworthy as they seemed, the peeling and rotting wooden hulls and ramshackle rafts kept afloat, carrying their human cargo across the sea. After the war, many of those who survived said they wished the boats had simply sunk and that everyone on board had drowned. Death at sea would have been a welcome escape compared to what was to come next.

A few did manage to escape, including David Balestra, a young Corfiot Jew who jumped overboard and swam to safety on the shores of Lefkada. After the war he settled in Israel, making a living as a children's swimming instructor.

But for Nino Nachshon, escape was not an option. At 19 years old, Nino was a gregarious young man whose laughter filled his family's home, even when their stomachs were empty, which was often. Nino's father died when he was a child, leaving his mother to raise him and his three siblings. His was a poor family and life in the Jewish quarter was difficult. Yet for Nino, living on Corfu, even in the ghetto, did have its advantages. Nino spent endless hours in the sea with his friends and was a strong swimmer, strong enough to jump off the decrepit boat and make it to safety.

As his heavily weighted raft sat low in the water, Nino looked out across the sea where the sky meets the water's surface. He knew he could do it. He knew in his heart that he could easily throw himself overboard and swim to the safety of shore. But he wasn't the only one; Nino's mother knew this as well.

"Save yourself," Nino's mother, who'd leaned in closer to him, whispered. Even as she clutched her daughter and youngest son to her, Nino's mother pleaded with her eldest child. "Save yourself," she said again.

Nino sat silently beside her. As they floated farther and farther away from shore, his mother's words became commands. "I know you can do it," she insisted. "I know you can. Save yourself. Leave us. Do it."

But even as his mother pleaded with him to go, Nino's younger brother clung to him. "Please don't leave us," he begged. "Please. Don't leave me."

That day, as the ramshackle boat floated farther and farther away from Corfu and toward an uncertain future, 19-year-old Nino did something he had never done before. For the first time in his life, Nino Nachshon defied his mother's wishes. Nino watched others slip into the water and swim away to safety as he sat firmly fixed in place, scared and hungry, crammed between his mother and siblings on a rotting death boat.

From the boats, Nino and his family were brought to Patras, where they were placed on trains bound for Athens. They spent several days in the Haidari camp, just outside of Athens, before being crowded together, one on top of the other, into cattle cars with no water, little air and almost no chance of survival. While Nino and his mother and siblings all survived the transport, most of Corfu's Jews never made it to the gates of Auschwitz-Birkenau.

When Nino's transport arrived, he, his brothers and sister were sent to the barracks. That very first night, Nino's mother was sent to the gas chamber.

Like Nino, 17-year-old Rebecca Aaron also survived the transport. But there were so many times she wished she hadn't. Rebecca and her family had escaped from the ghetto and found refuge in the small village of Kouramades in central Corfu, just six miles from Corfu Town. Then the signs were posted, reminding Christians of the penalty for hiding and helping Jews. Those posters proved to be Rebecca's family's death certificate. A town official, likely seeking favor with the German soldiers, alerted the Nazis the Aaron family was hiding in a small mountain-side shack, just outside the village. Rebecca and her family were immediately captured, the last of Corfu's Jews to be herded into boats.

As the doors of her transport were opened upon reaching Auschwitz, Rebecca watched helplessly while her family was separated for selection. Before the sun set on that very first day, 40 members of Rebecca's family were murdered, including her mother and siblings.

The working business model of the Nazi death camps was straightforward. Those who were fit to work were sent to the barracks and put to use. Those who arrived sick, frail or feeble were sent immediately for disposal.

Lasting almost a full month, the journey from Corfu to the gates of Auschwitz was one of the longest, most difficult trips that any Nazi prisoners had to endure. That, coupled with the mild Greek climate, meant that Corfu's Jews were ill-equipped, unprepared and often had little chance of surviving the transport. Often, when the doors to the Greek transports opened, SS soldiers were met by nothing more than silence.

And sometimes even those who survived the transport chose death rather than what the SS soldiers had in store for them. Four hundred and thirty-five men from Corfu survived the journey, but willingly went to their death rather than join the Sonderkommando, a unit of Jews who were chosen by Nazis to dispose of the dead bodies.

In all, 1,795 Jews were deported from Corfu. Of those, only 121 survived the war.

Of course, some managed to escape deportation, like Daniel Soussis, by hiding in plain sight. Stories of betrayal, like the fate of Rebecca Aaron's family and Daniel Soussis's mother, were quite common. While the majority of Jews and Christians on Corfu lived side by side in harmony, there was an undeniable taint of anti-Semitism on the island. In the 1400s, Venetian rulers set the tone by segregating the island's Jews from their Greek Christian neighbors, establishing the ghetto where Jews were required to live. In an eerie foreshadowing of what was to come centuries later during German occupation, small yellow buttons were manufactured and issued to the community. The yellow buttons had to be affixed to the lapels of Jews 13 years or older who were traveling outside the ghetto.

In 1891, a blood libel fractured the community further when an eight-year-old girl's murder was falsely blamed on members of the Jewish community. Rumors swept the island that her blood was spilled in a ritual Passover sacrifice, Christian blood a sacred and sordid ingredient required to make unleavened matzo bread. An investigation proved that this story and rumors of a ritual sacrifice were unequivocally false, and that the murdered girl was in fact Jewish, and not Christian. But the truth came too late, the damage already done. Even the passing of decades couldn't fully rid the community of the taint of distrust and suspicion. With the German occupation, those who had whispered their hatred of Jews under their breaths finally had a platform and vehicle for their hate.

And then there were those who turned on their Jewish neighbors, driven by nothing more than pure greed. There is a story long whispered about among the outdoor cafés and kitchen tables of Corfu. It is the tale of two friends, one Jewish and one Christian. In a desperate final effort to save his daughter, a Jewish man smuggled her to a Christian acquaintance. The Jewish man implored him to save his girl, and gave him all the money he had, to ensure his daughter would be hidden and provided for. He pleaded with the Greek Christian, begging him to take his girl, pass her off as his own and take his money as thanks for saving his child's life. The Christian man took the child and the money—and promptly turned the child over to the Nazis, keeping the money for himself, forever sealing his fate and that of his family. But while civility and morality appeared to be blinded by greed, karma kept her watchful eye. From that day forward, the man's family was stalked by tragedy, his own children dying at young ages.

While history books are filled with tragic dark stories of the Holocaust like these, there are also often little known stories of sacrifice and salvation. It is estimated that 200 of Corfu's Jews managed to escape deportation and death. For most of them, salvation came at the hands of Christian Greeks. Despite the danger, despite the threat of death by the Germans, these Christians put everything at stake to do the just and moral thing, risking their lives and those of their families to save their Jewish friends.

My yia-yia, Avgerini, was one of those Christians.

chapter three

YOU ARE ORPHANS NOW

Erikousa
September 1943

Although they were Christian and miles removed from the horrors unfolding in the Jewish ghetto, the islanders of Erikousa knew that they were not immune to the dangers posed by the Nazi threat. Yia-yia found some comfort in knowing that the extended Erikousa family would help her while her husband was away in America. But she also knew she needed to take matters into her own hands and to do all she could to protect herself and her children.

"Who died, Mama?" my father's sister, Agatha, asked. She sat on the bed and watched as her mother, my yia-yia, dressed not in her typical gray skirt and blouse but instead in head-to-toe black. Mourning clothes.

Yia-yia straightened her pleated black woolen skirt, buttoned her simple black blouse and knotted the black head scarf that obscured her center-parted and plaited hair.

"Who died?" my father, Anastasios, echoed, growing impatient now.

They wanted to get going and get on their way to school already. It was not that they so much cared about getting to school on time; it was that the teacher had a habit of smacking children who were late. But then again, children were often smacked on Erikousa during those years, by parents, teachers, relatives, strangers even. A swift backhand or tug of the ear to a child who displayed any precociousness or insubordination—or sometimes for no reason at all—was simply as much a part of the culture as greeting someone by saying "*yiasou*" or making the sign of the cross as you walked past a church.

It didn't matter that they might be late for school. Yia-yia insisted the children sit still. She had something to tell them.

"You are orphans now."

"No, we're not," Agatha said.

"What are you talking about? We are not orphans," my father chimed in.

Clearly they were not orphans. Their mother was standing right in front of them and their father, my *papou*, was away. It had been years since they had seen him, but he was still very much alive. Papou had left Erikousa before the Italians, and then Nazis, came. The plan was for him to work and save enough money for the family to join him in America. But then war broke out, making it impossible for him to return. He sent envelopes, stamped "from the USA"

43

and stuffed with dollar bills hidden between handwritten pages, though they had been arriving less and less frequently now. And never had they been needed more. But once every several weeks those letters and dollars did arrive, proving that Papou was still very much alive and thriving in America, while Yia-yia waited out the war and did her best to survive on Erikousa.

"Yes," Yia-yia insisted. She grabbed them both by the arms and yanked them to attention. "Yes, you are orphans. If the German soldiers ask where your father is, you tell them that he is dead. You never tell them he is in America. Do you understand? Never." It wasn't that Yia-yia was well versed in the minutia of war, politics or what drove the Allied powers to align against the Germans. But Yia-yia knew enough to understand that the Germans hated the Americans. She knew that if the Nazis learned that her husband was living in the United States, she and her children would likely be targeted as the family of an American man. It was a risk she was unwilling to take.

Agatha was just seven and my father just nine, but they too understood even before she said the words out loud. "They will kill us all if they hear your father is in America."

"Yes, Mama." Agatha and my father both nodded their heads in agreement. But a simple promise was not enough to convince Yia-yia.

"Swear," she insisted, grabbing the icon of Saint Spyridon, Corfu's beloved patron saint, from its place on the wall. "Swear on Saint Spyridon." She held the icon before them.

They knew better than to mess with Yia-yia or the saint. Each was regarded with equal parts reverence and fear. Agatha and my father each placed the thumb, index and middle finger of their right hand together and made the sign of the cross three times before kissing he icon.

Finally satisfied now, Yia-yia opened the door and scooted them outside. My father and Agatha ran all the way down the hill from their home, down the dirt path overlooking the sea, to the one-room schoolhouse located beside the church and in the shadow of the old cemetery.

Yia-yia stepped outside into the morning sunshine where her sister-in-law, Agathe, was waiting on the terrace. Agathe lived in the simple home adjacent to Yia-yia's with Papou's brother, Costa, and their five children. Just as there were no property lines between the two homes, there was no separation between the two families. Before Papou left, he entrusted his family to his brother, a responsibility and a role Costa took on with pride and care. The children were more like siblings than cousins, and the sisters-in-law more like sisters. The women actually felt closer than sisters, the circumstances of their lives bonding them in ways even tighter than familial bonds or blood ties. What they lacked in material goods, the two families made up for in love for one another. Agathe, a petite woman quick with a smile or a smack when the children acted up, and my yia-yia, raven-haired with black-olive eyes, shared everything between them—food, chores, supplies and worries.

That morning, the sisters-in-law did what they rarely afforded themselves the luxury of doing. The two women sat outside together on the terrace, as the freshly hung laundry flapped in the breeze above them and the chickens clucked and pecked in the coop behind the patio.

They were not wealthy by any means, and their homes were rustic and simple in every way. But oh, that view! Theirs was a view worth thousands if not millions of drachmas. From the cracked terrace they could see past the hulking, verdant ancient olive trees. Even from this far up they could make out each and every individual fruit of the giant yellow lemon trees down the hill in the grove, lemons that might pass for grapefruits were it not for their telltale sunburst of color. And down the slope, past the trees and farther down the dirt road, past a handful of primitive stone and whitewashed homes, the women could see straight to the beach and to the tiny port. The port was empty now, except for a cluster of small wood-hulled and weather-beaten fishing boats that bobbed up and down on the sea with the tide.

But Yia-yia and Agathe had heard the news. And they knew what was coming. They knew the Italians had surrendered and that sooner or later there would be German ships docked in the port. And no one knew exactly what that would mean, only that things were about to get worse.

She was poor, provincial and barely literate. Like so many Greek women of her generation, my yia-yia Avgerini was a woman born to serve, first her parents and her church, and then her husband, children and grandchildren. There was no indication that Yia-yia or her life was anything remotely outside the ordinary. It would take almost 70 years for anyone to realize just how extraordinary she really was.

Yia-yia lived on the tiny, remote island of Erikousa, just seven miles but worlds away from comparatively cosmopolitan Corfu. Erikousa lies at the northwestern tip of Greece, within a few miles of the shores of Albania, whose sandy beaches you can see with the naked eye from the island's dense, green hills.

In the 1940s, and even decades after that, Erikousa was secluded, with few phones, little electricity, no indoor plumbing and no police, doctors or shops of any kind. The islanders lived simple and primitive lives, boarding little fishing boats bound for Corfu whenever they needed anything that could not be farmed, fished or made with their very own two hands.

Erikousa was an island society where modesty and morality were paramount. Often, young girls were married off as teenagers, a bloodstained sheet hung from an olive tree the morning after a wedding as confirmation of a young bride's purity. Despite the fact that they lived on an island, women and girls were never taught to swim. Donning a swimsuit and bathing in the sea was seen as immodest and scandalous, bringing shame to a girl's family. Seldom, if ever, was a girl of my yia-yia's generation sent to Erikousa's tiny one-room schoolhouse to learn. Cooking, cleaning and tending to the livestock and garden were the only skills that mattered, and these were taught at home, under the watchful eyes of mothers, aunts and grandmothers.

Socially and spiritually, island life revolved around the tiny church of Saint Nicholas, where Sunday services, holidays, weddings, sacraments and name days were observed. Located adjacent to the old cemetery and steps from the one-room schoolhouse, the small icon-adorned house of worship was truly the heart, soul and center of island life. Deeply faithful, Yia-yia and the islanders would also make periodic trips from their island home to visit Corfu's Church of Saint Spyridon. There they would pray beside the island's beloved patron saint, whose mummified remains lay in a silver casket adorned in gold-embroidered red velvet robes and slippers.

Born in Cyprus in 270 AD, Saint Spyridon was a shepherd known for his humility, pure heart and charitable works. He was ordained a bishop after the death of his wife and came to be known around the world as the "Wondermaker," for the many miracles attributed to his name. Three hundred years after his death, Saint Spyridon's body—said to be still intact after all those years—was removed from Cyprus and brought to Turkey sometime during the seventh century. The saint's remains were kept in a Constantinople church until the fifteenth century, when the city was invaded by Turkish troops. After the fall of Constantinople, a priest carried the saint's remains to Corfu, where he has rested and been revered ever since.

Each person born with ties to Corfu is told that from the moment of their birth, Saint Spyridon will walk beside them and protect them. Once a year, the saint's priests open the casket to change his robes and shoes. And each year, it is said, they find seaweed entwined in his robes and that the soles of his shoes are worn through. The faithful believe that each night the saint rises, walking the shores and streets of Corfu, protecting his beloved island and her people. Corfiots believe that in the 1700s it was the saint who saved Corfu from the Ottoman invasion, rising from his silver casket to defeat the attacking Ottoman troops. The devout believe it was Saint Spyridon himself whom Turkish ships spotted standing atop the old fort, his lantern ablaze and raised to the sky, commanding the sea to rise up and swallow the invading ships.

In 1944, as Nazi soldiers raced to eradicate the Jewish community, Allied bombs fell on Corfu, destroying much of the old town except for the saint's resting place. While the surrounding buildings burned and fell into rubble, Saint Spyridon's church, with its icon-adorned marble altar, ornately painted ceiling that dripped with silver lanterns and imposing bell tower, remained untouched and intact. Countless more miracles around the world are attributed to Saint Spyridon. Many believe that what happened on Erikousa during the war is simply one more.

Despite the poverty and uncertain times, Yia-yia and her fellow islanders considered themselves lucky. Unlike the hundreds of thousands dying from famine across war-ravaged Greece, even the poorest of Erikousa's families, those with no livestock or income, could farm the island's fertile land and stave off starvation with octopus, lobsters, sea urchin and fish, all plentiful and free from the brilliant blue waters of the Ionian Sea. As the war raged on across Europe, Erikousa's remoteness, the very thing that kept this small island, her infrastructure and her people so antiquated and isolated from the modern world, proved to be her salvation.

Even during the Italian occupation, the Italian soldiers who looted villages across Europe never bothered the islanders of Erikousa. With the island so close to Italy, many of the local fishermen spoke Italian, and the island's dialect was infused with Italian words. The Italian soldiers looked kindly on the people who were so familiar in custom and language, for the most part leaving the islanders in peace.

Life for our family went on as it did for the rest of the island and generations before. Yia-yia tended to her home and children, molding Agatha to be a modest and devout Greek Orthodox girl while teaching her the skills she would need one day to be a successful wife and mother. My father spent his days running with the boys across the island, swimming, exploring and catching porcupines for the Italian soldiers, who viewed the prickly animal's sweet meat as a delicacy. The soldiers traded chocolates with the young hunters in return.

But then the Italians surrendered, German occupation began, and life on Erikousa, as Yia-yia and the islanders knew it, ceased to exist. At ten years old, my father went from running across the beach with his friends and savoring the sensation of melting chocolate on his tongue to stepping over the bodies of dead Italian soldiers in the sand, victims of German mines. He went from falling asleep to the rhythmic sounds of crashing waves and crickets to being woken by the sound of Nazi boots stomping outside his window and fists pounding against the door, demanding to be let in. Agatha went from sitting by her mother's side as she learned the secrets to rolling out paper-thin phyllo dough with a broom handle to hiding behind her mother's skirts whenever she caught sight of a Nazi soldier or heard the sound of German being spoken. And Yia-yia went from living a quiet life of obedience, obligation and reverence to one of defiance, danger and resistance, risking her own life and those of her children to defy the Nazi soldiers and help save the lives of a Jewish man and his girls.

That man was Savvas Israel, the Jewish tailor from Corfu.

chapter four

PASS THE LAMB.
WE SAVED THE JEWS.

Easter Sunday
New Rochelle, New York
1984

At this rate there'll be nothing left by the time we sit down for dinner." My uncle shook his head and laughed as he stood at his perch beside the spit, hand-turning the baby lamb over hot coals. Several of my uncles had been at it since 7 a.m., each taking a shift, turning the handle slowly round and round as the lamb cooked to perfection. By now the skin was crisp and charred, perfect for picking off a nibble as everyone congregated around the spit, enjoying an alfresco appetizer while waiting for dinner to be served.

"But this is the best part," my brother said as he reached his hand out and tugged at the lamb, peeling off a perfect morsel of the crunchy skin and moist meat.

It was midafternoon by now and the lamb had been cooking for hours. While the women held court in the kitchen, the men had gone out back early in the morning and impaled the entire animal on the spit, then taken turns slowly turning the handle as they smoked cigarettes and sipped dark, thick Greek coffee, which by afternoon was replaced by whiskey. Every 15 minutes or so, they dipped a cluster of rosemary twigs into a marinade of lemon, olive oil and garlic, bathing the entire lamb in the intoxicating mixture over and over again.

By now the air throughout the neighborhood was perfumed with the heavenly scent of the garlic-and-lemon-infused roasted lamb. Friends and neighbors up and down the block woke to realize we were at it again. The Greeks were celebrating Easter.

When the lamb was finally done, our entire family crammed around the dining room table. There were no bunnies, chicks or pastel colors to be found at our Easter table. Year after year, the centerpiece was always the same: a bowl of brightly dyed, deep crimson eggs. After being dyed and cooled, the eggs were rubbed with an olive-oil-soaked paper towel and buffed to shiny perfection. The eggs were always red and only red, to symbolize the spilled blood of Christ. Beside the bowl of red eggs were the lit candles we had transported home from the midnight Resurrection church service the night before. If the scent of cooking lamb didn't announce to the neighborhood that it was Greek Easter, the caravan of Greeks attempting to drive home from church at 1 a.m. with a car full of lit candles was always a dead giveaway.

We crammed around the table elbow to elbow, having scoured the house for every available chair. The table was covered in platters and serving dishes. What didn't fit on the table was piled high on the kitchen counter. There was enough food to feed a small village, or the entire island back home on Erikousa. And yet, as I scoured the table, I wondered what on earth I would eat. The food was rich, with complex flavors and sauces, but hardly anything appealed to my suburbanized palate. I had grown to prefer peanut butter fluff sandwiches to any element of traditional Greek cuisine. Even doused in lemon and garlic, lamb always smelled musty to me and tasted of old socks. As for feta cheese, a staple of any Greek meal, I couldn't stomach the fetid scent or stand the sight of its milky brine.

"Are you sure you're not adopted?" my cousins would always joke.

The first course was always the same: *magiritsa*, the traditional Easter soup. Or as I liked to call it, guts soup. Literally, it was a soup made from the guts and internal organs of the lamb. Every year, a few days before Easter, I would wake up to the distinct scent of intestines and other organs being cleaned and boiled. Yia-yia always seemed happiest standing at the sink, cleaning things I imagined more appropriately used to fertilize a garden than in a meal. But those intestines, simmered in broth with lemon, scallions and dill, were a tradition and the highlight of the meal for the rest of the family. And as always, a large bowl of it was placed before me on Easter Sunday as the entire table burst into laughter.

"Come on, Yvette." My brother laughed. "You know you want it."

"No thanks." I simply shook my head.

As everyone dug into their meal, the conversation was always the same. No topic was left unexamined; current events, news and politics were dissected with the same gusto as the latest island gossip or scandal, of which there was always plenty. And always, the chatter ended up right back where our family's story began, on the tiny island of Erikousa. Without fail, my father's sister, Agatha, was one of the most animated at the table.

"They were mean, mean, like animals, I tell you," Agatha announced. "Ugly people. Not nice to us like the Italians. One time I was walking by one, and I looked up. He was big, wearing his uniform. And he looked at me and lifted his arm and said, '*Heil Hitler*.'"

"And what did you do?" a cousin asked.

"What did I do?" Agatha's voice grew louder as she took another drag from her Virginia Slim light cigarette, her red lipstick staining the tip.

She flicked the ashes in an ashtray placed on the table beside the platter of roasted lamb and finished her story.

"What did I do?" she repeated. "I did nothing. I didn't know what to say or do. He wanted me to say, '*Heil Hitler*,' but I didn't know that. I was seven years old. So he hit me. He threw me to the ground and he kicked me. That mean bastard! And then I'll never forget it: an Italian soldier came over to me and he knelt down and said, '*Bambina, bambina.*' That's the Italian word for baby, you know. And then he took me to the café and he got me a slice of bread with marmalade. I still remember how delicious that bread and marmalade tasted. It was the best thing I had ever eaten."

"How many Jews were hidden on the island?" another cousin asked.

"Let's see. It was Rosa, Nini, Julia, Spera and Savvas," my aunt responded.

"Rosa was the littlest one," my yia-yia added. "She was the granddaughter."

"Yes. Rosa was just a little older than me," Agatha continued. "She was my friend. We would climb into my mother's bed, you know, when the adults were in the next room. We could hear them whispering. Right, Tasso?"

"Yes," my father replied. "I remember. We tried staying quiet. We would get hit if we weren't quiet."

"Well, we had to be quiet," Yia-yia added. "We never knew who was listening and who would tell the Germans."

As my yia-yia, father and aunt spoke of life under the Nazis, Easter dinner continued uninterrupted around them. And then, as quickly as the subject had come up, it was gone. Plates were piled high with seconds, more wine was poured, cigarettes were lit and life and the meal simply went on, the story of the Jews who were hidden on Erikousa no more significant than the story of whose teenage daughter was running wild and scandalously dating a non-Greek or which family was feuding over property left to them on Erikousa.

"Who's ready for dessert?" Agatha asked as she and the other women stood and began clearing the dishes from the table.

chapter five

PAPA SAVVAS, THE JEWISH TAILOR OF CORFU

Savvas Israel was by all accounts a gifted artisan, respected businessman and, above all, a true gentleman. With his piercing eyes, imposing mustache and immaculately tailored suits, Savvas was a man respected by Jews and Christians alike. His tailor's shop, located in the heart of the Jewish ghetto in Corfu, was a hub of activity, a place for conducting business, catching up on news and socializing with dear friends, both Orthodox Christian and Jewish.

He was nicknamed Papa Savvas—The Priest. At first it was a good-natured joke among his Christian friends. The moniker was a nod and a wink and a window into his character; Savvas was a wise man, kind and benevolent. But what began as some gentle ribbing among friends eventually stuck and grew over time to be how he was known by everyone: Papa Savvas, the Jewish tailor of Corfu. But the irony of Savvas's nickname was not the only paradox of Savvas Israel's life. While every garment Savvas made was said to be perfectly and immaculately crafted, the Jewish tailor's specialty happened to be clerical robes for Corfu's Greek Orthodox clergy.

Savvas Israel was not alone in his tailor's shop. His four daughters, Nina, Julia, Vittoria and Spera, were never far from each other or their father's side. Having lost their mother, Rosina, when they were young girls, Nina, Julia, Vittoria and Spera were particularly close and protective of each other and their father.

Nina was the eldest of the girls, and it seemed she took after her father in every way imaginable. By all accounts Nina, affectionately called Nini by her friends, was as kind, loving and exceedingly warm as she was talented. It was Nina who did the majority of the delicate, intricate embroidery Savvas's shop was so well known for. While her father specialized in clerical garments, it was Nina who Corfu's brides turned to when they wanted something exquisite for their wedding dress or trousseau. When Rebecca Aaron's aunt was getting married, she insisted that her friend Nini, and Nini alone, create her wedding gown. The dress was said to have been something of a dream, with beautiful lace trim and detail that no machine could ever replicate. It was the type of dress that isn't worn just once, the type of dress that becomes a family heirloom, handed down through the generations. But then the Nazis came, and those future generations, and the dress, were lost forever.

Spera and Julia, like their father and eldest sister, were known for their perfectionism and talent. It was Spera, headstrong and vibrant, who loved to socialize and test boundaries. It was Spera who turned heads with her beauty and made tongues wag with her many admirers. Maybe it was envy, maybe it was merely small-town gossip, but among the young ladies of the Jewish community, Spera's many flirtations and many suitors provided endless hours of gossip and speculation.

Like her sisters, Julia was devoted to her father and her family. Perhaps a bit more guarded than the other girls, Julia was the quietest. By all accounts she kept her thoughts, and her emotions, tightly under guard. But like her sisters and their father, once you had earned Julia's trust, there was no truer or more devoted friend to be found.

Usually, in both Greek and Jewish tradition, the eldest daughters were married first. But in the Israel household, it was Vittoria, the second youngest of Savvas's girls, who was the first to leave home. With curly dark hair and the same piercing eyes as her father, Vittoria had moved to Trieste, Italy, shortly before the war to be near her husband's family. It was left to Julia, Nina and Spera to care for their father and each other while learning the family trade. There, in Savvas's shop, the unmarried girls learned to sew and honed their craft, becoming skilled seamstresses under their father's watchful eye.

Having a new article of clothing made was a special occasion for my yia-yia and all of the islanders of Erikousa. It wasn't often that they could scrape together enough money for a new dress, suit, skirt or shirt, but when they did, it was an event. They would board those small fishing boats bound for Corfu, making the seven-mile journey from Erikousa's tiny port to the port of Sidari on Corfu's northern tip. From there they traveled by bus for the 23-mile journey down twisty and precarious mountain roads to the center of town to visit Savvas's tailor shop.

But it wasn't just the clothing and craftsman-ship in Savvas's shop that kept the islanders of Erikousa coming back. After so many years of doing business together, Savvas and many of Erikousa's inhabitants became friendly, exchanging much more than drachmas for garments. And while Savvas was respected and revered by the men of Erikousa as an artisan, businessman and friend, Spera, Julia and Nini became quite close with my yia-yia and many of the community's young women. It didn't matter that they were Jewish and the islanders were Christian; Savvas, Nina, Spera, and Julia were defined by their character, not religion, customs or traditions. The deeply devoted Greek Orthodox Christians of Erikousa and the traditional Jewish tailor's family grew to love and trust each other.

Despite their outward differences, they shared and valued the common bonds of morality, decency and integrity, even as the feverish contagion of anti-Semitism raged and the world around them went insane.

In June 1944, as the Germans rounded up all of Corfu's Jews in the lower square, Savvas Israel and his daughters Spera, Julia and Nina all managed to escape the carnage, along with a young girl named Rosa, who Savvas introduced to the islanders of Erikousa as his granddaughter. With her big, almond-shaped brown eyes and dark, cascading curls, Rosa bore a striking resemblance to Savaas's daughter, Vittoria, the beautiful olive-skinned girl who the islanders of Erikousa remembered from years of visits to the tailor's shop in Corfu.

In all their shared years of business and friendship, Savvas Israel had always been a man of his word. So when he arrived on Erikousa claiming Rosa was his grandchild, there was little reason to believe otherwise. But little Rosa, the shy, quiet child, was not who Savvas Israel claimed she was. Savvas would take Rosa's true identity to his grave. It was a secret he kept even from the friends who ultimately risked their own lives for his. He was so secretive about it that it took many years and much searching before I discovered who the little girl really was.

Somehow, almost miraculously, Savvas, Nina, Spera, Julia and Rosa managed to escape the chaos of Corfu and make it across the treacherous mountain roads and across the sea to the quiet, remote shores of Erikousa. They knew the risk of running, and there was no question of the threat. Stories of betrayal, like those of the families of Rebecca Aaron and Daniel Soussis, reverberated across the Jewish ghetto. The islanders of Erikousa had proven to be trustworthy friends through the years. But that was before the Nazis came, before befriending a Jew became a crime punishable by death.

And yet, they took a chance and they went, not knowing whether they would find salvation or betrayal. But Savvas, Julia, Nini, Spera and even little Rosa soon learned that what the islanders of Erikousa lacked in material goods and formal education, they more than made up for in integrity, bravery and honor.

Once Savvas, Julia, Spera, Nini and Rosa set foot on Erikousa, they were immediately taken in by their Christian friends, including my great-grandfather, Anastasios, who was an unofficial mayor of Erikousa and ran the fishing boats that ferried islanders back and forth to Corfu. The young women of the island—a small circle of friends and family, including my yia-yia Avgerini, her sister in-law Agathe, 15-year-old Theodora Musakiti and 23-year-old Amalia

Katehi—sprang into action, altering their clothing and appearance, assuring that Savvas and the girls would blend as seamlessly as possible into the rhythms of life on Erikousa. Spera, Nini and Julia were outfitted in plain buttoned blouses, skirts, dresses and aprons, the simple uniform of the Erikousa women. Their hair, worn inches shorter than the long braids traditionally worn by the Christian islanders, was parted in the center and combed straight. Each was given a head scarf to obscure their shorter hairstyle. Their own modern and beautifully crafted dresses were hidden away until it was safe to wear them again. Savvas's meticulously tailored suit was discarded as well. Instead the Jewish tailor was dressed in the threadbare shirt and pants typical of Erikousa's fishermen and farmers. Even little Rosa was dressed in a well-worn hand-me-down dress, long outgrown by a Christian child of Erikousa. The Jewish family appeared like they were native to the island. Just another poor Greek Orthodox family living day to day by God's grace.

Once dressed in the simple clothes of the islanders, Savvas and the girls were brought by their friends to the *keli*, the home of the island's priest. The islanders remember the priest at the time was a kind and gentle man named Father Andronikos who did all he could to help the villagers of Erikousa hide their Jewish friends.

Greek Orthodox archdiocese records show there was another priest on the island at that time as well, Father Achilas Kangas. A widower, Father Kangas was a kind and generous man known for helping others. Despite everyone's best efforts to piece together the details of what happened in those initial hours and days, the memories and minutia have blurred with the passage of time. While the islanders do clearly remember Father Andronikos taking the lead and doing all he could to help the Jewish family, it is clear that Father Kangas also played a role in this.

The *keli* was a tiny house, located behind the old grain mill, just a short distance from the port. Elevated on a small hill, it offered a perfect view of the nearby church and schoolhouse, with a stunning vista of the sea and Corfu in the distance. Without hesitation, Father Adronikos offered his prayers and promised to help the Jewish family any way he could. Again and again, Savvas offered to reimburse the priest, insisting he be allowed to pay at least a small amount of rent for the inconvenience they had caused. But Father Andronikos wouldn't hear of it. The priest refused any sort of reimbursement, insisting that it was his honor and privilege to help the family. For Father Andronikos, it was enough to know that he was helping to provide a place where Savvas and the girls could hide and practice their faith and traditions in private, away from inquisitive eyes and the danger of island gossips.

While the actions of Father Andronikos and Father Kangas on Erikousa were bold and brave, they were not unique. The heroism and selflessness of these two simple priests was part of a larger call to action taking place all across Greece. It was Bishop Damaskinos of Athens who set the tone and example for Greek Orthodox clergy throughout the country. Upon hearing of the Nazi deportations of Jews from Greece, Bishop Damaskinos stated, "I have taken up my cross. I spoke to the Lord, and made up my mind to save as many Jewish souls as possible."

Damaskinos used his pulpit to publicly denounce the Germans' campaign against Greece's Jewish population. He urged clergy all across Greece to help their Jewish brothers and to hide Jews in their own homes. The bishop issued thousands of false baptismal certificates and worked with the Athenian chief of police to issue false identity papers, which saved thousands of Jewish lives.

Learning of Damaskinos's insubordination, the German command sent a letter to the bishop, stating that they were fully aware of his actions and he would be shot and killed if he did not immediately cease and desist. Bishop Damaskinos boldly replied, "In our church our prelates are hanged and not shot. Please respect the traditions of our church."

The Germans were said to be so shocked by the bishop's reply that they did not follow through with their threat. Bishop Damaskinos, like the thousands of Jews he is credited with saving, survived the war. Of all the high-ranking Christian leaders across Nazi-occupied Europe, Bishop Damaskinos of Greece was the only one who publicly stood up to denounce the Nazis' deportation of Jews. It was with this courageous spirit that clergy all across Greece took it upon themselves to help hide and save their Jewish brothers, including on the tiny island of Erikousa.

While German soldiers never occupied Erikousa, they would come periodically, searching homes for valuables and Jews. Erikousa's remoteness, the fact that she was merely a tiny speck of land on the horizon and was rarely found on any map, was not enough to keep Nazi soldiers from completing their mission. They were single-minded in their focus and intent: to hunt down and exterminate each and every Jew from Corfu, and any Christian who dared help them.

Unlike the Italians, who were kind to the islanders of Erikousa, the Nazis were any-thing but. Once they reached Erikousa's shores, the Germans looted the island of any valuables that they could find, just as they had all across Europe. But being on a remote island had its advantages. The islanders could see the Nazis approaching. Erikousa's many hills and cliffs provided a perfect vantage point to spot approaching German boats.

With few telephones, the warning system was primitive but effective. When the German boats were spotted, the islanders would fan out, alerting each other that it was time to hide anything of value. Hoping to catch the villagers off guard, the Germans tried approaching the island in the dead of night. But fishermen, up before the dawn, spotted the approaching boats and set out to warn friends and family.

Hearing the warnings, my yia-yia would shake my father awake and tell him to head out across the island in the darkness to tell my great-grandfather to hide his guns. At 10 years old, shaking with terror and praying with every step that God and Saint Spyridon keep him safe, my father raced across the island in his nightshirt with nothing more than the moonlight and his memory to guide him.

But it wasn't just valuables and guns the Germans were hunting on Erikousa. The Nazis had their lists. They had their weekly census. They knew that 200 Jews were missing from the transport, among them Savvas, Julia, Spera, Nina and little Rosa. And there was little doubt the Nazi soldiers would stop at nothing to find them.

It was too dangerous for the Israel family to

stay in the *keli* when the Germans came to the island, so each time Nazi boats approached, my yia-yia, Agathe, Theodora, Amalia and a small group of islanders would mobilize. They gathered up supplies, blankets, food and water, and sent Savvas, Nini, Julia, Rosa and Spera to the uninhabited and wild side of the island called the *sandartho*. There, Savvas and the girls would hide, sleeping in a long-abandoned shed, wrapped in blankets for warmth and cooking food in a small pot placed over a fire dug into the ground. They survived on the fish, fruits, vegetables and supplies that their friends would bring to them each night after dark, without the aid of lanterns or candles, so as not to alert the Germans. Savvas and the girls stayed hidden in the *sandartho* until their friends would once again make the trip across the island to tell them that the soldiers had left and it was safe to return home.

But even when the Germans would leave empty-handed again, Savvas never allowed himself a false sense of security. The man who was so meticulous in his work was just as careful and measured in safeguarding not only his own life, but the lives of his girls and those who risked everything to help them. Week after week, Savvas insisted that he and the girls stay hidden and indoors during the daylight hours. He understood that despite the best efforts and intentions of his Erikousa friends, some secrets can't stay hidden for long. He knew full well that his life and the lives of everyone on the island hung in a delicate balance. The source for their exposure could have been any number of things—a poverty-stricken father willing to trade information for a loaf of bread to feed his family, a desperate mother willing to give up another man's child to save her own, or simply the innocent mistake of a child mentioning the name of Savvas, the gentle man with a mustache resembling a giant caterpillar, or that of Nina, Spera, Julia or Rosa, the kind girls who loved nothing more than to play with the island's children when they were not hiding in the shadows.

Each Friday at sundown, Savvas, Julia, Nini, Spera and Rosa would close all the windows and doors of the *keli* and privately and quietly keep the Sabbath. Lighting candles and softly reciting kiddush in hushed tones, they did their best to keep to themselves while keeping their traditions intact.

And each Sunday, the Orthodox Christians of Erikousa would file into the tiny Church of Saint Nicholas. The melodious chants of ancient prayers would be carried across the island on the soft morning breeze and through the opened windows of the *keli*. The Jewish family could hear their friends worshiping out loud, as they prayed they too would be able to do again one day.

"Why don't you convert?" my yia-yia and the other women each asked again and again. "If you become a Christian they won't hurt you."

"No." Nini was the most vocal. She was always the first to answer and refuse to renounce her faith.

"Here." One of the women removed the cross from her own neck and handed it to Nini. "Put this on."

Nini smiled and shook her head. "No," she said again. "Thank you, my friend. But I was born a Jew and I will die a Jew."

It didn't matter that Friday evening's hidden prayers and Sunday morning's melodious chants were in different languages, reflecting different traditions and religions. Christian Orthodox cr Jewish, Greek or Hebrew, at the end of the day, the prayers were all the same. Everyone on that tiny island asked God for the same thing. They prayed for peace and for safety, that the Germans would soon be defeated and that the secret of Savvas would remain just that.

chapter six

THE NIGHTLY KNOCK
AT THE DOOR

Erikousa
Summer 1944

"This doesn't taste like fish." It was a chorus of voices, all of the cousins talking over one another, saying the same thing.

"It's fish," Yia-yia and Agathe insisted. "Eat your dinner."

"But it doesn't taste like it." The protests continued. The meal was delicious, but confusing.

The slap was stealth, as always. Agathe smacked one of the children across the head. It didn't really matter which one. There was no precise target. Whichever child was within arm's reach would do. All it took was one well-timed and positioned smack to send a message to all of them. The protests and comments stopped, and the eating commenced.

The children were right, it was not fish they were eating, but Yia-yia and Agathe would never admit to it. The Germans were spending more and more time on Erikousa now and food was becoming more and more scarce. The soldiers went from home to home, helping themselves to any food they found or anything of value. Chicken coops and pantries were raided at will. Often the scent of a meal cooking over an outdoor kitchen fire was enough to summon the soldiers. It was not uncommon to hear the knock at the door, a family's meal confiscated by Nazis as the family was preparing to sit down for dinner. Families hid what they could, burying canned and jarred food along with guns, silver and jewelry, or hiding them down wells.

The children were hungry and their complaints were growing louder. Of course there was always fish. They would never starve like the hundreds of thousands across Greece who lived inland with no access to the sea. But the cries of a hungry child, frustrated with eating fish for every meal, will make a mother do things she never imagined.

Yia-yia and Agathe had conspired together and had come up with a plan. A family down the way kept quail out back. They decided they would take just a few, just enough to feed the children. A little protein would be good for them. And, of course, if any fuss or mention was made of the missing birds, it would be so easy to blame it on the Germans.

After dinner, the dishes were washed with water pulled from the well. The terrace was swept with a broom made from twigs bundled together with old twine. Finally, Yia-yia and Agathe went inside their respective homes and the children were tucked away in their beds.

Not long after dark came the gentle knock at the door. *Tap, tap, tap.*

Yia-yia sprang from her seat. Agatha and my father heard the noise and jumped from their beds, knowing what that soft knocking meant.

Yia-yia threw open the door. It was the first time Agatha and my father had seen her smile all day.

"Come in, come in," Yia-yia said, welcoming Spera, Nini, Julia and Rosa inside. "I'm so glad you're here. I was hoping you would come tonight. I saved you something."

Yia-yia went out to the kitchen and returned with a plate. "It's not much, but it's all we had." She placed a plate before the girls. It was fish, skin crisp from being fried in olive oil, a few roasted potatoes and a small morsel of the quail. "Eat, eat," she insisted. The girls divided the food, always saving the largest portion for Rosa.

The lessons commenced when Agathe was summoned from next door. The doors were locked, the windows shuttered, the lights and their voices kept soft and dim. Once everyone was seated in Yia-yia's small living room, Nini took the lead. Yia-yia and Agathe looked on like eager students as the Jewish girls taught their Christian friends to sew. In that dimly lit room, as the women huddled and chatted together, stitches were perfected, dresses were hemmed, socks were darned and blouses, aprons and skirts were crafted from old bedsheets and sacks. But it wasn't just clothing the women were creating night after night in that dimly lit room. As they sewed and chatted, whispering to one another their shared dreams and fears, meaningful friendships and lifelong loyalties were formed and cemented.

In the next room, as my father read mythology books filled with gods and heroes, Agatha and Rosa snuggled side by side in Yia-yia's bed. Together the girls shared secrets, dreams, and even their greatest fears. Rosa confided that she feared her family was gone. Agatha confided that she feared her father would never come home again. Snuggled together for warmth and comfort, Rosa and Agatha eventually fell asleep, each comforted by the friend sleeping beside her and the sound of the women whispering in the room next door.

Today, at 81 years old, with his health and memory failing, my father still remembers those nightly visits so clearly.

"Sometimes it was the only thing that would make my mother smile," he recalls. "She would be quiet and withdrawn all day, especially times that we had no news from my father. And then she would hear that soft knock on the door and her face lit up. It just lit up and she had this big, beautiful smile on her face."

But Savvas's girls were not the only people who sometimes came after dark. Sometimes the Nazis showed up. To this day my father can still viscerally feel the danger, how unsettled and nervous he felt as they waited to hear Nazi boots stomping outside their windows, the pounding of fists on the door. "I'll never forget it, *bam, bam, bam*. You could hear the boots. You could hear them walking, *bam, bam, bam*. Those heavy, heavy footsteps."

Sometimes, the Nazis came in. One night in particular stands out to him.

"I remember my mother just standing there. There was nothing we could do." His voice grows softer for a moment as he stares off across the room. And then my father looks at me and tells me what he remembers of that day, and I finally understand why he never had any interest in going back to Erikousa. It never quite made sense to me. All of my cousins had fathers who joined them on Erikousa each summer, those cherished family vacations spent together in Greece. But not mine. Each summer my father happily purchased my ticket, drove me to the airport and sent me on my way with notes on which relatives I needed to make sure to visit. He always claimed he was too busy to join me, that it would be impossible for him to leave the restaurant for a summer vacation. Now I know otherwise. Now, as an adult, I can understand the power of childhood memories. How those memories and experiences can mold us, shape our future and who we are, often propelling us forward, but sometimes also holding us back.

"We just stood there," he recalls. "There was nothing we could do. The Nazi just stood there yelling at us in German. I stood with my mother, who had her arm around me, protecting me. He was in her bedroom, just tearing everything apart, yelling, *'Where are the Jews? I know you are hiding them. Where are the Jews?'* We didn't say anything. We just stood there and watched as he ripped apart the house. There was nothing we could do but keep quiet. I thought he was going to kill us all."

While my father's most vivid memory of this time is of the fear and uncertainty, his sister, Agatha, most clearly remembers the love. "My mother loved those girls," Agatha recalls. "Nina was her favorite. She was really the nicest one. So sweet, and so kind. And for me it was Rosa. She was my friend."

Unlike my father, Agatha has gone back to visit Erikousa many, many times. And even today, with an assortment of health issues, Agatha is a fiercely outspoken spitfire, single-minded in determination. "Of course I'll get back to Erikousa," she insists. "Why wouldn't I?" she adds, as if I were insane to think otherwise. "It's my home."

Everyone on Erikousa, including my yia-yia, knew the risk. They knew the Nazis would make good on their threats to kill anyone found helping Jews, along with their entire families, and burn down the entire island as punishment. Even as German soldiers tore apart my yia-yia's house, even as they did the same across the island, to house after house, family after family; even then, no one on Erikousa gave up the secret of Savvas. Not one person on Erikousa told the Nazis that a Jewish family was hiding among them. Not one.

And Savvas, Julia, Spera, Nina and little Rosa all survived.

———————

British soldiers arrived in Corfu in October 1944, liberating the island from German occupation and answering the collective prayers of Christians and Jews alike. But even the end of German occupation was not enough to ensure the safety of Jews returning to Corfu. What was once a vibrant community was reduced to ash. Those who managed to survive the deportations and the Nazi death camps returned to the ghetto to discover just how difficult postwar life would be. They found two out of the three synagogues destroyed, countless homes reduced to rubble, and those shops and homes left standing were stripped bare by looters.

Realizing how difficult it would be to rebuild their lives on Corfu, Savvas chose instead to stay on Erikousa, surrounded by the friends who had risked their lives for his. Savvas, Julia, Nini, Spera and Rosa were finally able to come out from the darkness and live in the light. Finally they could throw open the doors and windows of their home and invite their friends to their Sabbath table without fear that they would be murdered for practicing their faith.

After the war ended, Savvas lived just long enough to see that his girls were safe, that the Nazis were gone. He knew that despite the evil he had witnessed, the islanders of Erikousa were living proof that humanity and civility still could and did in fact exist.

Savvas died of natural causes on Erikousa shortly after the German defeat on Corfu. He was buried just outside the Christian cemetery wall, behind the Church of Saint Nicholas and in the shadow of the Ionian Sea. Those who loved Savvas argued that he was one of their own, an islander, and therefore should be buried within the walls of the cemetery. What did it matter, Christian or Jew, his friends argued. All that mattered was that he was one of them, a man who loved their island and community as much as any man ever could. My great-grandfather and yia-yia listened to the arguments, adding their voices among those who professed their love and respect for the Jewish tailor. But the fact remained that Savvas Israel risked his life and that of his family, fiercely protecting his faith and traditions. Like Nina had stated when they first arrived on Erikousa, Savvas Israel was born a Jew and died a Jew. And, as such, he should not be buried within the walls of a Christian cemetery.

With no rabbi on hand, the islanders buried their friend, respecting his traditions as best they could. Nina, Julia, Spera and Rosa placed stones on the burial mound, as centuries-old Jewish tradition states, so that Savvas's memory might be eternal. The islanders, adults and children of Erikousa, showed their love and respect the only way they could, picking wildflowers and placing them on the grave of Savvas Israel, Jewish tailor and friend to the islanders of Erikousa.

After the war, like countless Jews across the globe, Nina, Julia, Spera and Rosa faced the daunting task of rebuilding their lives after having lost everything and everyone. Yia-yia struggled to build a new life for her own family as well. She moved with my father and Agatha to Athens, where they lived for a few more years until Papou was finally able to bring them to America. Yia-yia never forgot her Jewish friends, but after moving to Athens, she never did see them again. Yia-yia often wondered what happened to the girls who filled her home with love and laughter even in the darkest and loneliest moments of the war.

Years later, after she moved to America, Yia-yia heard that the girls had in fact returned to the island. They came back to remove Savvas's bones from his Erikousa grave so they could bury him in Israel, a final and fitting resting place for the gentleman tailor from Corfu.

On Erikousa, those who had loved Savvas and his girls savored the knowledge that they had helped the family in some way. They prayed to Saint Spyridon that Spera, Julia, Nina and Rosa would go on to live full lives and have families of their own. The islanders sometimes spoke of the Jewish tailor, but not often. As if they were still protecting their friends, the islanders kept the story of Savvas to themselves, the names and stories from a difficult and dangerous time occasionally whispered about, but after a time, mostly forgotten.

chapter seven

YIA-YIA NEVER TOLD

New York
1950s–1990s

After the war, like thousands of recently arrived immigrants, Papou and Yia-yia reunited and the family settled just outside of Manhattan, in the Bronx, New York. It was a life far from the dirt roads, outhouses and chicken coops of Erikousa. At long last, everyone was together and safe, food was plentiful, the war was over and the Nazis were gone. It was everything Yia-yia had dreamed about and prayed for.

In New York, as in Greece, the newly emigrated Erikousa community stayed close. It was a society no longer separated from the modern world by miles of sea, but insular nonetheless. They settled along the grand boulevards of the Bronx, crammed into the railroad apartments of Chelsea, and along the bustling avenues of upper Manhattan beneath the George Washington Bridge and in the shadow of the Church of Saint Spyridon, their beloved patron saint.

In New York, as in Greece, life revolved around the church community. Each Sunday, the Church of Zoodohos Peghe on Bruckner Boulevard in the Bronx overflowed with the transplanted islanders. The men, women and children of Erikousa filled the church pews, kneeling together in prayer and singing ancient hymns side by side, just as they had in Greece. Each Sunday, they stepped up to the altar, standing in line, one behind the other, until it was their turn to receive Holy Communion. Again and again, as the sound of ancient chants filled the church and the musky scent of incense wafted through the air, the priest dipped a golden spoon into a chalice filled with sweet red wine and bits of bread, the blood and body of Christ. When the almost two-hour service ended, the parishioners lined up again, this time to kiss the priest's hand as he gave each of them a piece of *andithero*, the blessed bread, which signaled the service was over. After church they would congregate together in the parish basement, catching up on news and gossip over coffee and tiny plastic shot glasses of Metaxa brandy.

No matter what their circumstance—who was struggling, who was suffering or who was having difficulty making ends meet—each Sunday the entire community showed up for church dressed in nothing less than their finest clothes.

School-aged children attended the Greek American Institute, an elementary school adjacent to the church, where they would learn

Greek history, traditions and language along with their American history and lessons in English. To this day, the Church of Zoodohos Peghe and the Greek American Institute are still the thriving epicenter of life for Erikoushoti-American families in New York.

Each day the men would go off to work, many dressed in white collared shirts and pants—the uniform of restaurant workers. They were always meticulously put together, their clothes starched and ironed to perfection by their wives. The men favored perfectly slicked-back hair and filtered cigarettes, which dangled perpetually from their lips. Whether they were leaving for church or for a 16-hour shift in the diner, the men of Erikousa were always immaculate in their appearance. They doused themselves in Old Spice cologne when they left home as the sun came up each morning. And each evening they returned home hours past sunset, the scent of hot grease permeating their skin, clothing and hair.

While my papou, father and even aunt Agatha adapted to their new hybrid lives, learning English and going off to work and school, Yia-yia, like the other newly emigrated wives and mothers of Erikousa, was left in charge of keeping a traditional Greek home. These same women who had so bravely defied the Nazis back home on Erikousa were terrified of losing their Greek identity now that they were in New

York. Determined to keep their culture and traditions intact, Yia-yia and the other women rarely ventured outside their safe circle of Greek-speaking friends and family. They socialized only with other Greek families, urging, and often insisting, that their children do the same. Assimilation was simply not an option. Many, like my yia-yia, lived in the United States for decades and never learned to speak English. It always seemed to me as though Yia-yia possessed some secret immigrant superpower. I never could quite understand how she barely spoke a word of English yet still managed to decipher every detail of what was happening on *All My Children* and which *poutana* was sleeping with whose husband.

When I close my eyes and picture the three-story attached house on Eastchester Road, I can still see Papou standing out front, watering the tiny patch of garden and hosing down the hot pavement, a giant smile plastered on his face, belly hanging over his belt, eyes squinting in the sun under those wild Manessis eyebrows that grew up and out and in every imaginable direction. To this day, that deep earthy and smoky, almost acrid scent of water cooling hot concrete always takes me back there. I'm transported to that front stoop, laughing and talking with Papou as he hosed down that little patch of his American dream. There was a lush green fig tree out back, painstakingly cared for and insulated with blankets fixed in place with duct tape each fall, insurance against the impending Bronx winter. The grape arbor next to the fig tree buzzed with fat bumblebees, providing a heavenly patch of shade in the summer and a backyard fragrance as sweet as Papou's homemade wine.

Inside, I picture Yia-yia standing at the kitchen sink, her shiny black hair freshly dyed from a box purchased at Woolworth's, her modest dress protected by an apron as she leaned not over, but into the sink with the full weight of her body. I can still see her smiling and chatting incessantly as she peeled potatoes, scaled fish or did whatever prep work needed to be done for that night's feast.

And it was always a feast. Yia-yia and Papou loved nothing more than to have a house full of family and friends, eating and drinking, talking and laughing. The vinyl maroon banquette against one wall made the room look like a saloon, always packed with visitors who would slide in and over to make room when the next guest arrived. When not covered in platters of pastas, stews or Yia-yia's signature pitas, the dark wood oval table overflowed with ashtrays and glasses of ouzo and whiskey. Papou was happiest when holding court, seated at the head of the table playing cards or feasting with friends or family. Yia-yia occupied the seat to his right, but never actually sat down. She was always too busy scurrying about, refilling plates and glasses and making sure every detail and guest was tended to. It didn't matter that she never sat. To have a house full of friends and family and plates brimming with home-cooked food was what made Yia-yia happiest in life.

Even when it was just the two of them, Yia-yia never cooked anything less than a full pot of food that could feed a small village. It was as if she were still waiting for that gentle knock on the door announcing that guests had arrived. While the scent of hot, wet pavement and sweet grapes dripping from the arbor perfumed the outside, inside, the savory scent of stews, cinnamon-infused tomato sauce and rosemary-and-oregano-encrusted roasted meats announced that you were home.

Papou was the life of the party, the consummate host, jokester and storyteller. Yia-yia had a quick and broad smile that made you at once feel warm and welcome. She never asked if you were hungry. It didn't matter if you had just eaten. In Yia-yia's house a hot meal was placed before you the moment you sat down.

We never lacked for food, laughter or company on Eastchester Road. There was always a house full of Greeks, most of them newly arrived from Corfu and Erikousa. I sometimes wondered if there was anyone left on the tiny island when they all seemed to be congregated in Yia-yia and Papou's house, crammed onto that maroon banquette and around the oval table.

While life was certainly not perfect, there was a moment in time when life on Eastchester Road was closer to idyllic than Yia-yia or Papou ever thought imaginable.

They spent winters in New York and summers on their beloved Erikousa, the island I had heard so much about yet had never visited. And then finally, in June 1980, when I was 12 years old, our family planned what was to be the summer of my life. We were finally going to Greece, to spend the summer with Yia-yia and Papou so my brother and I could see and experience Erikousa for ourselves.

But our perfect summer was never to be. Papou died just weeks before our scheduled arrival. He suffered a massive heart attack while visiting Corfu to purchase supplies for the indoor bathroom he was installing with his own two hands so we didn't have to use the outhouse.

My brother and I never made it to Greece for the funeral. Our freshly minted passports did not arrive in time. Papou never got to show me his beloved Erikousa and I never got to say good-bye.

We finally arrived on Erikousa a few weeks after Papou's death. Instead of being greeted by the sounds of his deep and infectious belly laughs reverberating through our home, I listened as Yia-yia cried for her husband in the traditional singsong mourner's wail that always made my hair stand on end. All of the women in our family, including my mother, dressed in head-to-toe black for the official 40 days of mourning. They sat on the patio, one after the other, black dress after black dress, looking to me like a row of black crows perched on a telephone line. My mother never got to wear the cute vacation outfits we had shopped for together at Bloomingdale's. My grandmother never wore anything but black for the rest of her life. And again, just as life changed for Yia-yia when Papou left her alone on Erikousa during the war, it changed for all of us when he left us for good.

That difficult summer, it seemed like everyone on Erikousa came together for us, as they have come together for one another throughout the generations. Knowing the heartbreaking circumstances of our papou's death, it felt like the entire island made it their mission to make sure my brother and I enjoyed our summer as best we could. If my papou could not show us the beauty of Erikousa himself, his beloved friends, family and island community would do it for him. Each day, along with a posse of our relatives and cousins, my brother, Emanuel, and I walked down the cypress- and olive-tree-lined dirt paths to the beach. The pristine caramel-hued sand spilled into the water, where the color shifted from palest blue to deep turquoise and then cobalt blue before our very eyes. We swam for hours in the bathwater-warm Ionian Sea and dove for spiky black sea urchins in the crystal-clear waters. We went for boat rides around the island on old fishing boats that our sun-weathered, Greek-fisherman's-cap-wearing uncles had long ago named for their wives. They let us help them pull up the evening's fishing nets, telling us we were good luck when the nets overflowed with red mullet, sea bream and lobsters, always sending us home with the largest of the fish for our dinner. Aunts and uncles took us by the hand and brought us to the island's one tiny grocery store, where they bought us giant ice-cream cones that dripped down our arms in the heat no matter how fast we licked. Each time we walked past the port, we made sure to stop and say hello to Stavroula, the developmentally challenged islander who always sat at the port's entrance to greet everyone as they came and went. She was around the same age as my yia-yia and dressed in widow's black, but Stavroula was mute and hid her lame arm under a black scarf. She hugged and kissed us again and again and shook her head up and down with joy each time we stopped to say hello. And every day, my brother and I took turns riding Jack, our donkey. Day after day, we attempted to ride Jack to the beach or to the port, but Jack was stubborn, as donkeys can be. Despite our attempts to navigate, Jack only wanted to travel from our house to the garden, the same route he traveled day after day, year after year, with my yia-yia and her beloved friend and sister-in-law, Agathe.

And each evening, one of our many aunts would prepare the most delicious meal for us over an open fire on the patio. It was the simplest of food: fresh potatoes fried in oil, stewed vegetables picked just that morning from the garden, a whole fried fish or even just freshly hatched eggs simmered in fresh tomatoes with olive oil, salt and fresh basil over crusty peasant bread.

That summer, my very first summer on Erikousa, I fell in love with our magical island. I arrived on Erikousa with a broken heart. And while nothing would ever heal the pain of missing my papou, I experienced firsthand the healing power of community and the ethereal nature of Erikousa's hospitality and kindness.

After that first summer on Erikousa, I could never get enough of our island and went back summer after summer, as often as I could. No matter what was going on in my parents' lives, no matter what financial hardships they faced, there was never any question that they would do all they could to make sure I was able to return to Erikousa each year. But then, after I graduated college and began to earn my own living, things got a bit more complicated. I had become spoiled and used to spending the entire month of August in Greece, along with all of my cousins and the Erikousa community. And while Europeans are accustomed to taking the entire month of August off, summer sabbaticals are not exactly a common American business practice.

I walked into my boss's office and asked to take a month off for summer vacation without blinking. Matter-of-fact, like it was the most normal thing in the world to ask of one's boss in a busy New York City newsroom. It never even occurred to me how absurd this request was. Maybe it was better that way. Ignorance was in this case not only bliss, but perhaps my saving grace. And, by the grace of God, my vacation was somehow granted.

I was going back to Erikousa.

For an entire month.

I could not wait.

The last year had been an absolute whirlwind, a constant blur of school and work. I was completely exhausted, but I knew better than to complain. Every day in journalism school, students are reminded that if they want to make it in this very competitive industry, they'll need to move to small-town markets and work their way up the journalism job ladder. Those who are incredibly good, and also incredibly lucky, may one day make it back to New York City, the number-one market in the country. This trajectory was not exactly a popular subject with my overprotective Greek parents, who at first didn't even allow me to move into the dorms at college. At the time, in most Greek immigrant households, a young woman's path was still typically to move from her father's house to her husband's.

"You can't move away from home," I was told again and again.

"NYU is forty-five minutes from home."

"Greek girls live home with their families."

"This is America," I reminded my parents.

Finally, after endlessly pleading my case and wearing them down, my parents gave in and let me move into the dorms at New York University. I realize now that they probably just got tired of my incessant grumbling and complaints and knew it was the only way to get me to stop badgering them. This tactic has served me quite well through my entire life.

In the end, we probably spent more time together when I lived at NYU than when I lived at home. While my father liked to come visit and catch up over dinner, my mother was known to drop by the dorm, sit on my bed and have coffee with my friends and me. There were also times she would show up and whisk me off to a night of theater, drinks and, in one case, to a male strip club with a gaggle of just-arrived-from-Greece aunts, who came prepared with a stack of crisp dollar bills. In our family, while the Greek immigrant women were incredibly traditional, they were also quite fun.

My job in the Fox-5 newsroom began as an internship the summer before my senior year at NYU. I was three weeks into the internship when a job opened up and was miraculously offered to me. I wasn't sure if my colleagues even knew how old I really was. There's a time-honored tradition of working in a newsroom: everyone heads to the bar after a breaking news story or to celebrate a job well done. Each time we went across the street to the Irish pub for a celebratory drink, I worried that the bartender would ask for my ID, embarrass me and kick me out of the bar in front of my colleagues.

My day began at 6 a.m., pulling file tape and research for reporters and producers. Despite how difficult it was for me to balance school and work, I loved everything about working in the newsroom. There's an adrenaline rush that comes with working on a live newscast or being on the ground floor of a breaking news story. It's addictive, it's challenging and it's so much fun. The newsroom itself becomes electric, a buzz of activity that to the outsider likely looks like chaos, with people yelling and running in all directions. But actually, the frenetic movements in a newsroom are a carefully orchestrated symphony of moving parts—crews, reporters, writers, producers and technicians that all work together to get a news broadcast on the air. I knew within weeks of taking the job that this was what I wanted to do with my life. I wanted to make news and break news. It's said that information is power. I quickly learned that not only is it power, but digging for that information is also a whole lot of fun, and that adrenaline rush is incredibly addictive.

After a full day of working in the newsroom, I would jump on the subway and head to school, where I finished my senior year with a double major in journalism and classical civilizations. It was an extremely difficult and stressful year. Although I loved my job in news, there were at least a dozen times that year I called my mother in tears, telling her it was too much for me, that I was going to quit.

"It's all right," she would say in that quiet, comforting way of hers. "You can do this. You can do anything. Just go to sleep; you'll feel better in the morning."

When my alarm rang at 5 a.m. I was always tired, but I always went to work.

Somehow I survived that year. School was finished. I had a degree and a job, and I was headed to Greece for August. Life was good!

While my parents wanted me to move back home after graduation, I wouldn't hear of it. Thank you, but no thank you. I was a career woman now. I was going to pay my own rent and make my own way. Despite our disagreements on where I would live, they were always supportive and generous.

But there was one problem: entry-level jobs in television news don't pay much. After spending most of my paycheck on rent, there was very little left. Desperate to save money and finance my trip to Greece, I stopped ordering takeout with my colleagues in the newsroom and began cooking my meals in my tiny apartment's tiny kitchen.

As I started to cook, I found myself gravitating to the Greek spices, techniques and recipes of my childhood. Chicken breasts were marinated in garlic, lemon and oregano. When I craved soup, I would bypass the cans and instead simmer a whole chicken with carrots, celery, an onion and several bay leaves, adding lemon juice and orzo to the broth. My salads were always dressed simply with olive oil, salt and red wine vinegar and dried oregano from the mountains of my mother's village in Greece. Pasta sauce was never from a jar, but made from crushed tomatoes cooked with onions and garlic and also a cinnamon stick for added depth of flavor.

In one month alone I managed to save over

$500, enough to have spending money for Greece. I realized then that I could save tons of money just by cooking at home. But I also realized something else. Despite all those years of wanting to be like my friends, of craving all-American comfort food, there was something so comforting to me about the scents and tastes of our very ethnic home. All those years that my mother and yia-yia pleaded with me to sit and cook with them, I couldn't be bothered. Whenever they asked me to help, or offered to teach me how to make a traditional dish, I was infamous for disappearing into the bathroom, feigning a migraine or insisting I had too much homework. But despite my best efforts, and without even realizing it, it turns out I had been learning from them all along.

It was as if a cultural osmosis had taken place.

It was the same with the story of Savvas.

That summer on Erikousa was like all summers on Erikousa—magical. Together with an extended posse of cousins and friends, my brother and I spent our days lounging on the beach and our nights dancing until sunrise.

We were young, free of responsibility and surrounded by an extended family who loved nothing more than to cook for us, smothered us with affection and lived to see us enjoying ourselves on Erikousa. Aunts, uncles, even elderly grandparents—it was as if they were living vicariously through us. Our joy and laughter became theirs. Seeing our love for Erikousa, watching as we returned each summer, it all seemed to validate the sacrifices and struggles our elder family members had endured during those difficult years on our tiny, magical island.

My friends back home and in the newsroom thought my vacations in Greece were about summer flings and flirtations, but they were not. They were about being surrounded by my family and cousins who were also my best friends. Night after night we would sing at the top of our lungs to favorite Greek songs and belly dance on the beach, on crowded dance floors, on banquettes, even on tabletops. There was something so visceral and joyous about the music and the company. A simple chord from a Greek bouzouki or the first droning notes of a traditional Greek syrtaki had us on our feet, lost in the music and the moment. Night after night we were a jumble of tanned limbs, arms hoisted into the air holding cocktails, long dark hair swaying with the music.

Each night, we'd stumble home down Erikousa's dirt roads as the sun came up over the Ionian Sea, the silhouette of Corfu's hills revealing themselves slowly across the horizon. One of those nights, walking home after a bonfire on the beach, my cousins and I decided to go home the back way, up the hill past the cemetery and church, instead of navigating the dozens of old, precarious stone stairs by the mill.

"That's the *keli*, right?" I pointed to the priest's small house as we lumbered toward home. "Where the Jewish family was hidden?"

"What Jewish family?" a cousin asked.

"The ones that were hidden here during the war. You know, the ones that were all saved. My yia-yia told me the story."

"My yia-yia never said anything about a Jewish family."

"Neither did mine."

"Oh yeah, I think my papou mentioned that," said another cousin.

"His name was Savvas. He was a tailor," I said.

"Nope. Never heard of him."

We continued walking home past the *keli* and past the church. I remember thinking how funny it was that not everyone knew about the story of Savvas. Most of these cousins and friends spent even more time on Erikousa than I did. So many of them came back each summer, for the entire summer, with both of their parents and siblings. From the nonchalant way my yia-yia always spoke of the story, I assumed it was just common knowledge, that everyone on Erikousa knew what happened.

And again, as always, as quickly as the subject of the Jewish tailor came up, it was gone. This was a night of drunken revelry, not a history lesson.

"Hi, Papou," someone called out.

I looked up to see whose papou could possibly be on the road at 5 a.m.

"Hi, Yia-yia," someone else called out.

But there was no papou or yia-yia out at that hour. As we stumbled home past the cemetery, one by one, the grandchildren of Erikousa called out to their grandparents, buried in marble family crypts one after the other behind the cemetery wall. Linked arm in arm, we continued on our way just as the dawn's first light bled through the darkness and a rooster's crow mingled with our laughter, down the dirt path toward home.

Revisionist history can be a tricky thing. Time passes, memories fade, oral history muddies, and transgressions, while sometimes subconsciously, are conveniently rewritten.

It would be so very easy to now say that I was an eager and attentive audience, the dutiful granddaughter lapping up every last detail of her grandmother's life and stories. It would be so very simple to say that I sat with her and talked for hours, asking if she was lonely when Papou left for America, afraid when the Nazis ransacked her home or hesitated before opening the door to welcome her Jewish friends inside. But that isn't the case. Not even close.

Unable to live alone after Papou died, Yia-yia came to live with our family in the suburbs of New York. Her bedroom was next to mine. Yia-yia's walls were adorned with crosses and icons of her beloved Saint Spyridon, mine with pictures of Rod Stewart and Duran Duran. Night after night I would walk past her door and catch a glimpse of her as she stood before her wall of icons. She would make the sign of the cross and give thanks, even when it was difficult to find something to be thankful for.

The house on Eastchester Road was no longer a hub of activity, of card games and parties. It was empty during the week, but my parents sent me there to spend weekends with Yia-yia so she could have the comfort of being in her own home.

For Yia-yia, those weekends were a reminder of the hard-earned life she savored, if for too short a time. For me, those weekends were forced exile from the life I wanted, from my American friends back home and the "normal" life I craved. I came to dread those endless days as Yia-yia's companion, where the minutes of the clock refused to move no matter how hard or long I stared. I wanted to be anywhere but there, surrounded by more women dressed in black, who ate large pots of snails and fish stew, spoke only in Greek and depended on me for shopping trips and translation.

As I grew into adolescence, my world expanded beyond my family's own immediate immigrant circle. I spent more time with my American friends and realized just how different our family and traditions were.

I longed to have the all-American home life I saw on television and in the homes of my classmates. While my friends vacationed in Hawaii and the Grand Canyon, our holidays were spent in smoke-filled Bronx apartments where the men played poker and drank ouzo. The women congregated in the kitchen cooking *loukoumades*, fried dough balls, which made my hair and skin smell like I too had worked a 12-hour shift in a diner. While my classmates spent their Saturdays and Sundays swimming at country clubs, I spent hours in churches, parish basements and catering halls. Each weekend's activities were dedicated to celebrating the christenings, weddings and memorial services of the Erikousa community. Back then, I didn't see how rich with culture and tradition those moments were, only that they were so mortifyingly different. I wanted what my American friends had. I wanted a homogenized life.

As a child, I wanted a grandma who had her hair set once a week, wore frosted pink lipstick and wintered in Miami. I wanted a nana who took me shopping at Macy's and made peanut butter fluff sandwiches and Rice Krispies treats. Instead, I had a yia-yia who dressed in black, spoke no English, sucked the eyeballs out of fish heads and wailed and beat her chest when something upset her. I was embarrassed each time I had a friend over who asked why my grandmother had a black scarf tightly knotted under her chin when it was 90 degrees outside. Yia-yia would always sit there and smile, greeting my friends with "*hello, dally-mou*," her Greeklish way of saying "hello, darling," and then ask in Greek if they were hungry, heading to the stove before they had a chance to answer.

In New York, as in Greece, and throughout her entire life, she was generous to a fault and loved without bounds. All Yia-yia ever wanted was my company. She wanted me to sit and talk, to share with me the stories of a life so different from my own. To teach me lessons that can't be learned from books.

And every now and again, she would mention the story of Savvas, the Jewish tailor from Corfu. With a smile on her face and a faraway look in her eye, she would recite the names of her friends, Savvas, Nina, Spera, Julia and little Rosa. She told me how the girls taught her to sew, and how the islanders of Erikousa taught the Jewish family that despite the evil they had experienced, kind and decent people did in fact still exist. She told me how the Nazis came to her door and searched the entire island for the Jewish family, but that she and the other islanders never betrayed their friends. I would sit and listen for a little while but eventually find some excuse to run off, usually to go lock myself in my room and listen to records. I never took the time to stop, to really pay attention and to really listen. I never took the time to stop and think about what Yia-yia's story meant, what she had lived through and sacrificed for.

During the time I was at NYU, I came home one weekend to please my parents, study in quiet and recharge with some home-cooked meals. One night I passed by Yia-yia's door, as I had countless times before, but this time I stopped and I watched her for a moment. She was lying there, propped up on her pillows, holding a child's mythology book in her hands. It was the book of my favorite myths—about Persephone, Arachne and Medusa—that my mother had read to me night after night when I was a child. I watched as Yia-yia struggled to read it, mouthing each word out loud and slowly turning the page. I took a step toward her room, but then stopped. I had work to do. I went back to my room, closed the door and studied for my degree in classical civilizations as my yia-yia lay in her bed next door, struggling to read a children's book of myths.

Yia-yia died when I was 24 years old, and even in her final days, my attention was elsewhere. I remember how waxy her skin looked and how labored and shallow her breathing had become when she was hospitalized that final time. But then my 27-year-old brother was admitted into the hospital as well, with an excruciating headache, the cause of which went undiagnosed for days. As my brother's health continued to decline, so did Yia-yia's. She died while my brother was still in the hospital. My father somehow found the strength to honor his mother's final wish, taking her body to Erikousa to be buried with Papou.

My mother and the rest of our family dealt with the details back home, the stream of friends, family members and mourners who filed in and out of our house. Day in and day out, I stayed by my brother's side in the hospital, refusing to leave him, barely acknowledging that Yia-yia was gone. My brain, my heart and my body were not equipped to handle all of this at once. I went into survival mode, compartmentalizing my emotions, focusing only on my brother and not allowing myself to think of Yia-yia. And again, just as when Papou died, I never really said good-bye.

In Greece, after the burial on Erikousa, my father stopped at the Church of Saint Spyridon on Corfu and said a prayer, for both his mother and his son, who was still in the hospital, not getting better and not getting any answers. While my father was in Corfu, I sat in my usual spot, the chair beside my brother's hospital bed, desperate for answers and a glimmer of hope. And then the doctor came in with his morning update, the same doctor who had days before spoken in hushed tones that scared me. The hospital staff had called the doctor at home that morning with news about my brother. He then raced into the hospital to see for himself. The doctor hovered over my brother, checking his vitals, standing close and examining his eyes. And then he said it.

"It's a miracle."

I stared at him from my seat, not understanding what was happening. My brother sat up a bit taller.

"Someone must be praying very hard for you," the doctor said. And then he told us that there was a marked improvement and my brother would recover from the meningitis and encephalitis that threatened to take him from us.

I knew in that moment that this was indeed a miracle. But what I didn't know is that my brother's recovery was also a long-ago promise fulfilled.

As we celebrated the good news, my mother told me a story. While my father's family is from Corfu, my mother's family is from a tiny mountain village north of Athens, where the villagers are familiar with Saint Spyridon, but he is not revered the way he is on Corfu. My mother said that when she was newly married, Yia-yia sat her down and shared with her new daughter-in-law stories of her beloved Saint Spyridon and his miracles. My mother, unlike me, sat patiently and listened. Months later, when she was pregnant with my brother, my mother had a dream. In it, Saint Spyridon came to her on a white horse and said, "I know you don't truly believe in me now, but you'll see. One day, twenty-seven years from now, there will come a day that you will. You will believe."

After that, we all believed that Saint Spyridon saved my brother. But although I have never doubted that his recovery was indeed a miracle, there is one question I've often wondered about. Could Yia-yia have known that by leaving us, she would leave us in Saint Spyridon's hands?

When I was younger, I was embarrassed by how different Yia-yia was, not realizing that's what made her so very special. Later, I was too busy to stop and sit still and to pay attention. There I was, the budding journalist, consumed with chasing stories, researching, investigating and exposing the truth. But all that time, all those years I spent telling other people's stories, I never stopped to realize that the most extraordinary story of all had been in the bedroom next to mine.

It wasn't until years after Yia-yia was already gone, as a veteran journalist who now wanted to try her hand at writing a book, that I remembered my yia-yia and her story of Savvas. Everyone I asked said the same thing: the number-one rule of writing is to write what you know. I thought about that for a while. I realized that what I knew best was what it was to be a daughter of immigrants. I knew what it was to be a grandchild whose grandmother lived on a tiny Greek island where the people are poor, yet so kind, so extraordinary and exceedingly generous, that they would risk their own lives to save their Jewish friends.

It is my yia-yia's story of Savvas and his girls, their story of sacrifice, friendship, secrets and survival, that was the heart and soul and inspiration for my first novel, *When the Cypress Whispers*.

While steeped in truth, *When the Cypress Whispers* is a work of fiction. Writing a novel about the magical bond between a yia-yia and her granddaughter was cathartic for me. In the book, the granddaughter, Daphne, spends endless hours sitting and talking with her yia-yia about her life, asking questions I wish I had asked, sharing secrets I wish we had shared.

But as I was writing *When the Cypress Whispers*, I realized it wasn't enough for me to simply fictionalize my yia-yia's story. I needed to finish it, to find the family she risked her life to save.

Because despite the Nazis' warnings, the danger and the threat of death, Yia-yia never told.

And I had never bothered to ask.

PART TWO

chapter eight

SEARCHING FOR SAVVAS

Corfu
June 2011

Time passed, I grew up and got married, but my heart never left Erikousa. From the first moment he stepped foot on our tiny island, my husband, Dave, instantly grew to love our tiny island as much as I did. Hand in hand, each summer Dave and I walked into the Church of Saint Spyridon. It was our tradition each time we visited Corfu. Together we would light candles at the church's entrance and then walk inside to kiss Saint Spyridon's silver casket. We would thank him for our blessings and ask him to watch over our family. We had so much to be thankful for.

Dave and I had been married for 15 years. We had two healthy children and two thriving careers. Life was busy, sometimes too busy to catch our breaths, but it was good. Before the children were born, Dave and I continued my tradition of visiting Corfu and Erikousa each year. While Dave had not been born into a Greek family, he certainly took to marrying into one with gusto. We often joked that at times he seemed more Greek than I was. No matter how many times he tried to get me to taste them, I still couldn't stomach lamb or Easter *magiritsa* soup. My mother looked on, beaming, every Easter as he ate enough for both of us.

As much as Dave and I both loved our yearly trips to Greece, once the children were born, finances and careers made it impossible to return every summer. But finally, in 2011, we made it happen. It was the first time we brought our children to Greece. We were home.

Christiana was 10 and Nico was 7, and they loved Corfu and Erikousa as much as we did. Watching them splash in the sea and pick blackberries from the roadside bushes made my heart burst with joy. I finally understood how the elder generation of Erikousa felt as they watched my cousins and me return to enjoy the island each summer.

We were spending two weeks in Greece. And while it wasn't quite the monthlong vacation I remembered from my youth, I knew our family would make the most of every moment. I knew how fortunate I was to have even two weeks off, as taking more than a week off at a time is a rarity in television work. After Christiana was born I had transitioned from being a hard news producer to lighter fare, producing for the Syndicated Entertainment News show *Extra*. The excitement and adrenaline of television was still there, only now instead of covering a crime scene or fire, my beat was celebrity news, red carpet events and movie premieres. Just two months before, in April, I'd spent a week in London covering the royal wedding of Prince William and Kate Middleton. Working in entertainment television and covering celebrity events certainly had its perks. But of all the wonderful places I had visited around the world, Corfu and Erikousa were by far my favorites. And of all the incredible stories I had heard and uncovered throughout my career, there was one story I still could not get out of my mind. It was the secret of Erikousa, my own yia-yia's story of Savvas the tailor and his girls.

"Here. I think it's down this way." I took Dave by the hand and led him through the narrow alleys of Kerkyra. By now, he knew those twisty back alleys and roads as well as I did. "Here."

I had passed this area dozens of times over the years and never stopped to think what had caused the damage to the decrepit building. The walls were partially collapsed, the roof completely opened to the sky. Within the hollowed-out frame, weeds and brush had grown thicker with each passing decade.

"This is where the Allied bombs fell, while the Nazis were holding the Jews at gunpoint in the *platia*," I said. "They never rebuilt it." More than seventy years later, the school building was still a mere shell.

"I think the synagogue is down here." We walked farther down the street of the Jewish quarter, stopping when I saw the Star of David on the door and on a plaque affixed to the front of the building. The last time Dave and I had been on Corfu together, 10 years before, we had stumbled upon the synagogue by accident. "Let's go see if anyone knows anything about the Jewish family on Erikousa," I had said. But the synagogue was locked that day and we simply went on our way.

Back then, I was curious whether anyone remembered the story of Savvas, but it was a mere coincidence that we had happened upon the synagogue. Now, a decade later, learning more about Savvas and his girls had become my obsession. We'd come here to find out whatever we could about the family.

Fortunately, this time the synagogue door was open. We stepped inside. There was a small cluster of people gathered around and two women seated behind a small folding table in the entranceway.

"Excuse me," I said in Greek. "I'm hoping you can help me. My yia-yia lived on Erikousa and she was friends with Jewish girls during the war. Their names were Nina, Spera, Julia and Rosa. The father's name was Savvas. He was a tailor.

The family hid from the Nazis on Erikousa. I was hoping someone here might know more. I'm trying to find the family."

The women looked at me and then at one another. "No. I'm sorry. I don't know the family. I don't think I ever heard this story."

"Do you know anyone else I can ask?"

"You can try some of the shops down the street. Someone in the community might remember something. But I don't remember ever hearing this."

We left the synagogue and continued farther down the way, stopping into a few of the crowded tourist shops that lined the street.

"I'm trying to find a Jewish family. They were friends of my yia-yia's," I said again and again.

And again and again I was met with blank stares, a simple shaking of the head, or on occasion, even a full sentence. "Sorry, I don't know them."

At the time, it was estimated that there were 60 members of the Jewish community still living on Corfu. Someone, somewhere, had to know something. I knew those girls could not have simply vanished after the war. I was more determined than ever to find them.

———————

After that day when Dave and I visited the synagogue and Jewish quarter of Corfu, I asked everyone we knew on Erikousa what they remembered about Savvas and the girls. Again and again I heard the same details. Everyone recited their names—Savvas, Nini, Julia, Spera and Rosa. Everyone said that no one on the island gave up the secret to the Nazis. Everyone knew that Savvas had died and been buried on Erikousa. But no one could agree on what happened to the girls after the war.

"They went to Israel," said one aunt.

"No, they took Savvas's bones to Israel," corrected another.

"They lived in Corfu. I saw Nina just a few years ago," insisted yet another family member.

Everyone on Erikousa that I spoke with offered to help. Everyone was excited about the idea of reconnecting with their old friends. Everyone promised to call me immediately, as soon as they had any news, which they were certain they would have for me very shortly.

But no one ever called.

Then one day, my father announced that my uncle had called him. "He said he can get Spera's number, that she had a house on Kerkyra and she may still be there," my father said.

"Are you serious?" I couldn't believe what I was hearing.

"Your uncle said he knows how to reach her," my father said.

"Do you really think so?" I was afraid to get my hopes up. None of it made sense to me. They

had been through so much with their friends on Erikousa. How could they not have stayed in touch? How could they just have gone on with their lives as if it never happened? As if my yia-yia and the others didn't risk everything for them? I simply didn't understand.

"Yes. He said he was confident," my dad insisted. "He said he'll call me in a day or two with her number."

That phone call never came. I was getting nowhere.

One morning a year and a half later, I was having a breakfast meeting with a publicist. I had had hundreds of meetings like this before. I'm a television producer, so publicists are always asking for meetings, to pitch a client or to find out if there is any way for us to work together. Sometimes those meetings are productive; sometimes they are interesting; sometimes they are a total waste of time. Sometimes the publicists are just hoping that I'll share a bit of insider celebrity gossip. I wasn't sure what to expect from this meeting. I had never met this publicist, Chris Powell, before.

"He's a great guy and a good friend. Just go meet with him," my friend Tammi Fuller said. Tammi was also a producer at *Extra* and had collaborated with Chris on several stories throughout the years. "He has a new client," she told me. "It's a family genealogy website, and with all the family history in your book, maybe there's something there for you. Just meet him. You never know."

And so, with Tammi's encouragement, I set off for a breakfast meeting with Chris Powell, a publicist for MyHeritage.com.

Chris explained that MyHeritage was a popular website where people around the world could research and build their family trees. Based in Israel, the company was working with Chris to expand their reach and business in the United States.

Over coffee and eggs, Chris and I chatted about possible story ideas and how we might be able to work together.

"Wouldn't it be great to find a celebrity willing to have MyHeritage.com research their family tree, and then feature the story on *Extra*?"

We ran over the possibilities, tossing out names of celebrities who might be interesting or willing to work with us on such a project.

"But it's about more than family trees," Chris explained. "They are really interested in preserving history and culture, traditions like family stories and recipes."

"That's amazing," I said. "Believe me, I know how important that is."

"Yeah, Tammi told me you wrote a book about your own family in Greece," Chris said.

I explained that *When the Cypress Whispers* was fiction, based on my grandmother's life. I told him how the book was steeped in all the tradition, legacy, recipes and oral history that seemed to be so much of what MyHeritage's mission was all about.

"Maybe we can work together somehow, to help you with your book," Chris said.

"You know, I've been trying to find the family my grandmother helped save," I said. "So far I've got nothing. No one in Greece knows anything and there are no records on the island. I know how we can work together. Maybe you can help me find the family."

"Of course." He said he would contact the MyHeritage offices in Israel and report back on our meeting, and my search to find Savvas.

Chris explained how the website worked: you simply typed a name into a database and waited for a match of the more than one billion profiles registered on the site. There were also researchers within the company that could work with you to do a more detailed search.

As soon as I got back to my office, I immediately logged on to MyHeritage.com. I typed the names and what little information I had into the database . . . and I waited.

I tried every name, every variation, every detail I could think of and every possible spelling.

Nothing. No matches. No information. Again.

chapter nine

RIGHTEOUS AMONG
THE NATIONS

In my novel, *When the Cypress Whispers*, Yia-yia explains to her granddaughter, Daphne, that when she is lost, or in need of guidance, the answers to life's mysteries can be found by listening to the voices of our ancestors whispering to us and guiding us, softly singing to us between the rustling leaves of the cypress trees.

It had been 12 years since Dave and I first stumbled upon the synagogue in Corfu. At first it was simply happenstance, a wrong turn down an alley that brought us to the synagogue. A spur-of-the-moment decision to knock on the door. But over time, the question of what happened to Julia, Nina, Spera and Rosa had become more than a just passing curiosity. Finding the girls and fleshing out their story had become a full-on obsession. I knew how my yia-yia and my father and aunt felt about the girls, what they'd told me about those dark and difficult times. I remembered how my father said that often, when that soft tap came, when Yia-yia threw open the door to welcome the girls inside, those were often the only moments that brought a smile to her face. I wondered if Savvas's girls went on to have children of their own and if so, what they told their own children about my family, about those nights in Yia-yia's home and their time on Erikousa.

Again and again, I came up empty. Everyone I asked on Erikousa and Corfu, and even the islanders who had moved to the United States after the war, all told me the same thing. There were no records, no proof, and there was no way of finding Nini, Julia, Spera and Rosa with nothing more to go on than an old story and some names.

But then I finally stopped and thought about the very words I had written in my novel, the sage advice of a wise old yia-yia to her granddaughter.

Sometimes our salvation is right there, just waiting to be heard. The cypress whispers are right there for us, just waiting to be heard.

And then I realized that perhaps like Daphne, my own answers could be found among the trees.

In 1989, at the height of the Intifada, the first Palestinian uprising, I spent a college summer semester in Israel studying journalism and Mideast history. While my friends studied abroad in more traditional places like London and Paris, I visited Christ's tomb, the Western

Wall and the Dome of the Rock. While my friends spent their summers lifeguarding and babysitting, I visited Palestinian and Jewish homes, interviewing families and learning about their faith and their fears. When the Palestinians inquired about my ethnicity, I would tell them "I'm Greek." "You're one of us!" they would respond, hugging me close and inviting me home for tea. When Israelis asked the same question, I would again say, "I'm Greek." And again, I was met with broad smiles and hugs and invitations into their homes.

"You're one of us."

Palestinians and Jews had both claimed me as their own. The irony was not lost on me.

It was during this time that I visited Yad Vashem, the Holocaust museum in Jerusalem. I remember walking through the Garden of the Righteous Among the Nations, where trees are planted to honor righteous gentiles, non-Jews who risked their lives to help save Jews during the Holocaust. I remember reading the names of those who had helped save their Jewish friends, marveling at their courage, amazed that beauty and grace can indeed exist in the face of such evil. Walking through that beautiful space, I never stopped to think about what my own yia-yia had done, what had happened on our little island—that something beautiful had happened there.

It wasn't until years later, after Yia-yia was

gone, frustrated by my unsuccessful search for Savvas's family, that I remembered my trip to Jerusalem and that lovely garden. And in that moment, I finally realized that my own yia-yia's story was just as remarkable, significant and beautiful as those I had read about under the shade of those magnificent trees in the garden at Yad Vashem.

I thought about emailing Yad Vashem's Righteous Among the Nations, the department that researches and recognizes gentiles who risked their lives to save Jews during the Holocaust. I started and stopped writing the email so many times, thinking it would be yet another waste of time. After all, Erikousa was nothing more than a tiny speck of dust on a map, when you could even find it on a map. I had nothing more than fragments of an almost 70-year-old story and the names and profession of a Jewish family. I had no records, no documents and no proof. No one in the Jewish community of Corfu even remembered the family. It seemed hopeless.

Finally, late one evening, in a fit of wine-fueled frustration, I drafted an email and hit send. I figured these world-renowned researchers would never pay attention to me or my story.

I couldn't have been more wrong.

Less than two weeks later I got a reply from Gili Diamant, a researcher with Righteous Among the Nations. For Gili, working at Yad

Vashem researching the stories of Jews hidden and saved by Christians during the Holocaust was deeply rewarding, at times challenging and always profoundly personal. Gili herself had grown up listening to her own grandmother's story of how she and her family were hidden and saved from the Nazis by a poor Christian family in Poland. The names of her grandmother's rescuers are etched into the Wall of Honor, just down the way from Gili's office on the museum's Jerusalem grounds.

While Gili enjoys the detective work and relishes diving into challenging investigations, that's not what she finds most rewarding about her work at Yad Vashem. For Gili, seeing firsthand what the Righteous Among the Nations department means to the survivors themselves is what drives her. For so many survivors, the trauma of what they endured during the Holocaust manifested itself in silence. The department serves for many of these survivors as a "bank of memories," as Gili calls it. Even those who never spoke of their experiences, who never uttered a word about the Holocaust even to their families, often feel compelled to break their silence and document their stories with Yad Vashem's Righteous Among the Nations. Witnessing the power of gratitude as these survivors come forward to document the stories of their saviors, to publicly acknowledge and thank them, is for Gili the most rewarding aspect of her work.

And while working with Righteous Among the Nations can be tremendously gratifying, there are other aspects of Gili's work that are incredibly difficult. Writing to inform someone that there is not enough information or evidence to submit a case to the Righteous Commission for review is always difficult.

Such was the case with the email Gili found herself drafting to me.

> **Dear Ms. Corporon,**
> **Thank you for your email and my apologies for this delayed response.**
> **I would be very happy to try and help you find the Savvas family, but I must admit that this is not a lot of information to go by . . .**

From that day on, Gili and I corresponded and exchanged dozens of emails. She asked me for photos. I had none. She asked me for first-person testimony from Savvas's family. I had none. She asked me for any proof or documentation showing that Savvas and the girls had in fact been on Erikousa during the German occupation. I had none.

Gili searched databases, survivor testimonies and Holocaust records, cross-referencing names and dates with any documentation she could find. She reached out to Holocaust survivors from Corfu and all across Greece. She placed ads in newspapers and on social media, asking for any information and help in finding the Jewish family who were hidden and saved on Erikousa.

While Gili searched from her office in Jerusalem, I continued exhausting every avenue, contact and possibility on Erikousa and Corfu. At this point my relatives were pretty much sick and tired of me asking the same questions over and over again.

"I already told you everything I know," they would say.

"It was seventy years ago, Yvette. What more do you want me to tell you? You're driving me crazy." Agatha in particular feigned frustration, but I knew she secretly loved sharing her memories, even if they were the same ones, over and over again.

Gili and I corresponded every few weeks. She would check in, always asking if I had any new leads or information, assuring me that she was continuing to dig on her end.

And then, after a year of research and correspondence, I received another email.

Dear Yvette,
 I hope you are well. I was wondering if you had any new infor-

mation from Corfu . . . I'm afraid that I've come to a dead end here.
    Best,
    Gili

Reality set in. I had nothing new. I'd never find the girls or the ending to Yia-yia's story. Accepting that this was indeed the end, I thanked Gili for her time and asked her to share what little information she had found, however insignificant.

In Rehovot, Israel, the Hassid brothers, Avraham and Peretz, were searching for answers as well. Their mother, Rosa, had passed away, leaving boxes of old black-and-white photos, documents and countless unanswered questions. Rosa had been widowed when the younger brother, Peretz, was just two years old, and she never spoke of her family or her past. She made it clear that the past was too painful to revisit, and the brothers didn't want to hurt their mother further by dredging up painful memories.

Tall and olive-skinned, Avraham Hassid is a man with a personality and heart as big as his stature. He is always impeccably turned out, with a chain dangling around his neck, pristine sneakers cleaned and buffed to perfection and shirt crisply ironed and tucked in. At first glance, with his hulking physique and steely gaze, Avraham might appear a bit intimidating. But to spend one moment in his presence, to see the mischievous smile slowly snake across his face, hear his infectious laugh or a perfectly timed joke—usually at the expense of his brother—is to fall in love with this gentle giant.

Peretz, the younger and more fair-skinned of the brothers, seems at first more reserved than his elder brother. But while first impressions can sometimes be misleading, they can also be layered. While he is outwardly more quiet and reserved than gregarious Avraham, Peretz's well-timed jokes and sarcastic remarks are equally as funny and hit their mark with the same exacting precision. Having lost his own father when he was just two years old, Peretz relishes his role as husband and father to his three beautiful girls. Theirs is a home where people love fiercely and laugh often. It's a warm home where Shabbat is spent sharing stories around the dinner table, playing intensely competitive board games and laughing together.

Avraham and Peretz live just down the street from one another, in the city of Rehovot, where Avraham is a municipal worker, tending to Rehovot's gardens and greenery. The entrance-way to Avraham's apartment is lined with lush and thriving potted flowers and trees that he prunes, waters and cares for as if the plants were members of his own family. It is with the same pride and meticulous attention that Avraham cares for the papers and photos his mother and aunt Nina left behind. Inside, the apartment is bursting with family mementos that make you feel as if you have walked into a three-dimensional family scrapbook. The walls are covered in these old black-and-white pictures, showing his mother as a young woman, on her wedding day, and posing with the three women simply known as "the aunts." Their names, the brothers know, are Nina, Spera and Julia. Avraham and Peretz never knew exactly how the aunts were related to Rosa, only that they were very dear to her and the women often spoke in Greek when they were together.

But there is another photo in Avraham's apartment as well. It is a large, framed portrait of a man. He is immaculately dressed, with piercing eyes and a manicured mustache. Neither Avraham nor Peretz knew who this man was. All they knew was that the well-dressed man was very important to Rosa, and that their mother had loved him dearly.

Seven years had passed since Rosa's death before the brothers were finally ready to ask the questions they were never allowed to ask when their mother was alive. They wanted to know where Rosa grew up, how she survived the Holocaust, what happened to her family and who the man in the portrait was. And Avraham and Peretz Hassid had no idea where or how to begin.

I knew Gili had reached a dead end, but I refused to give up. I had asked her to share with me what little information she found, however insignificant. When the email with that information popped up, I braced myself for another disappointment.

Gili wrote that she had located a Holocaust survivor from Corfu named Dannie Talmor, who said the names Spera, Nina, Rosa and Julia rang a bell. Gili did some digging around and learned that Dannie left Greece on July 30, 1946, on board the *Henrietta Szold*, which was an illegal refugee ship carrying immigrants from Greece to Israel, which at the time was called Mandatory Palestine. The ship and refugees were denied entry and instead sent to a British refugee camp in Cyprus, where they were interred for several months. Dannie said he recalled quite clearly that two girls named Spera and Rosa from Corfu were in the camp with him. Dannie often traveled back to Corfu from his home in Israel and began asking his friends and family on Corfu what, if anything, they knew about the Jewish tailor and his girls. Finally, after a bit of digging within the small community of Corfu's survivors and their families, Dannie reported back what he learned.

And finally, through Dannie, we at last had our first glimpse at the lives of Savvas's girls after the war and after they left Erikousa. In her email to me, Gili wrote:

> Julia moved to Athens and possibly later immigrated to the US; she never married and had no children. Nini married an older man by the name of Rahamim Levy. They did not have any children. Spera married a man by the name of Vittorio Moustaki, also a native of Corfu. They divorced later and did not have any children. Rosa was adopted by her older sister Nini; she married and had children, but we have no names. She used to live in the city of Rehovot here in Israel.

I read the email over a few times. Gili said she had come to a dead end, but her email turned out to be just the beginning.

I honestly didn't expect to find anything when I typed the name Vittorio Moustaki into the database of MyHeritage.com. Since my meeting with Chris a few months before, I had tried several times to find Nina, Julia, Rosa and Spera by using the site. Every few weeks I would try again, hoping that maybe someone, somewhere, might have added a family tree that would unlock the secret of what happened to the girls.

Each time I tried I was met with nothing. No matches.

But that morning, as I typed the name of Spera's husband, Vittorio Moustaki, into the database, something different happened. This time, a family tree instantly appeared on my screen, each branch filled with those familiar names— Julia, Spera and Rosa. I clicked on each name, each individual branch, and there they were, black-and-white photos, faces staring back at me.

I looked at my screen, where a beautiful wedding photo appeared. An elegant family, ladies all seated in front, dressed in beautifully cut and draped gowns. The women all wore their hair side-parted and bobbed. Their arms overflowed with lush bouquets. Seated in the center was the bride. She wore an exquisitely embroidered dress, her chicly styled hair tucked under a cloche hat, embellished with a delicate flower on one side. The dark-eyed men all stood behind the women, outfitted in suits, with boutonnieres pinned to their lapels. Unlike the other men, who wore standard ties, the groom wore a bow tie.

I couldn't believe my luck or my eyes. Identified in the photo were the names I had been searching for. Vittorio Moustaki. Rosa and Spera.

I must have stared at that photo and family

tree for at least a few minutes, numb, mute, in complete shock. But then the initial euphoria began to wear off when I noticed a problem—a very big problem. The names were the same, but the family tree on my screen showed that this family was from Trieste, Italy. Savvas's family was from Corfu, Greece. And then, on further inspection, I looked closer at what made the photo so exquisite: the fashions. While I'm certainly not a fashion expert, the gorgeous, flowing draped dresses looked to me more like something someone might wear in the 1920s or '30s, and not the 1940s, when Vittorio and Spera were likely married.

Immediately, I dug deeper, searching through more pages until I found the contact for the family, the man who had so meticulously documented his family's history and uploaded this beautiful wedding photo. His name was Manuel Osmo. I used the MyHeritage messenger tool to message him right away.

Hi Manuel

I found your family tree and I am hoping you can help me. I am looking for the family of Vittorio Moustaki from Corfu, Greece. Vittorio married a woman named Spera who was hidden from the Nazis along with her family on the island of Erikousa.

Can you please tell me if this is the correct family? Thank you so much.

Within minutes, in his perfectly imperfect English, Manuel responded.

Hi
   We are from Corfu to
   I'll ask my old parents and get back to you
   Have a nice day
   Manuel

Manuel did get back to me in a few days, as promised. After speaking to relatives in Israel and in Trieste, he confirmed my fears. The family members in that beautiful wedding photo were not the Spera and Rosa that I was searching for. Within the small, tight-knit Jewish communities of Corfu and Trieste, Spera and Rosa were common names often found in family after family. The beautifully dressed girls in the wedding photo were not our Spera and Rosa.

But while the wedding photo proved to be a false positive, getting in touch with Manuel proved to be the best thing I could have done. Manuel confirmed that yes, his uncle Vittorio Moustaki had indeed been married to a woman named Spera from Corfu. They were in a refugee camp together and eventually made it to Israel with a young girl named Rosa.

The couple had divorced a while later, Manuel confirmed, and no one in his family knew what happened to Spera after the divorce. However, Manuel said, there was one person who might be able to help. Manuel promised he would be in touch soon, right after he spoke to his uncle, Nino Nachshon, a Holocaust survivor from Corfu.

In Los Angeles, television executive Michelle Mendelovitz was quickly climbing the corporate ladder at CBS. Born in California to an Israeli-immigrant mother and Mexican-American father, Michelle will be the first to tell you that hers was not a typical Jewish upbringing. In Michelle's home, Passover seder might consist of matzo and brisket, served alongside fresh tortillas. Each December, Christmas tree lights twinkled festively beside the candlelit menorah.

Michelle's mother, Rachel, who had rich auburn red hair and a penchant for chic clothing, raised her daughter with an independent spirit, a deep devotion to family and an interest in celebrating her family's rich hybrid cultural history. She had grown up in Israel, the youngest of three sisters, and it wasn't always easy for Rachel, raising her daughter in Los Angeles where gang violence, drugs and crime were obstacles of everyday life. But even in the most challenging moments of her childhood, Michelle was grounded by the love and support of her family.

Each Saturday, Michelle would visit with her grandparents Meir and Tikva, pretending to serve them tea from the antique tea set they kept on the side table. Their home was always filled with the aromas of Michelle's favorite foods, which Tikva lovingly prepared for her granddaughter. Sweet almond cakes were drizzled with just the right amount of honey. Savory Israeli *shashuska*, which Michelle could never pronounce but simply referred to as tomato eggs, simmered away on the stove.

While she was never deeply religious, Michelle was very culturally aware and proud of her dual heritage and history. Frustrated with the challenges of life in her hometown and at the expense of a college education in the United States, Michelle found herself at a crossroads. She decided to clear her head by spending two weeks vacationing in Israel, her mother's childhood home.

That two weeks turned into seven years.

Michelle instantly felt at home in Israel, drawn to the energy and culture of the tiny country, which is just about the same size as New Jersey. She felt a kinship with the citizens of Israel, a people who know what it is to suffer, to survive, and because of all they have endured, to celebrate each and every moment of life as if it were a gift. But no matter how hard she searched, there was one thing that Michelle just could not find in Israel. Throughout the entire country, in every town and city she traveled to, Michelle could never find honey-drizzled almond cakes as delicious as the ones her grandmother, Tikva, made.

During her time in Israel, Michelle fell in love literally and figuratively, marrying an Israeli Air Force pilot and carving out a new life with her husband. But after seven years abroad, after being changed by her experiences in Israel, Michelle felt it was time to return to the city of her own childhood, Los Angeles.

Settled now in California, Michelle was raising her own children, and family secrets began to emerge. Rachel told Michelle that one time Tikva mentioned to her that there was a family who saved her, and they should go visit them. Rachel pressed for more information and asked what Tikva meant, saying of course they should go visit this family. But Tikva waved her away and told Rachel to forget it, that it was too far a trip to make. She never spoke of it again.

Michelle and Rachel never learned who or what Tikva was referring to or what she meant by being saved. Tikva took this secret to her grave.

———

It was spring of 2014 and in Tel Aviv, 88-year-old Nino Nachshon was going about his daily routine. On any given day, that routine included yoga, a trip to a nearby park to feed the birds and hours spent swimming in the local pool—his favorite pastime. The years hadn't dulled Nino's love for the water. He still remembers those magical days he spent swimming in the Ionian Sea with friends, growing up on the beautiful island of Corfu. But that was before the Nazis came and everything changed.

Nino refused to listen to those who told him to forget the past, to never speak of the Nazis and those terrible years. While Nino's brother, Isaac, never talked about what happened, Nino felt it was his duty. He felt he had an obligation to share the story of his mother, who was murdered the very first night of their arrival in Auschwitz, and his sister, who survived the camps, only to die of typhus just two days after liberation. He felt the guilt shared by so many survivors, a responsibility to the millions of others who never returned home. Nino had come so close, so very close to being counted as one of the six million who lost their lives. But somehow he had managed to survive Auschwitz and a near-fatal case of typhus. Nino shared every detail of those hellish years with his children, grandchildren, extended family and anyone who would listen. As a tribute to his grandfather, Nino's grandson tattooed Nino's Holocaust number on his own arm. That number, A-15510, once a symbol of hate, now transformed into a symbol of survival, strength and love.

For as far back as he can remember, Manuel Osmo cherished every moment spent in the company of his uncle Nino. Even as a small boy, Manuel loved nothing more than to sit and listen to Nino share stories of their family and life back in Trieste, Italy, where the family lived before moving to Corfu in 1938 to escape the fascists. Just six years later, in Corfu, there would be no escape from the Nazis.

Hanging on the wall of Nino's Tel Aviv home is an old, framed, hand-drawn family tree chart, circle upon circle resembling a sunburst or a multitude of rings on an old tree. Nino explained that this type of circular family chart hung in the home of nearly every Corfiot Jew, before the Nazis came and destroyed everything and everyone. It was Manuel, dedicated to passing down their family's stories and legacy to his three sons, who sat with Nino and painstakingly transferred the handwritten chart, converting it to a digital family tree on MyHeritage.com. It was this that led me to the name Vittorio Moustaki in Manuel's family tree.

When Manuel Osmo phoned Nino and told him of the email he'd received from me, of my search for Nina, Rosa, Spera and Julia, Nino immediately sprang into action. Of course he knew the girls and was well aware of their story.

Each year, on Holocaust Remembrance Day, Israel's surviving Jews of Corfu would meet for a memorial and commemoration ceremony. For many years after the war, Nino would see Savvas's girls at the gathering. Nino knew Rosa had lived in Rehovot and had two sons. He had not seen her in quite some time, but Nino was confident he could help. After all he had lived through, seen and survived, Nino was ready to take on his latest challenge, finding Rosa.

And with that, 88-year-old Nino Nachshon set out to locate an old friend and help solve a 70-year-old mystery.

chapter ten

WHATEVER YOU DO, DON'T CHALLENGE HIM TO A GAME OF CHESS

Israel
Spring 2014

Gilad Japhet, the founder and CEO of MyHeritage, loves nothing more than a twisty and difficult genealogical mystery.

After a stint in Silicon Valley, Gilad had returned home to Or Yehuda, Israel. The plan was to take some much-deserved time off and spend it with his family in their lovely cottage home behind a picturesque picket fence. From his garage office, Gilad planned to use some of his newfound free time to research and document his own family's history. But what started out as a hobby soon morphed into so much more. Unsatisfied with the family history tools he found available, Gilad decided to create his own, writing code he would develop into MyHeritage.com. At first he began with just one employee, and then there were more, working from every corner of his home. In just a few short years, Gilad would grow that garage startup into

MyHeritage, a global leader in family genealogy and family trees, with hundreds of employees and almost 100 million users around the world.

Even as a child, Gilad had always been interested in genealogy, understanding that his obsession with family history was about so much more than family trees. In fact, Gilad's single-minded determination and tenacity helped him accomplish what the German and French governments had tried and failed to do again and again. After he founded MyHeritage, Gilad's genealogical detective work helped reunite dozens of Jewish families with property and art that was stolen from them by the Nazis. He had seen an article one morning as he was having breakfast. Time was running out for the families to reclaim their property, the headline declared. The German government had been looking for the rightful heirs of owners of thousands of stores and factories in eastern Germany that were confiscated by the Nazis. They had exhausted all their leads and declared that statutes of limitation would soon set in, and the money set aside by the German government to compensate the victims would be forfeit. Gilad was angered by this and took it upon himself to search through family trees, Holocaust documents and historical records for all the names on the list, finding many of the rightful owners and their descendants. With great pleasure, Gilad picked up the phone each time he found a match to personally deliver the news to the families.

A *New York Times* reporter who had heard about Gilad's success in Germany asked him to help her find the rightful heirs of works of art on France, as the French government had been unable to do so. Originally looted by the Nazis as part of what was probably the world's largest art robbery during World War II, the priceless paintings were now hanging in the best museums in Paris. The French authorities were successful in reclaiming the looted paintings from Germany, but fell short when it came to locating the French families from whom those paintings had been originally stolen, many of whom were Jewish. Again, Gilad took up the challenge and discovered the owners of all the targeted paintings, successfully restoring them to their rightful owners as a mitzvah, a good deed in Hebrew.

That's the way it is with Gilad Japhet. Once he sets his laser focus on accomplishing even the most daunting task, he will not rest, or sleep, or think of anything else until it gets done. Never issue a challenge to Gilad without expecting it to be taken on and met. Never present a problem to Gilad without expecting it to be solved. And from what I'm told, you should never, ever, challenge him to a game of chess. Don't say you weren't warned.

Aaron Godfrey, vice president of Marketing

for MyHeritage, understands all of this quite well about his boss. Aaron, a father of four young boys, had recently moved to Israel with his wife, Gaby, from their home in Britain when he met Gilad. With a wicked sense of humor, an infectious laugh and an uncanny resemblance to James Corden, Aaron was perfecting his Hebrew and figuring out his next career move when he was called to the cottage for an interview. Driving up to Gilad's house, Aaron at once noticed the beautiful picket fence and the company's intimate setting. It was literally a company about families, operating out of the boss's home. Aaaron fell in love and signed on right away.

After our initial breakfast meeting, Chris Powell had reported back to the MyHeritage offices in Israel, sharing the story of my search with Aaron and introducing us via email. That email led to a phone call, which led to another phone call, and then a few Skype chats. Ultimately, Aaron booked a flight to New York so we could meet in person. Aaron was at once consumed with the story of Savvas and how close I had come to finding the family through Manuel Osmo's MyHeritage family tree. He immediately understood that if anyone could help me solve this mystery and find Savvas's family, it was his boss. And so Aaron pitched the seemingly impossible quest to Gilad: find the family members who vanished 70 years ago from a tiny Greek island and are known by almost nothing but first names. Gilad at once took up the challenge, determined to at last solve the mystery of what happened to Spera, Nina, Rosa and Julia. But it wasn't enough for Gilad to find only the girls. He understood that to truly bring the secret of Erikousa to light, Gilad also had to find the final resting place of Savvas Israel, the Jewish tailor from Corfu.

Gilad asked Aaron to collect and send him all of the available information.

After reviewing the material, Gilad wrote in an email to his staff:

There is little information here, some of it contradictory. My chances of finding relevant information through the available data are unfortunately less than 0.1 percent.

Despite the odds, or perhaps because of them, Gilad Japhet dove right in.

Fueled by the challenge, Gilad stayed up late, poring over documents and data. That very first night he searched through the records of all the women in Israel named Nina who had moved there from Greece after the war. In a mountain of records, he found one Nina with the last name of Israel who was born in Greece in 1915, immigrated to Israel in 1965 and died in 2000.

Her last address was listed as Meor HaGola Street in Tel Aviv. It was a seemingly insignificant detail that Gilad filed away in his mind for later.

After searching through cemetery records, Gilad located Nina's headstone in the Kiryat Shaul Cemetery in Tel Aviv. On a windy weekend, he drove to the cemetery to physically find the gravestone. Normally cemetery records would be available online, but the cemetery's computer system was offline for religious observance. Not one to let minutia get in the way, Gilad scoured the grounds on foot, examining thousands of headstones until he found the one he was looking for.

On Nina's headstone was written her father's name, Shabtai, the Hebrew name for Savvas. Buried beside her was her husband. His name was Rahamin Levy—the same name from the last email I received from Gili at Yad Vashem.

Gilad had found Nina.

He found the final resting place of the woman who hid with my yia-yia in the shadows, who taught her to sew behind locked doors and shuttered windows, and whose whispers lulled my father and aunt Agatha to sleep.

Gilad had found the final resting place of my yia-yia's friend.

As exciting as this discovery was, Gilad knew

it wasn't enough. Not even close. While there is history in headstones, there is legacy in family. Yes, the story of what happened on Erikousa was powerful and extraordinary on its own. But what of the family bloodline? Were there people alive today because of what happened on Erikousa during the war? Had the simple islanders of Erikousa saved future generations with their kindness and compassion? Energized by his discoveries and not content to stop with mere headstones, Gilad pressed on and focused his attention on Spera.

I remember glancing down at my phone when I heard the distinct ping, alerting me that I had a new email. I looked down to see a message from Gilad, with a note at the top: *please make sure you are sitting down when you read this.*

I was sitting down. But even so, I felt out of body, as if I were floating. I scrolled down, not fully processing what I was reading.

I believe I've found Spera and if I'm correct, we have living descendants of her. I found her granddaughter who now lives in the Los Angeles area, and works for CBS!

I must have read that line three or four times over again. And then I read on, not believing what I was seeing, not able to fully grasp what this meant. The email continued:

I said to myself: the name Spera comes from Espera and the full name is Esperanza. She would not use the name Spera in Israel. That's a very foreign name, scarcely used in Israel; only a handful of people in Israel ever went by the first name of Spera, and none of them from Greece. So what is Esperanza in Hebrew? It means "hope." As a linguist, I know the meaning of many names. "Hope" in Hebrew is חקוה which is pronounced Tikva.

My assumption was that if Spera ever made it to Israel, she would have changed her name to Tikva. So I looked for women in Israel called Tikva who were born in Greece.

Fortunately, only 9 results came back. The first one had me absolutely speechless.

That very first Tikva on Gilad's list had an address listed on Meor HaGola in Tel Aviv, just a few doors down from where he'd found Nina. Gilad reasoned that after all they had been through, it made perfect sense that Nina and Spera would want to live near one another. And he was right.

He did it.

Gilad had found Savvas's girls.

chapter eleven

I THINK OUR GRANDMOTHERS WERE FRIENDS

April 10, 2014

My hands shook as I dialed Michelle Mendelovitz's office.

To get her number, I had reached out to my old college friend Kim Izzo-Emmet, who works at CBS, where I myself had worked as a news producer for five years. When I told her that we had found Savvas's girls, Kim was thrilled, and then floored. Kim told me that she knew Michelle and they used to work together. She had Michelle's phone number and email address. Our worlds had not only gotten smaller, they had collided.

The phone rang four times and then went to voicemail.

"Hey Michelle, this is Yvette Corporon—I'm a producer with *Extra*. If you have a moment can you please give me a call? I'm calling about something personal, not business. I think our grandmothers may have known each other and I wanted to just reach out and see if this is the correct family. If you could call me back, that would be great."

I sent an email as well, just in case she might see that sooner. In the subject line I wrote, *I think our grandmothers were friends.*

And then I did what I'm not very good at doing. I waited.

————————

In Los Angeles, Michelle looked down at her computer, reading the subject line, *I think our grandmothers were friends.*

At first, Michelle didn't know what to make of the odd email. As a television executive, you get a constant stream of requests, claims and pitches flooding your in-box. She thought this email was simply one more, another request from a stranger who wanted something from her—until she read the signature at the end of the note. Seeing that I was a senior producer with *Extra*, Michelle thought twice about it. Still, she wasn't quite convinced, not exactly 100 percent sold. But the fact that I also worked in television at least gave her a glimmer of hope. Maybe, just maybe, I wasn't just another kook with a crazy request.

Michelle took a leap of faith and picked up the phone to dial my office.

At the offices of *Extra* in New York City, it was all hands on deck. My colleagues on both coasts had lived through every moment of the search with me. They all knew the story. They knew how long I had searched and how desperately I wanted to locate the family of the girls my yia-yia helped save. They all knew how much was riding on receiving this call from Michelle.

So when the phone rang in the New York bureau of *Extra* and the caller asked for me, announcing that it was Michelle Mendelovitz, my colleagues went into overdrive. I had asked everyone in the office to find me at all costs if and when Michelle called, and my coworkers weren't taking any chances.

"You can take my number," Michelle said. "She can call me back."

"No. She told me to find her. Hold on. Don't hang up," the assistant countered as she called out for me and sent a search party to hunt me down.

"Really, it's okay. She can call me back."

But my friends and colleagues wouldn't have it. "She told me to find her. Just hold on. We're finding her. She told me not to let you go. Don't hang up. We'll find her."

Michelle laughed to herself on the other end of the phone. Intense and crazed television people. Something Michelle knows quite well. It seemed we had a lot in common already.

They found me in the kitchen, where I was making a cup of coffee. I ran to the telephone, picking off my manicure as I sat down. My heart raced as I cradled the receiver to my ear.

"Hello, Michelle."

"Is this Yvette?"

"Yes, hi."

"So you're looking into your family's history?" she asked.

"Yes. I actually wrote a book based on my family's history and that led me on a quest to find a family that my grandmother told me about. And we have reason to believe that it's your family."

I went on, in tears now, trying unsuccessfully to control my emotions and maintain my composure as I struggled to explain to Michelle my yia-yia's story of the Jewish girls who were her friends during the darkest days of the Holocaust.

"We have lots of reasons to believe that one of the women, who we knew as Spera, was actually your grandmother, Tikva."

"Yes, my grandmother was Espera Tikva Levy."

"Yes. Yes!" I shouted into her ear. I could not believe what I was hearing. It was her. We had found her. We'd found Spera. I couldn't wait to hear what Spera told her own granddaughter about Erikousa, the brave islanders who hid her. Maybe, just maybe, Michelle would have a glimmer of a story of a kind woman named Avgerini who sat with Spera night after night in the darkness. Wouldn't it be something if I could hear my yia-yia's story of their nightly visits, their nightly sewing lessons, from Spera's own granddaughter? But my euphoria would soon turn bittersweet.

"Did you know the story?" I asked.

Michelle had no idea what I was talking about.

Before her death in Los Angeles in 1997, Spera never spoke to her family about the war. Her whereabouts during the Holocaust were a mystery to the family, a puzzle Michelle had always wanted to piece together, but with the demands of her busy life and career had never gotten around to doing. Spera never spoke to her family of her father's tailor shop on the beautiful island of Corfu or the vibrant community of Greek Jews of which she was once such a vital part. Spera never spoke of her time on the tiny green island of Erikousa or of the poor islanders who risked everything to hide her from the Nazis. Spera never once uttered the name of her friend, my yia-yia, Avgerini.

I struggled to process what Michelle was saying. But before I could fully digest and comprehend what this meant, Michelle had another unexpected twist to deliver.

"Spera was my step-grandmother," she said.

This meant there was no blood relation.

Spera had loved Michelle as her own. She was the only grandmother Michelle had ever known. But there was no bloodline. There was no legacy tracing Michelle back to what happened on Erikousa, no future generations who owed their existence to the actions of my yia-yia and her friends.

"My mother was the youngest of three sisters. Her sisters were older when Spera came into their lives. They might know more. I'll call my mother and we'll ask them. I'll let you know as soon as I have any news."

Still shaking, I hung up the phone and immediately started praying that Michelle's mother and aunts might somehow remember some tiny details that connected Spera to Erikousa.

Just a few days later, at her family's Passover seder, Michelle shared with her family the story that Spera had kept secret for so long. Spera's family finally learned where she was during the Holocaust and how an entire island community loved her, protected her and risked their lives to save her.

Together, the family pieced together the missing details of their beloved Spera's life. Yes, Spera spoke Greek and had two sisters, Nina and Julia. Now the family finally understood the genesis of those Greek roots. By speaking to various family members, Michelle confirmed that Spera was indeed on board the *Henrietta Szold*, and she did spend time in a British refugee camp with a girl named Rosa. They were two young girls alone, without family and without a chaperone, and they were treated horribly. The few times Spera spoke of her time in the refugee camp she told her family that the conditions were terrible, and of hot water being thrown on them.

Michelle also learned that when Spera finally arrived in Israel, she was told to never look back, that she was reborn the moment she stepped foot on Israeli soil. After so much suffering, who could blame her for never revisiting the past and sharing those painful memories with her family? And so, even so many years after the war, even after the Nazis were long gone, Spera continued to keep the secret of Erikousa, never sharing stories of the tiny island or of the friends who had risked so much to help her survive.

That Passover, as Spera and Michelle's family sat around their seder table celebrating life, my own family was making funeral arrangements. That very weekend, on a rainy Palm Sunday afternoon in the parking lot of a Jewish community center in a bucolic Kansas town, my beautiful 14-year-old nephew, Reat, and his grandfather, Dr. Bill Corporon, were murdered by a neo-Nazi on a mission to kill Jews.

PART THREE

chapter twelve

REAT AND BILL

Kansas
April 13, 2014

On a street of beautiful new homes, the house at the top of the lane was one of the prettiest on the block. Mindy and Len had picked the street, and the lot, and then took their time with the builder and the plans. They wanted to make sure their family's new home would be a paradise for their two young sons, Reat, who was named for his great-grandfather on his father's side, and Lukas. Without question, it was.

Surrounded by the flat, open plains of Kansas all around, the house was built on the very top of a long, sloping hill, a rarity for this part of the heartland. Each morning as the sun rose in the yard, dawn's first rays bled through the leaves and branches of the woods that bordered the property. And each evening, the brilliant colors of a Kansas sunset reflected from the faraway horizon in the home's large front windows.

The hill itself proved a perfect track for bikes and ATVs, which the boys would ride and race up and down the street. They loved nothing more than to load up those ATVs with fishing rods and tackle and drive themselves to the pond down at the base of the hill. Seated on the dock, feet dangling in the water, the boys would bait their hooks, and if they were lucky, reel in a catfish before the sun went down and it was time to drive up the hill toward home.

As if the large yard out back and woods surrounding the property were not enough to make the home a boy's paradise, the house itself was every child's dream come true. With their parents' bedroom located downstairs, Reat and Lukas had the run of the upstairs. Their bedrooms were separated by a shared bathroom. This setup provided easy access and always a few laughs, as well as fistfights, when Reat would prank his younger brother by stealing his clothes and towels when he was in the shower. When Lukas would emerge from the shower and run naked after his brother down the hallway, Mindy knew the boys were at it again. Just down the hall, Reat and Lukas had their own private man cave, a perfect spot to watch movies or play Xbox, or wrestle, even when their parents yelled at them to stop.

All of Mindy and Len's meticulous planning and attention to detail had certainly been worth it. The home at the top of the lane was the perfect place for their boys to grow up.

But it wasn't just the physicality of their home

that made this such an enviable place to raise a family. It was Kansas itself. It was the shared all-American Christian values of a tight-knit community of neighbors and church friends. It was a place where the streets were freshly paved and clean, where families said grace before meals, children were taught to say thank you, ma'am and sir, and where people rarely locked their front doors.

Every day, Mindy thanked God for the blessings of her family. She knew life was good. She had worked very hard to make it that way. With deep dimples, a bright toothy smile and eyes that twinkle when she smiles, Mindy is the pretty all-American girl personified. She is a petite thing, but what Mindy lacks in height, she more than makes up for in determination and intelligence. The former Kansas City Chiefs cheerleader is athletic, spunky and a whole lot of fun. But Mindy also means business, and both Reat and Lukas knew that about their mother. The boys were both well aware that while their mom coud be their best friend, she could also be a no-nonsense disciplinarian who demanded they conduct themselves with the Christian morals and ethics that are the foundation of her belief system.

It was cloudy that Palm Sunday morning when Mindy went into Reat's room to wake him. She knew it wouldn't take much prodding to get him out of bed that day. As she leaned in to kiss him good morning, Reat told his mom that it was all right to hug him, but cautioned her about getting too close to his pillow, since he had drooled on it in his sleep.

Shortly afterward, dressed in his suit, tie and hat, Reat came downstairs into the kitchen. It was the day he had been waiting for. This was the first year he was old enough to audition for *KC Superstar*, the closest thing to *American Idol* in the Kansas City area. He had been working for months with his vocal coach to prepare for this audition. And he was ready.

Reat was a freshman at Blue Valley High School in Stilwell, Kansas. Reat was quick with a hug and a flash of his broad, toothy smile, which showed off those famous Corporon dimples. An Eagle Scout candidate, honor student, member of the debate team and church volunteer with a very active social life, Reat had a lot on his plate. But even so, even with everything he had going on, there was one thing this all-American boy loved to do more than anything else. Since that very first time he had stepped out onstage dressed as the baby elephant bird in *Seussical the Musical* when he was just four years old, this handsome boy had loved to perform. And above all, Reat Griffin Underwood loved to sing.

There was a lot going on in the household that day. But as always, Mindy had it handled.

The plan was for Mindy and Len to take Lukas to his lacrosse game. Mindy's dad, Dr. Bill Corporon, aka Popeye, would take Reat to the Jewish Community Campus, where the audition was being held. Everyone would meet for 5 p.m. Palm Sunday church services afterward, followed by a family dinner to celebrate Mindy's brother, Tony's, birthday.

It made perfect sense that Bill would be the one to take Reat to his audition. After all, Bill was Reat's grandpa, loudest cheerleader, musical coach and biggest fan. But Reat and Bill shared so much more than just a love of music. They had shared pretty much everything since Mindy's marriage to Reat's dad ended and Mindy moved back in with her parents when Reat was just four weeks old. From the very beginning, Reat knew even then that Popeye was so much more than just a grandfather.

It was Reat who began calling Bill "Popeye," a name fitting Bill's larger-than-life, take-no-prisoners, strongman personality. Mindy married Len when Reat was just a toddler, and Len stepped in to love and raise Reat as his own. But Bill always remained a father figure in Reat's life. When Mindy and Len settled in Kansas, Bill and his wife, Melinda, moved from their home in Oklahoma to Kansas too so they could be closer to their grandchildren. Bill's devotion to Reat became a running joke among members of the Corporon family. Our in-boxes were filled with long emails from Bill, documenting every milestone and moment of Reat's existence. The entire extended family laughed, shook our heads and sometimes rolled our eyes as we read pages upon pages of Bill's stories and the minutia of everything from diaper changes and potty training to teaching Reat to sing and to hunt. And while Bill's lengthy emails were a source of amusement for the family, there was no question that each one of us wished we had someone in our lives as devoted to us as Bill was to Reat.

As they waited for Bill to pick up Reat that Sunday morning, Mindy stood in the kitchen, admiring her handsome boy. Out back, the family's newly installed pool was filling with water. Reat couldn't wait to properly christen the pool and have his friends over for their first pool party. Mindy was just as excited as her son. Nothing gave her greater joy than to see Reat and Lukas laughing and living their lives surrounded by their friends, family and church community. It was everything she had worked so hard for, all she'd ever wanted—for them to be together as a family, living life in their home at the top of the lane. There was so much to look forward to, so much to be grateful for. The school year was ending and next month Reat would turn 15. He had auditioned and won a role in the *Tom Sawyer* production at the theater in the park and was also in Starlight Stars. It was to be a magical summer filled with friends, pool parties, Eagle Scouts and performances. While no one's life is ever truly perfect, their life was indeed blessed.

As they waited that Palm Sunday for Bill to arrive, Mindy asked Reat to run through his songs once again. You never had to ask Reat to sing more than once. He was always happy to oblige.

He'd prepared two songs for the audition and had been tirelessly rehearsing to make sure they were perfect. First he sang "On the Street Where You Live" from *My Fair Lady*. And then Reat sang the second song he had worked so hard to prepare.

When I'm gone
    You're gonna miss me when I'm gone . . .

Bill arrived shortly afterward, commenting on how nice the pool looked before he and Reat headed for the door.

"Good luck. I love you." Mindy kissed him good-bye.

"I love you too," Reat said to his mom.

Those were the last words Mindy heard her son speak.

Reat would never get to swim in his new pool.

He would never come home again.

Storm clouds rolled in and the skies above Stilwell, Kansas, turned a muddy gray that Sunday afternoon. Lightning was spotted in the distance, and as a precaution, Lukas's lacrosse game was cancelled.

Mindy looked at the time. As disappointed as she was that she would not get to watch Lukas play lacrosse, she knew this meant she could make it the short distance to the Jewish Community Campus in time to watch Reat's audition. Any other day, Mindy would have called Reat and Bill to let them know that she was on her way, but she didn't have her phone with her that afternoon. A week before, she had confiscated Reat's phone as punishment for a recent bout of teenage sass. When Reat needed a pitch pipe for his audition, Mindy downloaded one to her phone and gave it to him to use. Without her phone, Mindy had no way of reaching Bill and Reat to tell them she was on the way. If she hadn't confiscated Reat's phone, if she'd had her own phone with her, maybe Mindy would have called her son or her dad. Maybe they would have stopped to rendezvous somewhere and driven to the JCC together. Maybe they would have arrived through a different entrance, or maybe just a few minutes later. Maybe they would not have pulled into the parking lot exactly when they did. Or maybe Bill would have just headed home and not gone to the

JCC at all that day. Those maybes have haunted Mindy ever since.

The air had turned cooler by the time Mindy pulled her car into the parking lot. She spotted Popeye's truck right away, but something wasn't right. The doors to the red truck were opened and Mindy saw her father lying on the ground. She barely managed to throw her car into park before she raced across the parking lot toward him. As Mindy ran she felt a physical change in her body, a shift. And she knew. She knew he was gone. She thought maybe he'd had a heart attack. Maybe it was the fall that killed him. And then, once she'd stopped running, as she stood looking down at her father, Mindy heard a voice. The voice spoke to her. It was a full sentence, clear as day, as if someone were standing there with her, right beside her.

"Your father is in heaven. Go find Reat."

She knew immediately that this was the voice of God. She knew in that moment that Bill was gone from his body and from this earth. He was in heaven. Mindy is a woman of deep faith, and she knew these things with every fiber of her being. As she looked down to see her father lying on the ground at her feet, Mindy knew without a doubt that she would see him again one day, that they would be reunited in heaven.

But for now, here on earth, Mindy needed to find her boy. She needed to find Reat.

Mindy ran around to the other side of the truck, unable to comprehend what she was seeing. Reat was there. Her sweet boy was there. Reat was lying on the ground on a small patch of grass in the parking lot. He was being cradled by two men Mindy did not know.

"What happened? What happened?" Mindy screamed.

"Who are you?" a third man answered as he grabbed her from behind and pulled her away. She wanted to be with her son. The strange man was pulling her away and Mindy needed to be with Reat.

"That's my dad and he's dead and this is my son. Is he dead?"

"We're not sure. We don't know."

Another man came and pulled Mindy even farther back, even farther away from where she needed to be, there, beside her boy.

Mindy turned her head and saw the broken glass, the door of the JCC that had been shattered by gunfire. Those shards and fragments at once made the situation nightmarishly clear. It was not a heart attack that killed her dad. He had been shot. And Reat was there too, lying on the ground as strangers held him and tended to him. There were little drops of blood on his face.

The men sat Reat up. *That's good, that's good,* she thought, hopeful that this was a good sign, praying for her son, praying that this must be a good sign.

But then she watched as the men wrapped her sweet boy's head and her hopes shattered like the glass all around her.

"You have to call someone," one of the men said, and handed Mindy his phone.

———————

Len was driving Lukas home from the cancelled lacrosse game when his phone rang, showing an unfamiliar number. He answered the call to find Mindy screaming on the other end.

"You need to come to the Jewish Community Campus immediately. There's been a shooting . . . My dad's dead and I don't know if Reat is alive."

Len tried to comprehend what Mindy was saying, but it made no sense; Mindy's words didn't make any sense. Lukas looked at Len and asked what was going on, getting more anxious and scared by the moment.

"Something happened to Popeye and Reat and we need to get there immediately," Len said as he turned the car away from home and sped toward the Jewish Community Campus. Just a short while later he saw flashing lights and a police car and turned his car into the parking lot. Lukas and Len jumped out of the car and raced toward the scene. They saw a body on the ground.

"I think this is my family," Len told the officer.

But Len was wrong.

The body they saw lying on the ground was not Reat or Bill. This was not the parking lot of the Jewish Community Campus. In the chaos, Len had gone to the wrong location. He pulled into the parking lot of the Village Shalom nursing home. The person they saw lying on the ground was Terri LaManno.

None of them understood this at the time, but Reat and Bill were not the shooter's only victims that day. After he shot Bill and Reat, he then went to the nursing home and found his third victim. Terri was a devout Roman Catholic, a loving wife and mother of three. An occupational therapist who worked with visually impaired children, Terri was as deeply committed to her patients as she was to her family and her faith. It was Terri's belief in God, her unwavering devotion to her faith, that had helped get her through many challenging moments and guided her through life's most difficult decisions. And now, 25 years after the most difficult decision of her life, Terri's prayers had been answered. Just six months before, Terri's phone rang and she answered to hear the words "I think I'm your daughter." Terri and her husband, Dr. Jim LaManno, were reunited with the daughter they had given up for adoption before they were married, when as a young couple they were still unsure of their future together. Terri and Jim eventually married and went on to have two more children and build a loving home together. Yet they always dreamed of one day finding the daughter they loved so deeply but had not been prepared to raise. Their firstborn child, their beautiful daughter Jennifer, had finally found them. Terri and Jim's other two children were doing incredibly well and were exceptionally close to their parents. Their son, Gian, was thriving in college, and their daughter Alissa was on her way home that very afternoon, excited to start nursing school and spend time with her best friend, her mom. Terri and Jim had been through so much together, had worked so hard for so many years, and now it had all paid off. Their family was reunited, complete and happy. On Tuesday, Terri and Jim would celebrate their twenty-fifth wedding anniversary and all of the many blessings in their lives. They had so much to celebrate, so much to be grateful for and look forward to. But first Terri would stop at the Village Shalom nursing home to visit her ailing mother, as she did each Sunday, before meeting the family for Palm Sunday mass and dinner that evening.

Then a gunshot rang out in a second Jewish facility parking lot that Sunday afternoon, shattering another beautiful family, derailing so many dreams. They'd had only six months together, reunited as family, and now Terri was gone.

Len and Lukas stood in the rain and looked

down at the ground to see Terri lying there. In that moment they didn't know who she was or what had happened to her, only that this poor woman was somehow tragically connected to Bill and Reat.

Panicked now, Len desperately tried to make sense of what was happening. But then his phone rang again. It was Micky Blount, the man who had lent Mindy his phone. Micky told Len that he was at the wrong location, that he needed to come to the Jewish Community Campus. Grabbing Lukas, Len raced to the car and sped down the street to the JCC. By now the street was closed and there were more police and emergency vehicles on the scene.

Sitting in the car beside his father, Lukas wanted to cry, but he tried so hard to fight back the tears. He looked out the window and locked eyes with a young couple on the street. The young woman smiled at him, but Lukas couldn't smile back. He could only fight harder to keep the tears from coming. The previous night, Reat and Lukas had gotten into a fight, a full-on physical fight, as brothers do sometimes. That morning, when he woke up, Lukas was still mad. He saw Reat but didn't speak to him. He'd had the chance, but they never spoke. And now, sitting in the front seat of the car beside his father, Lukas would do anything, give anything, to see his brother again, to have a chance to speak to him again, to watch Kevin Hart videos together again. Lukas was 12 years old. He was supposed to be on a lacrosse field, laughing and playing with his friends, not in the middle of a crime scene, scared and frantic, searching and praying for his brother and grandfather.

As the JCC went into lockdown, the men insisted Mindy come inside the building for her own safety. There was still an active shooter out there. She turned to one of the officers and asked him to please cover her father with a tarp so her mother, Melinda, and the rest of the family did not have to see him like that when they showed up.

Len and Lukas arrived at the JCC. They saw the police cars and the flashing lights and there was no mistake this time: it was Bill's red truck amidst all those lights and officers. Lukas and Len ran to the front door. They had to get to Mindy to try and make sense of this madness. But none of it made sense.

In the chaos, Len called Melinda and Mindy's brothers, Tony and Will, and told them there was a shooting and they needed to get to the JCC immediately. But Len didn't tell them Bill was dead. He couldn't bring himself to say the words. Everyone had the same reaction to the news that there had been a shooting. Bill was a licensed gun carrier and an avid hunter. *There must have been some kind of accident,* everyone thought. Maybe his gun had gone off accidentally, or maybe Bill had shot someone. *Dear Lord, what if Bill shot someone?* Melinda thought as she raced to the scene.

There were so many unanswered questions, but there was one thing everyone knew for certain—the one thing of which there was no question. Bill would have done anything, shot anyone, or sacrificed his own life to protect Reat. Bill was a proud member of the NRA and had a licensed gun with him that day. But Bill was ambushed as he exited the car. He never had the chance.

Melinda was escorted inside, downstairs to the basement where Mindy was waiting, frantic. As she burst through the door, Mindy was at once overcome with unbearable grief and also guilt. "I'm so sorry. I'm so sorry," she repeated again and again and cried to her mother. *What if I had driven?* she thought. *If I had driven, then Dad would still be alive.*

Melinda struggled to make sense of what Mindy was saying, of what she had seen in the parking lot before she was ushered inside and to the basement. As she worked to comprehend what was happening, Melinda had one heartbreaking question for her daughter. "Is that your father under the tarp?"

And then another: "Where's Reat?"

"What do you mean, where's Reat?" Mindy replied. "He was outside on the grass."

But as Melinda pulled into the parking lot, she had seen an ambulance pulling away.

Tony arrived next. The skies had opened up and he was soaked from rain. Mindy and Melinda both felt sick, waiting for news, waiting to be taken back upstairs so they could find Reat. Tony punched a bathroom stall. Len and Lukas were ushered inside, downstairs to the basement where the family waited, desperate for answers.

As they waited, another man from the JCC approached Lukas and asked him if he wanted to play basketball or swim. *What an odd thing to say,* Lukas thought. But there are no instruction manuals for comforting a 12-year-old boy whose grandfather and brother have been shot in a hate crime at a JCC on a Sunday afternoon in a quiet Kansas town.

Again and again the family demanded to know what happened and where Reat had been taken.

It wasn't supposed to happen like this. Mindy was his mother. She was supposed to be the one beside him, holding his hand, comforting him, riding in the ambulance with him. She ran upstairs searching for answers, and for Reat. Two new officers were stationed at the door now, officers who had no idea who Mindy was, that it was her father under the tarp, her son in the ambulance.

"The adult who was taken to the hospital had

177

no ID on him," one of the officers said. "I'm sorry we can't tell you where they took him."

Mindy was screaming now. "That is not an adult! That's a fourteen-year-old boy! And he's my son!"

And then he was gone.

It was supposed to be just another Sunday, one activity among many scheduled that day. It was nothing more than a simple high school singing competition in a picturesque Kansas town. At a tan building surrounded by a parking lot, located on a long, straight road that cut through the heartland, just a short drive from the house at the top of the lane. Reat was supposed to be inside that building onstage, and Bill was supposed to be there, clapping and cheering him on from his seat.

Mindy should have been there too, on her feet, wildly cheering her son. Instead, as the rain turned torrential, she was ushered into a small private room at the hospital with Len, Lukas, Melinda and Tony. Mindy's eldest brother, Will, was driving in from his home in Oklahoma and had yet to arrive.

This is not good, Mindy thought. *You never want to be ushered into the small room.*

A rabbi came into the room with them. *We're not Jewish,* Mindy thought.

A surgeon entered the room next. His gray hair

was tied into a ponytail. And then the surgeon spoke, dividing life into before and after.

"The young man that we had in the ambulance lost his life. We couldn't . . . we could not save him. He lost his heart rate in the ambulance and we could not resuscitate him."

The room erupted into chaos. Lukas fell onto the floor. Last night they had argued. This morning they had ignored each other. Last night he had a brother. Now he was an only child.

Bill and Reat had always shared a special, inexplicable bond. From the time Mindy showed up at Bill and Melinda's home when Reat was just four weeks old, they had been inseparable. And now they were still together, but they were gone.

Mindy knew without a doubt that her son and father were together in heaven. But that didn't take the pain away, not even for a moment, not even for a woman of unwavering faith like Mindy. She wanted to be with them. She didn't want to be here, in this cold, small room without them. She wanted to be taken up to heaven with them. But even so, even through the horror and the pain and unspeakable grief, Mindy did what she always does. What her father had taught her to do, and what she taught her children to do. Mindy thought of others.

Reat was 14 years old and had recently got his driver's permit. On it, he listed himself as an organ donor. Even in those first devastatingly chaotic moments, Mindy asked the hospital staff about donating his organs. She was told that since Reat's heart had stopped, they could not honor his wish. In an afternoon of inexplicable pain, this wounded Mindy in a different way. This was too much. She became irate. Surely there had to be some way to make it work, to save a life or help another child. Even in the immediate moments following her son's death, Mindy knew that God must have a plan, there had to be a reason and a purpose. Something good had to come from all this horror and pain. After insisting and pressing the matter with the hospital staff, another nurse came in and finally she was told that yes, there was hope. Since Reat's heart had stopped in the ambulance not all of his organs could be donated, but they would in fact be able to make tissue donations and possibly some organs could be salvaged. Reat's wish to be an organ donor would be honored. The loss of his life would save others.

"Thank you," Mindy said, feeling some modicum of peace.

But that wouldn't be the last time Mindy put her unimaginable pain aside to help others through that terrible, terrible day. That evening, as their grieving and numb family and friends began to gather at Bill and Melinda's house, Mindy heard that teenagers were gathering for a prayer vigil nearby. She knew she had to go.

When Mindy was 15, her friend Kyle had passed away, and she remembered well the pain and the confusion. Even as she grappled with the overwhelming reality that she was now a mother who had lost a child, and also a daughter who had lost her father, Mindy still remembered the searing pain and confusion of being a teen-ager who'd lost a friend. She remembered the darkness, and wanted to tell those kids that despite what they felt in the moment, the sun would come up again. Despite the overwhelming swirl of emotions, life would go on.

Life had to go on.

The air had turned brisk and it was unusually cool that night. Mindy grabbed her father's beloved red Oklahoma University sweatshirt from his closet and pulled it on. A dear friend drove her to the vigil.

She sat there and listened as the adults spoke in an effort to comfort the teens. Mindy had been there too, and she knew. She knew their words were not helping and she knew what she had to do. "I need to speak," she told a friend. Dressed in her father's red sweatshirt, Mindy stepped up to the podium to comfort the students. These were the friends who should be laughing and swimming with Reat in their new pool, not crying and grieving the loss of a beautiful young man taken by a cowardly act of hate.

With one hand clutching the podium, the other

holding her friend's hand, Mindy spoke. She intended only to speak to those present, to the friends, classmates and their parents assembled in the room. What Mindy didn't know was that there would be television cameras trained on her that evening and that the impact of her words would reach far beyond that room.

"My name is Mindy Corporon, and I am the daughter of the gentleman who was killed and the mother of the son who was killed."

The gasps and cries reverberated across the room as she said those words. But Mindy paid no mind. She had a message, and she was intent on delivering it.

"I just want to be here with students. I wanted to tell you how much Reat loved school, and he loved acting and singing, and he was at the JCC to try out for a theater program for *KC Superstar*. My dad got elected to take him because my mom was busy with other cousins and I was with my other son at a lacrosse game. And we were in life. And we were having life. And I want you all to know that we're gonna have more life and I want you all to have more life . . . I just appreciate you being here. It's just very helpful. Thank you. God bless you."

Mindy went home that night and climbed into Reat's bed, laying her head on the pillow scented with the drool he had warned her about just hours before. She prayed for God to take her away, and bring her into heaven with her son and father. She felt out of her own body, as if physically willing herself there, into heaven. The pain on earth was too real, too consuming. There was no pain in heaven.

As night turned to day, Mindy finally drifted off to something resembling some sort of sleep. And that's when she saw him. Mindy saw him. She saw Reat. Reat was with Kyle, Mindy's friend who passed away when he was just a teen. Kyle had his arm around her son. Kyle had found Reat, just as Mindy knew he would. They were together in heaven.

And then the sun did come up again, as Mindy had promised it would.

Images of the petite, dimpled, heartbroken mother attending a vigil for her son and father, wearing a red sweatshirt and comforting a room of teenagers, were transmitted across the globe. Mindy didn't know it yet, but her calling from God was taking shape. Her son and father's deaths would not be in vain. Mindy's message of love had already touched millions around the world.

The first ripple had formed. And it was just the beginning.

chapter thirteen

WHEN WORDS DON'T MAKE SENSE

Massachusetts and New York
April 13, 2014

Dad said to pull over and call him."

I glanced over at Christiana, buckled into the front seat beside me. The last thing I wanted to do was pull off the highway and delay the three-hour drive home any longer. Several weeks ago, I had promised to drive Christiana and her two friends to Boston for a concert. It was one of those parental promises you make in the moment, then wonder why you ever agreed to as the day gets closer. It was the worst possible time for me to be away for an entire day. To say I was overwhelmed would be an understatement. I felt like I was drowning in work and had taken on too much. My book had just been released and I had a television interview scheduled early the following morning with my old friend Rosanna Scotto on *Good Day New York*, never mind the laundry that was piled up at home and the grocery shopping and cooking that still needed to get done.

But with all that I had on my plate, every unchecked box on my endless to-do list, there was still one thing that consumed me more than anything. I was so very close to finding Rosa's sons, the two people whose very existence could be traced back to the actions and bravery of the islanders of Erikousa. Since our initial phone call just three days before, Michelle and I had corresponded several times. She, like Nino, knew that Rosa had two sons who lived in Rehovot, Israel. And like Nino, Michelle was determined to help me find them.

I was still struggling to juggle it all when Christiana reminded me that I had promised to drive her to Boston that day. It was the last thing I wanted to do, but working mother's guilt got the best of me, yet again. No matter how busy I was in my life, there was never any question of my priorities. My children came first. They had to, always. And so there I was, in Massachusetts for the day with Christiana and her two best friends.

In the end, it turned out to be a fun and productive day after all. While the girls were inside the concert venue listening to their favorite band, I sat in a little booth at the adjacent Mexican restaurant, working on my laptop and waiting for the show to finish. As stressed as I was about everything, seeing how happy Christiana and her friends were made the trip well worth it. I worked on my computer for hours, taking breaks to dip in and out of the concert hall, checking on the girls and making sure they were safe. In between preparing for my interview the following morning and firing off emails, I scanned the latest headlines and noticed a story about three people who were killed in an anti-Semitic shooting in Kansas that afternoon. I remember seeing the photo, a haunting image of a red truck, windows shattered, surrounded by police tape in the rain. It made me think of Michelle and Spera and of Rosa's family, with whom I was so close to finally connecting. I thought of the devastation, suffering and death, of so many generations lost, for no other reason than because they were born Jewish.

Dear God, how are things like this still going on? Those poor families. How awful! How can people still, to this day, hate others so deeply just because they are Jewish? I thought to myself, glancing at the headline, not bothering to click on it or read the story. I had work to do. I was busy, far too busy to read an article about an anti-Semitic attack that happened so many miles away. Besides, those things only happened to other people.

And after all, we aren't even Jewish. It had nothing to do with us.

We were now on our way back home, and Christiana was a snapshot of 12-year-old bliss. Her brace-face smile was wide and on full display as she laughed with her two very best friends, who giggled in the backseat behind us. Christiana was happy, and therefore so was I. It was the kind of moment we mothers live for—a split second of time that you want to freeze and bottle and hold and go back to when your child is upset or distressed. But perfect moments in our children's lives can't be frozen. We can't keep them there no matter how badly we want to, no matter how hard we pray for the hands of the clock to move backwards so we can see those beautiful, innocent smiles again. Innocence is so finite, and so very fleeting. Sometimes the phone rings, shattering a perfect moment, drowning out a child's laughter. Sometimes the message you hear takes away their innocence, dividing life into *before* and *after.*

"Dad said to pull over and call him," Christiana said again.

I pulled the car over into a rest stop along the Massachusetts Turnpike and called Dave. Christiana and her friends were laughing and looking at photos and reliving every moment of what they had been up to till that moment, an afternoon of perfect memories.

In a controlled tone, Dave spoke. "Something happened in Kansas. There's been a shooting. Reat and Bill were shot."

It's a surreal thing to hear someone you love using those words to tell you about someone you love. It's as if you can hear what's being said to you, you can understand each individual word, but when placed together, the words don't make any sense. *Shooting. Shot. Gun. Accident.* Dangerous, ugly words. These are words you read in the newspaper or hear on the news, words I myself wrote countless times as a news producer. Words you use to fill a page, fulfill a word count, recount something that happened to *someone else.*

Other people's families. Not mine.

"Yvette, did you hear me? There's been a shooting. Reat and Bill were shot."

It's amazing how many thoughts can race through your mind, how many scenarios can play out within a mere moment of silence.

Bill and Reat are hunters. He must mean there was some type of hunting accident. Of course that's what he meant. I wondered if it was serious enough for them to go to the hospital. *Oh goodness, can you imagine what Dr. Bill is putting those poor doctors through?* I could picture him there, lying in a hospital bed, even if he'd injured himself, calling the shots and telling the attending doctors how to treat Reat. *There is no way,* I thought, *that Dr. Bill would let another doctor take the lead in treating Reat.*

Is Mindy even home? I wondered. Just a few weeks ago she'd told me about a trip to Mexico that she and Len were planning. *I hope she's back,*

I thought, thinking how horrible it would be for Mindy to be away if Reat was hurt. *I really hope she's back.* What could be worse for a mother than to be away when her son was injured?

No, she must be home by now. The Mexico trip was last week. I thought Mindy must be at the hospital right now, sitting at her son's bedside. I thought about how Reat was probably laughing from his bed, those dimples on display.

"Did you hear me? Reat and Bill have been shot."

Dave continued speaking words that made no sense, words that had no business being placed side by side in a sentence. Displaced rage flared up. How could Dave say this to me? What was wrong with him? This was supposed to be a happy day, a day of smiles and laughter. I watched Christiana's beautiful, bright smile turn before my eyes.

"Mom. What is it? What's wrong?" my girl asked. "What happened?"

"Yvette . . ."

"But they're okay, right?" I more insisted than asked, because they had to be. There was no other option.

Silence.

"Dave . . ."

Again, silence.

I didn't want silence. I wanted an answer. I needed an answer. I needed confirmation that everything was fine. That this accident was nothing more than an inconvenient blip. Something that wouldn't really affect this perfect all-American family living their perfect all-American lives. Because to me, that's what they were. They were the family I had dreamed of all those lonely afternoons when I was stuck in Yia-yia's basement surrounded by black-clad women speaking only Greek, eating food my American friends couldn't pronounce.

Dr. Bill was my husband Dave's first cousin. So technically, Reat wasn't really my nephew, but I never understood all this American "third cousin twice removed" stuff. In the Greek culture, older relatives are simply called aunts and uncles and younger relatives are called nieces and nephews. I had always considered and called Reat my nephew, no matter how many times Dave tried to correct me and tell me we were cousins. In that extensive Corporon clan, Dave had twenty-three first cousins. But in that large extended family, there were a few of Dave's relatives that I had gotten to know better and grown closer to than the rest. Dr. Bill was one of them. Maybe it was the endless emails he fired off to the family, pontificating about politics, world events and of course, every detail of Reat's life. Maybe it was the way he rocked his signature look, that bushy mustache and that loud patterned shirt stretched over his belly and those ever-present suspenders, that always made him stand out. Maybe it was the way he and Melinda gushed and oohed and ahhed and lapped up every morsel of the traditional Greek meal I cooked for them when they came to visit us in New York. Or how they opened their home to the entire Corporon family each time we converged on Kansas for a family reunion. I remember Christiana, at just three years old, sitting on the pristine white carpet of Dr. Bill and Melinda's brand-new home. Christiana's toddler fingers shoved juicy red cherries into her mouth, one after another, red juice dripping down her face, threatening to stain that perfect snow-white carpet. Bill and Melinda just watched her and smiled, asking if she'd like some more.

To me, they were a family of standouts. Reat, Mindy, Lukas, Len, Bill and Melinda and the entire family were Boomer Sooner and God Bless America. They were blue eyes and dimples, church picnics followed by football on Sundays, Kansas City barbecue and stars and stripes proudly waving in the yard. They welcomed me with open arms and made this daughter of immigrants feel like I belonged in their family. In our family. Accepted. Loved. One big American family.

But the Kansas Corporons were so much more than my version of Americana. They were goodness personified. Whenever we spent any time together, I walked away with the feeling that I wanted and needed to be a better person. *I need to be more like them,* I always thought. Dr. Bill was larger than life, an imposing man whose broad belly was as large as his personality and opinions. A doctor who loved the science of medicine and the psychology of helping people, a beloved and respected patriarch both at home and in the hospital. He had married his high school sweetheart, and he and Melinda looked forward to celebrating their fiftieth anniversary together in just a few months. He was a man who got down on the floor and played with his grandchildren, who got dirty and silly with them. He was a teacher, a straight shooter, an outspoken conservative Republican, a fiercely and proudly American card-carrying member of the NRA. He lived for his family and loved them without bounds. Bill and Mindy had always shared a special bond, closer than that of any father and daughter I had ever seen. It was the kind of hands-on, go-to-ballgames, do-things-together-and-talk-about-anything relationship I prayed Christiana and Dave would also have.

Mindy was the mother we all strive to be, loving, devoted, no-nonsense and yet really, really fun. I never knew how she managed to be so present in the boys' everyday lives and activities while still devoting so much of herself to volunteering and charity work, not to mention running her business. It's not that I spent tons of time with the Kansas Corporons. But I had visited with them a handful of times for family reunions. Each time I found myself in Kansas for another reunion, I felt like a fish out of water. It wasn't even so much the flat landscape or the strip-mall culture I found so hard to get used to. For me, the biggest culture shock of life in the heartland was the food. One time we went to a favorite aunt's home for lunch and were presented a first course of salad. That salad consisted of canned fruit in Jell-O served in a bundt mold. The entire Corporon clan thought my East Coast Greek-American confusion in moments like this was great entertainment. And although outwardly our lives and experiences had been so different, Mindy and I had grown close, forming a bond unique to working mothers. We understood each other, even when no one else did.

We had plans, Mindy and I. The last time we'd seen each other was just a few weeks before, when she was in New York on business and we met for coffee. We sat at the Starbucks near my office and talked about our futures, and the futures of our children. Her wealth management business was growing exponentially and my lifelong dream of publishing my novel was finally coming true. It was happening for both of us. All of our hard work and sacrifices were finally paying off.

That afternoon in Starbucks, Mindy told me

Reat was fascinated with my job as a television producer. We talked about how much fun it would be to have him come visit, to stay with us in New York and come out on a few shoots with me, maybe even to a red-carpet event. He would love that, Mindy said. And so would I. We talked about so many things that last time we met for coffee. I had always felt close to Mindy. She and I had always connected, but it's often hard to stay that way when you're both working moms running in a million directions with so many miles between you. Yet something had shifted recently. It was as if the two frenetic working mothers finally had a chance to sit and catch our breath, to be still for a moment, as if the finish line was finally in sight. When you're the mother of small children you live in the moment; it's so often hard to see past the next feeding or diaper change, often impossible to find time to sit and have a meaningful adult conversation. But our children were getting older now. It was getting easier. Mindy and I both felt the time had finally come. We could start making plans, travel to see each other more, spend more time together as a family. We talked about how tough the tween years could be and how wonderful it was that Reat and Christiana had bonded. Wasn't it amazing how social media managed to connect the kids, to bridge all those miles between them?

Mindy and I had so much to talk about. We

could talk for days. There was never any silence between us.

And now Dave was silent on the other end of the phone.

Silence only happens to other people, not hardworking, churchgoing American families from Kansas. Not my family.

Christiana was staring at me now. "Mom. What is it?"

"Yvette, do you hear what I'm saying?" Dave spoke slowly and deliberately. "No, they are not okay."

"Mom, what is it?!" Christiana demanded.

I had no idea what to say or do. The blood drained from my face. I felt like I was falling. I was falling deeper and deeper down a black hole as I sat in my car, buckled into the driver's seat at a rest stop in Massachusetts. If I didn't say it out loud, maybe it wouldn't be real. If I didn't repeat it, then it couldn't possibly be true.

"Yvette, are you hearing me?"

"Mom, Mom, what is it? Mom!"

I would have done anything, given anything if I didn't have to put those hateful words together.

I then looked at my baby girl. And finally, I spoke.

"It's Reat and Dr. Bill. There's been a shooting."

"Mom, are they . . ."

"Yvette, are you hearing me? Reat and Bill are dead."

"Mom, answer me. Is Reat dead? Mom!"

I stared at my little girl. Wordless. Silence again. She knew the answer before I uttered a sound.

"He died, honey. Reat died."

Everything was still.

Christiana and I locked eyes and the girls in the backseat gasped and reached for one another and for Christiana. My little girl screamed and started shaking and repeating the word *no* again and again. I reached out to hold her, to make it better, because that's what we do as mothers— we make it better. But there was nothing I could do to make this better, for Christiana, for Mindy, for Reat or Dr. Bill, for Lukas, for anyone.

"No. No. No. *No!*" Christiana screamed, and then she opened the car door and ran. She ran across the parking lot of a rest stop off the Massachusetts Turnpike as people slammed on their brakes to avoid her and others stared and pointed.

I ran across the parking lot after her and grabbed my little girl, pulling her to safety and holding her tightly to me. More people stared, more pointing and whispering as I begged her, pleaded with her, to get back in the car. When she was little, I would simply scoop her up in my arms and kiss the boo-boos away. I would sleep on the floor of her bedroom when she was sick and pulled her into bed with me, wrapping my body around hers to keep the monsters away, when nightmares woke her. Now in the parking lot, I held my broken girl so close to me, but I was powerless. I couldn't look under the bed or search the closet and convince her there was nothing to be afraid of. This time the monsters were real. I held Christiana close as she leaned into me and we walked together back to the car.

Before and after. It was as simple as that.

What was normally a three-hour drive home took seven hours that night. There was a fatal accident ahead of us and we sat, not moving, on the shut-down Massachusetts Turnpike for hours. Whenever I felt my rage or frustration flare up, I reminded myself that my children were safe. We would be getting home, no matter how many hours later.

My children were safe. Mindy's child was not.

When we arrived home at 1 a.m., Dave and I finally had a chance to talk, and he told me what he knew. This was a hate crime, an anti-Semitic attack. Reat and Bill and a 54-year-old woman named Terri LaManno were killed because the shooter thought they were Jewish. The shooter was a white supremacist who had a long history with the KKK and a deep, twisted hatred for Jews. His health was failing, and knowing he likely didn't have much longer to live, he wanted to know what it felt like to kill Jews before he died. He went to the Jewish Community Campus that day hunting for Jews. The parking lot was quiet, and after a while he got into his car to leave. But then Dr. Bill's car pulled in with Reat in the passenger's seat. Thinking this was his chance to kill more than one Jew, the shooter turned his car around and drove back into the parking lot. He shot Bill first as he was exiting his car. And then he shot Reat. He then drove to Village Shalom and shot Terri.

Police found him shortly afterward in the parking lot of a local elementary school. He asked the officers how many he'd managed to kill and then shouted "Heil Hitler!" as he was handcuffed and arrested. That monster murdered three people that day, Bill, Reat and Terri. Three beautiful people with blessed lives and families who loved them. He set out that day on a mission to kill Jews and failed, murdering three devout Christians instead.

Dave and I turned on the television and there it was, the red truck I had seen in the article that I had not bothered to read. It did not belong to someone else, some nameless, faceless victim, another anonymous crime statistic. That red truck with the shattered windows belonged to Dr. Bill, our Popeye. This was the truck Bill drove to church in, picked up the groceries in, took his grandchildren to school in and drove Reat to a singing audition in on Palm Sunday.

I saw Mindy on the news that night too. My Mindy, wearing a red OU sweatshirt, standing in front of a group of teenagers at a prayer vigil, assuring them that everything was going to be okay, even if her world would never really be okay again. But she put on a brave face to help others. That was Mindy, always thinking of others.

When I ask Nico about that night now, he doesn't remember much of it. He doesn't remember how I walked into his bedroom to find him still awake. He doesn't recall rolling over to face me or saying the words that pierced my heart. He can't remember the words I won't ever forget.

"I don't understand, Mom. You told me the Nazis were gone and the family was safe. How could this happen? How could they do this to Reat?"

As parents, we want to protect our children, keep them safe, cocooned from the news headlines and the often-dangerous realities of our world. But sometimes we have no choice. Sometimes it's impossible to shield them from the vitriol and violence, the hate, ugliness and danger of racism and intolerance that still exists today. It's still there. Sometimes it's in a story on television that we don't bother to watch or listen to, in a news article we don't take the time to read. Some sad and terrible thing that happened to a stranger. Someone else's problem. Always someone else's tragedy.

Then suddenly, without logic, reason or warning, fate decides it's our turn. It's our loved ones whose photos are flashed on the news. It's our loved one's car surrounded by police crime tape and our children who ask questions that reduce us to tears as we struggle to answer.

"How could this happen?" Nico asked again. "You told me the Nazis were gone."

I could spend endless hours discussing, dissecting the motives of the Nazis and of the neo-Nazi who attempted to destroy our family and countless others. I could explain the history of how and why people hate others simply because they are of another faith, because of the mere fact that they call God by another name. I could go on and on, but I won't. It makes no sense to the rational mind, because hate is not rational. Evil is not reasonable.

Seventy years ago in Greece our family helped save a Jewish family from the Nazis. What happened on Erikousa was proof that light and goodness can exist even in the darkest moments. *Look at what our family did!* I'd told Christiana and Nico again and again. *Your ancestors had the strength and moral courage to stand up to evil, to do the just and moral thing even in the face*

200

of danger. Be proud of your past. Learn from your history. Emulate them and always be sure to stand up for what's good and just.

But on April 13, 2014, everything changed. Teaching my children about standing up in the face of evil, finding hope in even the darkest moment and not allowing hate to have the last word, was no longer about our family's history. It was our family's present and it was our future.

Hate and evil had the power to take three beautiful people from us that day. It had the power to break so many hearts, to change so many lives, and in an instant turn Melinda into a widow and sweet, curly-haired Lukas from a brother to an only child. Hate had the power to do all that. But that didn't mean we were powerless.

Much of our family's story has already been written—the tears, the sadness, the fact that they are gone and that we miss them so terribly. The lives of Reat, Bill and Terri ended in a parking lot that rainy Kansas Sunday with the words of a neo-Nazi attached to their names, but that doesn't mean their stories end there. It can't. We won't let them. Just like my yia-yia and her fellow islanders 70 years before, we are determined to write a different ending.

chapter fourteen

TRAGIC IRONY

Back home in his native Great Britain, Aaron Godfrey was enjoying a much-needed vacation. Between spending time with his wife, Gaby, and chasing their young children around, Aaron was busy catching up with friends and family, filling them in on his new life in Israel and talking about all of the exciting developments at his new job with MyHeritage.

There was one project, he explained, that he was particularly proud of and excited about. It was the story of a tiny island in Greece called Erikousa, and how the islanders had all worked together, risking their lives to hide and save a Jewish family from the Nazis. Gilad had already located the family of one of the girls who was saved, he said, and they were so close to finding the sons of Rosa, the youngest girl who was hidden. Rosa's sons were the bloodline, the legacy and continuation of life that those poor, brave islanders had risked their own lives for. And Aaron explained to his friends and family that along with Gilad, everyone at MyHeritage was now vested in this story. Everyone in the office was determined to find them.

Although he was on vacation, Aaron still checked his email several times a day. Like Gilad, Aaron understood that his work with MyHeritage was about so much more than filling in the boxes of a family tree. When he glanced down at his phone that day, he could not believe what he was seeing. Aaron read my email over again several times to make sure he was reading it correctly. He did not believe this could actually be real, and attempted to wrap his head around the implications.

> **I am so sorry I have not been in touch. I have devastating news to share. 2 members of our family were killed in that horrific JCC shooting in Kansas yesterday.**

Aaron turned on the news. There it was, on television, the story of the three people killed in Kansas. And there it was on the screen, the name he had become so familiar with over emails and phone calls back and forth these past several months: Corporon. In shock, Aaron explained to his family the horrific connection that the anti-Semitic shooting on television had to the story he had just shared with them about the heroic islanders of Erikousa. He then forwarded the email to Gilad, who summed up what everyone was thinking:

Dear Yvette,

It is a tragic twist of fate that as we are exploring together a rare act of kindness and courage 70 years ago which saved a Jewish family, we have encountered an unthinkable, insane hate crime, which although was targeted against Jews, has killed beautiful people from the family of those who saved them.

Gilad

Seated around the television at Peretz Hassid's house, the family watched in horror as the photo of the handsome boy and his grandfather from Kansas who were killed was flashed onscreen. Peretz—Rosa's son—could not believe what he was seeing. The reporter explained that they, along with a married mother of three, were murdered by a neo-Nazi who thought they were Jewish.

Like every family in Israel, the Hassids knew all too well about the senseless loss of life and the dangers of anti-Semitism. They didn't know anything else about these victims other than what the newscaster read, but soon the Hassids would learn more about the handsome young man and his grandfather, and they would learn that they were connected to the tragic American Christians in ways they never wanted or imagined.

The island of Erikousa.

Effie Orfanou Photography

The port in Erikousa.

Effie Orfanou Photography

The Jewish quarter of Corfu.

Municipal Archives of Corfu

Jewish quarter bombed during WWII.

Municipal Archives of Corfu

My father and his grandfather about five years before the German occupation.

My family during the war. Left to right: my great-grandmother, Agatha, my great-grandfather, Anastasios, my yia-yia Avgerini. Center: my aunt Agatha.

Savvas Israel with his wife Rosina and one of their daughters. We are not able to identify which of the daughters this is.   Michelle Mendelovitz

This is the portrait of Savvas Israel that hung in Avraham's apartment. He had no idea who the man in the photo was until we told him.

Hassid Family

Rosa, center, with her brothers Gabriel, left, and Menachen, right. This was taken during Purim in Corfu before the Nazis came.

Hassid Family

Savvas Israel and his daughters. Left to right: Spera, Nina and Julia. This was found among Nina's photos after her death.

Hassid Family

Savvas Israel and his family before the occupation.

Michelle Mendelovitz

Spera with friends on Erikousa after the war. That's Spera on the top left, my aunt Netso and Theodora. Bottom are my uncles George and Nick.

Manessis Family

Rosa, left, and Spera, after they arrived in Israel.

The original flyer that was posted by the Mayor of Corfu celebrating the fact that the island was at last rid of the Jews.

211

My family, after the war, after moving to New York. Seated: my grandfather, Emanuel. Left to right: My grandfather's brother, Costa, Agatha, my father, Anastasios, and my yia-yia.

Manessis Family

My yia-yia and papou after moving to the Bronx, New York.

Aunt Agatha, my grandmother, and Agatha's husband Tasso.

My parents' wedding.

The photo that began it all. Manuel Osmo's grand-mother's wedding photo from 1933. This is the photo that popped up on my computer when I entered the name Vittorio Moustaki into the database of MyHeritage.com. That's Vittorio Moustaki, top left.   **Osmo Family**

The Corfu archives.   **Patrick Record**

Dr. Bill and Reat.

Mindy and Reat.

Reat doing what he loved best . . . singing.

Mindy, Bill, Lukas, Len, Reat and Melinda.

Israeli stamp commissioned by the International Raoul Wallenberg Foundation honoring Erikousa as a House of Life.

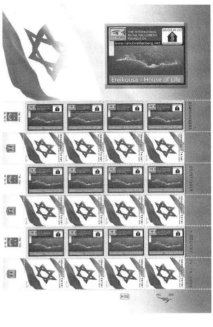

Yvette with Rosa and Spera's families on Erikousa.

Yvette and Avraham at Savvas's grave in Corfu.

Yvette's family and Rosa's family together on Corfu left to right: Effie, Inbar, Peretz, Mayaan, Sigalit, Sapir, Dave, Christiana, Yvette, Avraham, Nico, Linor and Emanuel.

chapter fifteen

HE PICKED THE WRONG FAMILY AND THE WRONG COMMUNITY

None of it made sense. None of it seemed real. I thought that maybe if I got myself up and went to work, went about my normal routine, then somehow the universe would correct this horrible mistake. I would somehow miraculously know exactly what to say to my children, how to answer their heartbreaking questions. I prayed that life would somehow fall back into place, find its way back to normal. But normal is hard to come by, frankly impossible, when a beautiful, kind 14-year-old boy with so much promise and potential will never have the chance to grow up, to thrive and to shine. You can't ignore or will that horror away. The truth is that you and your family are forever changed, forever trying to find and to adjust to a new normal that you hate with every fiber of your being. And my truth was that I did not know what to say or do, how to handle this. I had nowhere near the grace or strength that Mindy displayed.

I stood in the *Extra* newsroom the day after the shooting and glanced up at the wall of television monitors, like I'd done countless times before.

On CNN, the hosts and correspondents were talking about Malaysia Air flight 370, which had disappeared over the Indian Ocean with 239 people on board. Then the anchor announced that there was breaking news and they would be cutting away to a press conference underway right now, in Kansas City, where the mother of a 14-year-old boy who was murdered was speaking.

I watched as the pictures on the television monitors all changed, switching from generic shots of newsrooms, broadcasters and images around the world to ones I recognized. To faces I knew and loved.

"That's my family," I announced to no one in particular. I stood there in the newsroom, surrounded by television monitors. I stood there watching a tragic news story unfold on the screen, like I had done countless times before. But this time it was personal. My friends and colleagues all stopped what they were doing and watched with me.

First, Adam Hamilton, the senior pastor of the United Methodist Church of the Resurrection in Leawood, Kansas, stepped up to the podium. The day before, Pastor Hamilton had been in tears as he sat with his family at their dining room table. He'd still had Palm Sunday services to lead when he first learned of the shooting, and he could not rush to Mindy and Melinda's side until afterward. When he'd finished leading the congregation in prayer, he went to Melinda's house, offering a hug and spiritual support. From that very first moment, Pastor Hamilton helped Mindy, Melinda and the entire family navigate this exceedingly difficult journey both spiritually and physically. When media calls and requests for interviews began flooding his office, he offered to help organize a family press conference at the church.

Pastor Hamilton spoke briefly, introducing Mindy and her brothers, Will and Tony. Mindy then stepped up to speak. She was more composed than I ever imagined possible, her face almost obscured by a half dozen or so microphones, looking so very tiny behind that large podium. Will, Mindy's older brother, stood on one side of her, clutching tissues, and Tony, her younger brother, stood on the other.

In my own newsroom, and in newsrooms and homes across the country and across the globe, the millions of people watching all wondered the same thing—*how?* How did Mindy, Tony and Will have the strength to stand up there, to tell their story, to speak so eloquently of staggering loss, unwavering strength, unshakable faith and even hope. How?

As her brothers wiped tears from their eyes, Mindy maintained her composure and explained. Tony reached out to touch Mindy's back when he knew she needed a steadying hand, although outwardly she never wavered.

"This isn't easy. People keep saying, how come you're so strong? And I'm strong because I have family. I'm strong because I have faith."

"And we want something good to come out of this. We don't know what that's going to be, so we want people to let us know if they think that something good has come from it. You know, you have to reach to God, you have to reach to your friends and search your soul. And that's what it's about. It's about us who are living and it's about loving and caring for one another."

Mindy stepped aside and Will stepped up to the microphone to tell the world about his talented nephew, Reat, and his personal hero, his dad. Will shared with the world what we all knew, what anyone who had ever met Dr. Bill, even for a moment, knew in their very core.

"I know that my dad would have given anything if it could have just been him. He'd have stood up and just said 'take me,' if that would have been offered. And that makes it so much harder. My father leaves behind a legacy of faith and family and community . . . We do have a strong family, and boy it's being tested. We don't know why bad things happen to good people. Nobody does. We choose not to focus on the why or what happened or—it really doesn't matter to us. The fact remains that, you know, two of the people we loved most in our life are now not here with us. And we do take comfort that they were together."

Several reporters shouted out their questions. Will continued to stand at that podium, answering them with the grace, eloquence and strength he had inherited from his father, looking so very much like his father. A reporter asked about the shooter. Will made certain that the conversation and focus stayed exactly where they should be, on Reat and Bill.

"Well, it takes no character to do what was done. It takes no strength of character. It takes no backbone. It takes no morals. It takes no ethics. All it takes is an idiot with a gun."

Will went on.

"But we do hope that, you know, if there's any way possible that any little sliver of good, goodness, grace can come of this, then by the sheer grace of God, it will not have been just totally, totally for nothing."

I stood watching as the press conference ended, the screens again filling with random shots of broadcasters. I simply stood there, staring, trying to process what I had just seen and heard. I was in awe, complete and utter awe.

It amazed me that through their unimaginable pain, while still processing their visceral emotions in those 24 hours immediately following the shooting, Will, Tony and Mindy could be so focused and determined. Will had worked in broadcasting and he knew. He knew that no matter how hard it was, no matter how personally difficult, by his stepping out in front of the cameras and telling the world about Reat and Bill, the focus would remain where it belonged, on Reat and Bill, and not on the monster who murdered them. Will understood how the media works as well as I did. Give the press a story and they are less likely to go out and look for one.

Will's instinct had kicked in immediately. Even in those very first moments after hearing about the shooting, he went to work. As his wife drove from their home in Oklahoma to the Kansas hospital the night of the shooting, Will sat in the car, fielding calls and organizing a plan. The family had been advised to wait until morning to release any information, but Will wouldn't hear of it. He searched and searched and found what he was looking for, the photo of Reat and Bill, together, grandfather and grandson, smiling, arm in arm. He hit send on his iPad from the passenger seat in the car that very first night, even before he arrived in Kansas. This was not some random shooting. This was not some nameless, faceless crime. He didn't want some random producer or editor digging up his father's driver's license photo, using that sterile image to tell the story. This story was about Reat and Bill. *Our* Reat and Bill. Will understood that while they had no control over what had happened, they could at least control what happened next.

And so, with that in mind, the very last thought that Will shared during the press conference was that the family wanted something good to come from this. That if "any little sliver of good, goodness, grace can come of this . . . then by the sheer grace of God, it will not have been just totally, totally for nothing."

The pain was real. Nothing would ever take that pain and loss away. But Will, Mindy and Tony were Dr. Bill Corporon's children. From the earliest age he instilled in them, and in the entire family, the power of four words. *Love. Grace. Community. God.* And as they stood there, stoic and strong, the children of Dr. Bill and Melinda Corporon embodied those very words. I can only imagine how proud Dr. Bill must have been looking down on them in that very moment.

The press conference that afternoon proved so much about our family, but it also made crystal clear something about the shooter. That "idiot with a gun" intent on delivering a message of hate had picked the wrong family. He picked the wrong family, and he picked the wrong community.

The day after the press conference, I sat at my desk and stared down at my computer. Feeling sick to my stomach, I read the latest family email in disbelief.

This made no sense, absolutely no sense. Bill and Reat were devout Christians, killed by a man who hates Jews and blacks, who was also a member of the KKK. And now their funeral would be picketed by a group known for protesting against the LGBTQ community, Catholics, Muslims, Jews and just about everybody else. I had heard of the Westboro Baptist Church from their attempts to disrupt and protest at military funerals. Westboro members believe that God hates homosexuals. They also believe that when an American is killed, including members of our military, it is God's way of punishing Americans for our tolerance of gays. Just the thought of those people being anywhere near Bill and Reat's funeral was too much. It was so absurd, so very twisted and sickening. Hadn't our family been through enough?

On Good Friday, April 18, 2014, the lives of Dr. Bill Corporon and Reat Griffin Underwood were celebrated as they had lived and died, together, at the United Methodist Church of the Resurrection.

Despite the horrific reality that Reat and Dr.

Bill had been murdered, ambushed and ripped away from us; despite the fact that the hate-mongers from Westboro planned to protest their funeral; despite the deep, dark awfulness of it all, somehow, some way, a glimmer of light and love managed to pierce through all of that darkness. Despite all of it, something beautiful happened that day in Kansas.

That morning, numb, still in shock, unable to grasp that this was indeed reality, each of the family members filed into their cars for the unthinkable journey to the church. Mindy, Len and Lukas stepped out of their home, got into their car and began the five-mile journey to the church. They drove past their neighbors' homes, down the hill, past the fishing pond and down the long, straight familiar roads of their idyllic community. They drove past the lovely neighborhood developments near their own, and past the large plots of yet undeveloped land all around them. They all knew about the Westboro threat to protest the services, and they had prepared themselves. Well, as much as anyone could prepare oneself in that surreal situation.

Protesters from Westboro Baptist Church showed up to the funeral that day.

But as the members of the family made their way to the church, none of them saw one single Westboro demonstrator or message of hate. Instead, as Mindy, Len, Lukas, Melinda, Tony,

Will and the rest of the family looked out their car windows that morning, they saw instead a sea of love. An angel wall.

More than 2,000 people—friends, classmates, neighbors, strangers, Christians, Jews, Muslims, atheists—all showed up to stand side by side for the final two miles leading up to the church. They stood there, peacefully, quietly, purposefully, holding signs reading LOVE WINS. Others held handmade signs with Bill and Reat's names on them, covered in hearts and a rainbow of color. They were a living, breathing message of love, intent on blocking any message of hate. These angels successfully shielded the family from the protestors, once again proving how hate can be drowned out with love.

That theme extended inside the church to the funeral, which was profoundly moving.

First, Will spoke, telling the more than 3,000 people assembled in the church, and the 10,000 or so watching online, about his father's dedication to helping others, about the importance of community over self, and of Reat and Popeye's legacies. Stoic and strong, Will spoke eloquently of his father's dedication to Reat, and also to medicine and to helping others.

"In their honor today and every day, love one another more deeply. Look for ways to live with more civility. And above all, we want you to search for and hopefully find the kind of faith that will sustain you not only when the unthinkable happens, but when life happens. Because if you are able to find that faith, if you are able to live with that grace and peace in your life from day to day, this horrible, awful, unthinkable tragedy will have become the starting point for something much greater. This hate will have become something much different: it will have become a shining example of God's love in a world that so desperately needs it. And Reat and Dad would really like that."

After Will, it was Tony's turn to speak. Tony, who shared his father's wicked sense of humor, who following Will's eloquent eulogy quipped, "Will is ever the consummate politician, but I was the favorite."

Tony went on to share more stories of Reat and Popeye's amazing bond, again bringing laughter through tears as he shared some favorite memories.

Then it was Lukas's turn to speak.

"Can everyone hear me?" Lukas asked as he stepped up and leaned into the microphone, again bringing the entire room to tears of both laughter and pain.

"I recently went turkey hunting with my grand-father," Lukas said. "The funny thing is we didn't even hear a turkey. We just sat there for three hours doing nothing. But I just told him I was having a wonderful time with him and I was so glad that he took the time out of his day to spend with me."

Lukas continued, "My brother, Reat, was the best singer ever. He had big plans for his future. He was going to be a singing doctor and make a lot of money."

Again, the room erupted in laughter. Lukas looked up from his paper and smiled, as if fueled by the validation and support of everyone in the room. He went on, his voice cracking as he spoke. "I love you, Reat and Popeye. You'll always be in my heart."

Sweet, curly-haired Lukas stepped off the stage and into the arms of his mother. After giving Lukas a giant hug, Mindy stepped up to the podium. She was the final family member to speak, sharing more stories of her sweet boy, her firstborn whose death left a giant hole in her heart. And again, through the pain and the unimaginable loss, the same theme resonated as Mindy spoke of her precious son.

"Dear Reat Griffin, what an amazing young man. Something good is happening from this . . . Reat, there are too many dreams to mention that we will not capture with you. But your loving smile and the memory of hugs will help us move through life one day at a time and we will feel you with us. You were so beautiful inside and out."

Pastor Hamilton spoke next. The pastor's words

echoed Mindy's sentiment. They all wanted something good to come from this. It was Pastor Hamilton's words that assured and reminded us all that by the example set by Mindy, Will, Len, Tony, Lukas, Melinda and the rest of the family, something good already had . . .

"As a family, you've shared your faith and your courage with the rest of the country so that we can peer in. You've opened your hearts so we can peer in, and you've touched us and inspired us. Each of us has the power to do that, to push back the darkness in this world."

The service was a true celebration of two beautiful lives, a grandfather and grandson who were together always, even in death.

———————

Dave and his parents traveled from New York to Kansas for the funeral service.

I did not.

One of my greatest regrets is that I did not make the trip. At the time, it still all seemed so surreal, so very unreal. I wanted to be there, for Melinda, to hug Mindy and sweet Lukas and be present with them. But I just couldn't bring myself to do it. Something held me back. At the time I thought that staying behind was in some way protecting my children. It was too much to comprehend, too many emotions, too much loss. It was so very hard, especially on Christiana. I struggled to help her through the myriad of emotions, even as I grappled with my own.

I thought that maybe by keeping Christiana and Nico home with me, I could somehow shield them from the reality, the horror. I thought that by staying away I was saving them from the emotional trauma of facing those awful protestors, of seeing their hateful signs and hearing their vitriolic rhetoric. That by staying away I could somehow protect them from the cold reality of what happened to Reat and Bill.

When I was Christiana and Nico's age, I had only ever been to Greek funerals. These were always dramatic affairs, and people wailing, clawing at themselves and threatening to climb into the casket with the deceased tended to be the norm. Those funerals were always so emotionally exhausting, so difficult and very upsetting. I remembered the row of black-clad women on Erikousa all sitting and wailing together with my yia-yia after Papou's death. Those raw displays of emotion and dramatics had left an indelible mark on me as a child. I didn't want my children anywhere near that.

But Bill and Reat's funeral was so very different.

I sat at my desk and watched the funeral service streaming on my computer. It was like nothing I had ever seen or experienced. It was uplifting, cathartic and hopeful. The funeral was a true celebration of two beautiful lives, a testament to the entire family who had planned it so perfectly and meticulously.

Their loss was staggering, and so was their strength. I had never been more proud to call myself a Corporon. And I had also never been more ashamed. I was angry. So very angry and so very disappointed—in myself.

Just a few days before, when I first made contact with Spera's granddaughter Michelle, she had learned that her Jewish grandmother had been saved by Christians, and she sat in her office and cried.

Now it was my turn. I sat at my desk, attempting to make sense of the senseless.

A neo-Nazi shouting "Heil Hitler" had murdered Bill and Reat. Reat would never finish high school. Mindy would never get to hold her sweet boy again. She could never again ask her father's advice or lean on him when she needed strength. They were ripped from life because a man filled with hate thought they were Jewish. This was not a story in an old, dusty history book. This was now. This was today. It was real. It was us.

I sat at my desk as Bill and Reat's funeral played on my laptop and I cried. I wasn't like Mindy, stoic and unfaltering. I found no consolation in knowing we would be reunited in heaven. I found no comfort in thinking Mindy would get to hold and kiss her baby boy again when God called her to him. The senseless loss of life, the fact that a 14-year-old boy was ripped from his family so violently, made me question my own faith as Mindy's seemed to solidify and grow.

I took my husband's name when we got married. Corporon. I shared a last name with Mindy, the woman who, in the wake of unimaginable pain and loss, became a symbol of grace, strength and faith across the nation and around the world.

Avgerini. That's my name in Greek. The name I was given in honor of my yia-yia, the woman who despite the Nazi threats risked the lives of her own children to do the right thing and help a Jewish family.

Mindy Corporon. Avgerini Manessis. They were two women that I was blessed to know and have in my life. Two ordinary women, both demonstrating extraordinary selflessness and courage.

I sat at my desk and cried.

Because while I had the honor of sharing their names, it was painfully clear I had nowhere near their strength.

chapter sixteen

HE WAS WATCHING OVER THEM

On April 30, 2014, in Rehovot, Israel, the phone rang in Avraham Hassid's apartment. He didn't know what to make of the caller on the other end. He also didn't know that dozens of people in New York, Greece and Israel had been searching for him.

"We have information about your mother, Rosa. We need to meet with you," Aaron Godfrey announced.

Avraham quickly called his younger brother, Peretz, and filled him in on the cryptic phone call he'd received from the stranger who spoke Hebrew with a British accent and claimed to know secrets about their mother. The brothers were suspicious, but curious, wondering what this man wanted from them and how on earth he could know anything about their incredibly private mother or their family. Peretz then called his wife, Sigalit, who raced to Avraham's apartment with their three daughters in tow. The girls were frustrated, angry even, that some cryptic phone call from a stranger prompted their mother to literally drop everything and cut short their shopping trip to the mall.

The brothers agreed to meet Aaron outside, on the street in front of Avraham's apartment, in case Aaron turned out to be a liar or a lunatic. They would soon learn that he was neither.

As he sat in the audience of his daughter's dance recital that night, Gilad's phone buzzed in his pocket. It was Aaron calling. Aaron told Gilad that he had made contact with Rosa's sons and was on the way to meet them that very evening. I would be joining them as well, via Skype from my office in New York, with television cameras rolling to capture every moment.

It was no surprise that Gilad, the world-renowned linguist, immediately assessed the challenges inherent in what might, on the surface, appear to be a well laid-out plan. Gilad knew that neither Avraham nor Peretz spoke Greek or English. And while Aaron's Hebrew had improved dramatically since he'd moved to Israel from England just a few months before, he was still not completely fluent. Gilad at once recognized that without a shared fluent language between us, important details and nuances might very well be lost in translation. We had come so dangerously close to losing the secret of Erikousa to history. We had come so dangerously close to never learning if there was a Jewish bloodline that could be traced back to what happened on Erikousa during the war. Gilad understood that after having come so far, after having overcome incredible odds and so many obstacles in our way, we could not take a chance with anything less than perfect translation during this pivotal meeting.

A multi-hyphenate by nature, Gilad Japhet is many things: a linguist, businessman, lover of history and genealogical detective. But perhaps above all, Gilad Japhet prides himself on being a family man. Seated in the audience of his daughter's recital beside his wife, Gilad would never have considered leaving before witnessing his daughter have her big moment. But as luck, or fate, would have it, when Aaron called with the news of our imminent meeting, Gilad's daughter had just finished her dance. Gilad had captured every moment on his video camera, which was still fully charged. This was no longer just another work assignment. Gilad had become emotionally vested in finding Rosa's family and bringing to light the secret of Erikousa, so his wife urged him to leave the recital, to join Aaron in Rehovot and to personally see the story of Erikousa come full circle. Video camera in hand, Gilad sprang from his seat and drove to Avraham's house, which happened to be just a 10-minute drive from where the dance recital was taking place.

They met out on the street outside Avraham's apartment, and it took mere moments for Rosa's sons to realize that Aaron and Gilad were not involved in some elaborate ruse, but that these two men claiming to be from MyHeritage were exactly who they said they were. Rosa's sons also quickly realized that these two strangers could quite possibly hold answers to the secrets their mother had guarded so fiercely all their lives.

Aaron and Gilad were ushered inside and welcomed into Avraham's home. There, they laid the foundation for what was about to take place, explaining to the family that I had been searching for them for years, that their mother was hidden from the Nazis by the kind people of Erikousa and that they were alive today because of the bravery and sacrifice of the islanders. Aaron and Gilad also told the brothers that our common bond runs deeper than history, explaining that the grandfather and grandson they had recently seen on the news, the victims of the anti-Semitic attack in the United States, were members of my own family. Avraham and Peretz could not believe what they were hearing.

At the *Extra* TV studio in New York, my colleagues gathered with me in the large windowed conference room of our midtown offices. This was no longer just my story; this was our story. My *Extra* colleagues and friends in both New York and LA had lived through every moment of this journey with me, offering help whenever possible, encouraging me to keep trying when I was certain all hope was lost and picking up a camera to shoot when I wanted to document something on video. This was their moment and resolution as much as it was mine.

With my friends seated around the conference table behind me, I stood in the front of the room, just inches from a large television screen where the Skype session would take place. All around me, large windows looked out over the majestic skyline of Manhattan. It was a canyon of sky-scrapers as far as the eye could see. The skies above New York City were a jumble of gray, with dark, stormy clouds that brought nearly five inches of rain to Manhattan that afternoon. But no one inside that conference room paid any mind to the torrential downpour outside those windows. We were all transfixed on that television screen, watching as images of a family filled the screen. A family seated on a sofa in an apartment in Rehovot, Israel, along with Gilad and Aaron, surrounded by family photos.

And in Rehovot, that family was transfixed on the picture that appeared on their television screen as well. That picture showed a dark-eyed, dark-haired woman in jeans and a black top, nervously pacing in a New York City conference room, her face frequently erupting in a huge smile. Every now and then, she would run her fingers through her hair, turn around and say, "Can you believe this? Oh my God, can you believe this?!" to the people off camera, seated at a conference table behind her.

In that moment, as we first locked eyes and smiled at each other on Skype, across thousands of miles, several time zones and 70 long years, we not only defied the odds to find each other, but we also defied the natural laws of human relationships. Because in that very moment when we first smiled at one another across Skype, strangers not only became instant friends, strangers were instantly cemented as family.

"Yvette, these are Rosa's sons, Avraham and Peretz," Aaron announced.

I waved at the camera like a crazy person.

"And you'll see, like you found out with the other person, they don't talk much about what happened," Aaron added.

I stood in front of the large television screen not believing what I was seeing, what was happening. I started talking and couldn't stop, even with Aaron and Gilad reminding me to slow down so they could translate. Even then, my mouth was moving at warp speed. I had a lot to say, and I couldn't get it out fast enough. I told Rosa's family everything. I told them how I had searched for years to find them. I told them everything my yia-yia, father and Agatha told me about the Nazis in our home, searching for their mother. I told them how Rosa, along with Spera, Julia and Nina, would come visit my yia-yia at night, and how Yia-yia would take food out of her own children's mouths so that Rosa had enough to eat.

Overwhelmed with emotion, the brothers finally understood that when young Rosa's family was killed by the Nazis, Rosa had been taken in and protected first by Savvas, Spera, Nini and Julia, and then also by my yia-yia and the islanders of Erikousa.

Hearing our story, Peretz's wife, Sigalit, remembered an old school assignment about family history that her eldest daughter, Inbar, had interviewed Rosa for. Inbar had asked Rosa to share her memories and stories from the Holocaust. Even after all those years of keeping her silence, even after all those years of never sharing the secret of Erikousa, Rosa's life had changed when Inbar was born. It was as if the birth of this beautiful child, who shared the same birthday as Rosa, had brought light where Rosa had known only darkness. Even though she had never spoken to her own sons about the Holocaust, Rosa could not deny her granddaughter's request. And so, just three months before her death, Rosa sat with her granddaughter, Inbar, and shared with her a few details of her life during the war. It was the first and only time Rosa spoke of it to her family.

After listening to my story over Skype, Sigalit ran home to find that homework assignment.

Holding it in her hand, Sigalit returned to Avraham's apartment as she stared down and read Rosa's story in disbelief:

"The Germans came to the island of Corfu, where my grandmother lived. They gathered up all the Jews in Corfu, including my grandmother's family, her parents and her brothers, and killed them all. My grandmother and her three aunts were saved because they were hidden from the Germans by good non-Jews who helped them."

There, in black and white, based on Rosa's own words to her granddaughter, in a long-forgotten homework assignment, was confirmation of our story.

The entire Hassid family gathered around as Aaron picked up a photo from a stack that Avraham had been sorting through earlier. It was the unidentified portrait of the well-dressed man that had hung on Avraham's apartment wall for years.

"Hold the picture up to the screen," Gilad directed from his seat on the couch.

"Yvette, you are going to have to see something that we are bringing to the web cam now," Aaron said as Avraham stood up to bring the photo closer to the camera.

As the image filled the screen, I instantly recognized the face. Just days before, Michelle had sent me some old family photos that her mother had found in Spera's papers. One of the photos took my breath away. It was of Savvas Israel, the Jewish tailor of Corfu, and his family. The photo was exquisite. Savvas stood tall, a commanding figure with dark brows, piercing eyes and a thick mustache, dressed in a suit jacket. Beside Savvas sat his wife. She wore her hair pinned up, and a long dark dress with a white lace collar. She held on her lap a chubby-cheeked baby no more than a year old. The three young girls in the photo were dark-haired, and all wore exquisite white-lace-trimmed dresses. There was a wide-eyed little boy in the photo as well; he wore white knickers and knee socks, his hand placed on the lap of his mother. We were still sorting through birth records to try to identify the children, but there was no mistaking the handsome man. And now, as Aaron placed a black-and-white photo up to the screen, there was no mistaking the face of the man in the portrait.

"That's Savvas!" I shouted, and pointed at the screen. "That's Savvas from the photo Michelle sent me." I could not believe what I was seeing.

"She sent a photo of him with his entire family," Gilad said.

"Yes. With his family. But that's the same man!" I cried. "That's definitely him. Amazing."

Year after year, from his place on the wall, and without anyone ever knowing it, Savvas Israel, the Jewish tailor from Corfu, had continued watching over Rosa's family all along.

PART FOUR

chapter seventeen

THE ONES WHO STOOD UP

It was love at first phone call.

"Do you speak Greek?" Marcia asked.

"Yes, of course," I replied.

"I married a Greek. He was my second mistake."

"What was your first mistake?"

"He was Israeli."

And with that first conversation, that very first belly laugh, my adoration of Marcia Haddad Ikonomopoulos was cemented.

Marcia is the director of the Kehila Kedosha Janina Synagogue and Museum and also president of the Association of Friends of Greek Jewry. From everything I read about her, it seemed to me that Marcia was the world's leading authority on the Jews of Greece. When we first crossed paths, I thought it was a happy accident, but I soon learned it was nothing of the sort. As Marcia told me, our meeting was *beshert*, the Hebrew word often used to describe someone's soul mate. But *beshert* also has another meaning. As Marcia explained, *beshert* is also a divine destiny, something that was meant to be. And indeed our meeting was. Marcia would change my life, and the lives of every single person who was touched by the secret of Erikousa.

I first reached out to Marcia in September of 2012, as I was writing *When the Cypress Whispers*. Wanting to add some more historical context to the book, I began researching more about the Jewish community of Corfu and also the Jewish community across Greece. In article after article, document after document, I kept coming across the same name—Marcia's. Sorting through all of the articles, documents and research that Marcia had written or been cited in, I figured she would likely be located in Jerusalem, Athens or Thessaloniki, since that's where much of her research seemed to be centered. But it turns out Marcia was not located in Greece, Israel, in another country or even in another area code. Marcia's office was just few miles from mine, in a historic synagogue in lower Manhattan. *Beshert.*

Marcia soon became my Greek Jewish fairy godmother, and she also provided comedic relief when I needed it most. From her Facebook page, I learned Marcia has an affinity, more like a grandmotherly love, for the chickens she keeps in her Long Island yard. Those hilarious poultry-inspired posts offer keen insight into this extraordinary woman's character. Marcia Haddad Ikonomopoulos is a woman who lives with gusto, laughs out loud, often breaks into dance and always finds joy, celebrating life at every opportunity. She is also a woman whose every breath is dedicated to telling the stories of the millions of victims who lived and died in the Nazi camps and gas chambers. A woman who lives to remind us that while it is our obligation to never forget, we must also never forget to live. My friend Marcia is the living, breathing personification of the philosophy that each moment of life and freedom is a gift to be savored and celebrated.

It all began as a young girl's promise to her grandmother. Her grandfather, one of 11 siblings, left Greece before the Nazis came. Those who stayed—more than 112 members of his family from Thessaloniki and 12 from Kavala—were killed. When he learned about the fate of his family, all of the loved ones who were murdered, Marcia's grandfather went into a dark room and never spoke of what happened. He lived the rest of his life consumed with survivor's guilt, thinking that maybe, somehow, he could have been able to save his brothers and sisters if he had stayed in Greece with them. As far back as Marcia could remember, it was as if a black cloud and millions of unanswered questions hung over the family. Marcia was simply told to leave her grandfather alone, not to bother him or ask about the family.

But then, when she was grown, Marcia's

grandmother put her faith in her determined granddaughter and asked her to find out what had happened. Marcia promised she would. That promise laid the foundation for what was to become Marcia's life's work.

As a young woman, Marcia went to Greece to retrace the final steps of her family, and she learned the tragic stories of countless other families in the process. She soon realized that these were untold stories of a community forgotten by fellow Jews, by Greece and by history.

"Initially when the Jews of Greece came back from the concentration camps and told their fellow Jews what happened, no one believed them," Marcia explained. "And they said to them, 'Go on with your life. Forget about what happened. Go on and get married; have other children.' It took years before their stories came out. The more I found out, I realized what a responsibility I had to tell the story. You have to realize the story of Greek Jewry was very rarely being told. To this day I'm still amazed by how many people are not aware of what happened."

And so Marcia became a voice for the voiceless. She's a tireless reminder of the approximately 65,000 Greek Jews who were murdered, a community 85 percent exterminated and largely forgotten. Today, Marcia travels the world sharing the story of Greek Jewry with anyone who'll listen. As she explains, "Our story has become the orphan child of Holocaust studies, a footnote, an afterthought." But no longer, not if Marcia has anything to do with it.

"My grandmother was a very smart woman," Marcia says. "I think she was very wise in choosing me to find out about our family. I was always obsessive as a child, and this obsession finally became legitimized when I became a museum director. Otherwise they would have committed me long ago."

Kehila Kedosha Janina Synagogue and Museum is a small brick building. The facade is adorned with stained glass and Stars of David. Unchanged throughout the years, the building is located on Manhattan's Lower East Side, in what is now one of New York City's hippest neighborhoods, where it is nestled among trendy hotels, cafés and apartment buildings. The tiny synagogue is a designated New York City landmark and is the only Romaniote synagogue in the Western Hemisphere. The Romaniotes were Jews who, according to oral tradition, were put on a slave ship following the fall of the second temple in Jerusalem in 70 AD. The ship was bound for Rome, hence the name Romaniote. A storm threatened the voyage and forced the ship to come ashore in Greece, where the Romaniotes settled and lived for centuries. They spoke a distinctive language, a mix of Greek, Italian and Hebrew, and lived for centuries all throughout Greece, including Corfu. Through the years, Marcia has made several trips back to Corfu, both to study and research the Jewish community there and to swim in the crystal-blue water and dance under the stars. Our mutual love of Corfu was just one more bond that cemented our friendship from the very first moment Marcia and I met.

As the launch for *When the Cypress Whispers* approached, Marcia insisted she host an event for the book in that beautiful historic synagogue. That book signing became a turning point in my life and the lives of so many others. In that intimate setting, as I spoke about the inspiration behind *When the Cypress Whispers*, and the real-life secret of Erikousa, I looked out at an audience unlike any I had spoken in front of before. This was an audience filled with people who had been personally touched by the Holocaust: survivors, children of survivors, people who lost countless family members in the Nazi camps. I looked out at all of their faces, so eager to hear my story, and I felt a tremendous responsibility. Who was I to stand here in this historic synagogue and speak of the Holocaust and of bravery? I hadn't done anything heroic. I was a writer of fiction, retelling a story I had barely paid attention to for so long. I understand full well the power of storytelling and literature, but even so, I felt the stakes were too high this time to be confined to fiction. I looked out at the crowd gathered in the synagogue that day and I saw my father sitting among the audience, smiling up at me. In that moment I knew what I had to do.

"It's one thing to hear the story from an author, and another to hear it firsthand from someone who lived it. Daddy, would you come up here, please? I think everyone would rather hear this from you."

My father smiled as he stepped up to the microphone. And then he began to speak, and to share his memories with this very eager, attentive and incredibly special audience.

"I'll never forget how scared we were. Everyone was scared. But there was nothing we could do," he began.

"Louder!" shouted someone from the back of the room. "We can't hear you. Speak louder." They wanted to hear every word of what my father had to say. I unpinned my microphone and held it to my father's mouth as he spoke. He smiled at me again, and then went on with his story.

"I hid behind my mother and watched as the Nazi came into my mother's bedroom and tore everything apart," he recalled. "Those girls were my mother's friends. We loved them. My sister and I loved how happy they made my mother. Not everyone on the island felt that way, of course. There were those who wanted them gone, who thought it was too dangerous for them to be there. But even they never told. No one told."

He told the audience in the synagogue that day everything he remembered, how everyone on Erikousa loved and protected Savvas's family. My father's story was a stark, heartbreaking contrast to what so many of them, and their own family members, had experienced.

After the talk, dozens of people stood in line and waited. Yes, some wanted me to sign their books, but most waited and waited for a chance to speak to my father. They shook his hand and thanked him, and told him that he was a blessed man and his mother, my yia-yia, a blessed woman. One man, whose mother survived the camps but who lost so many other family members, kissed my father and hugged him. He then looked into my father's eyes and reminded us all what is written in the Talmud, reciting the words, "He who saves a life, saves the world."

Another man came up to me and said two words that stopped me in my tracks.

"Thank you," he said.

"Why thank me?" I replied. "I didn't do anything. It was my yia-yia and the islanders. My father. Not me."

"Yes. It was you. It is you. Thank you for telling this story. We all hear the horror and the evil. There are so many stories, my mother's among them, of all the evil things that happened, the inhumanity of that time. But we need to hear the good. We need to be reminded that good things happened too. My mother lived through hell in those camps. She needs to know that there were good people in the world too. It is so important to her, and to all of us."

I hugged this man and thanked him for his kind words, and for opening my eyes and mind to what this all meant. One act of kindness and courage so many years ago, touching so many lives, even today. One glimmer of hope and of light in that vast darkness, still resonating so many years later. History so often remembers and highlights the darkest moments. But what of the light?

That afternoon, as my father and I shared our story, each one of us was reminded that no matter how oppressive the darkness, it is our obligation to always seek out, remember and remind one another of the light.

It is a sentiment echoed by Marcia. "My feeling is that we should be teaching the next generation not the names of the perpetrators, may they rot in hell, but to emulate those who had the moral courage to make a difference."

Marcia stood in the front of the room beside my father and me and told us that the Association of Friends of Greek Jewry has an honor, similar to Yad Vashem's Righteous Among the Nations. It is an award given to gentiles who risked their lives to save Jews during the Holocaust. The honor is called the Award of Moral Courage. Daniel Soussis's rescuer, Errikos Sueref, is one of the dozens who have been honored with the award. Marcia announced that the Association of Friends of Greek Jewry would be presenting the Award of Moral Courage to the islanders of Erikousa for saving Savvas and his family. And not only that, to properly recognize and honor the islanders, the Association of Friends of Greek Jewry would like to host a ceremony *on* Erikousa and invite the entire island to attend. And, God willing, Marcia added, we would be joined by Savvas's family.

Marcia personally vowed to do all she could, to move heaven and earth, to ensure that we would all be together on Erikousa to celebrate the island and its heroic community. And also, Marcia added, she wanted to personally be on hand when the islanders of Erikousa at last welcomed the families of Spera and Rosa home.

"My feeling is that we should be teaching the next generation not the names of the perpetrators, may they rot in hell, but to emulate those who had the moral courage to make a difference."

I played Marcia's words over in my head again and again. Those words, words so powerful and so profoundly true about the past, were now also so incredibly prophetic.

Marcia's words echoed not only what happened on Erikousa during the war, but what was happening in present-day Kansas as well. From the very moment that their world was shattered, Mindy and her entire family had shown extraordinary moral courage.

The moral courage to make a difference.

They were words to live by and emulate, in our past, in our present and, so very importantly, in our family's future.

chapter eighteen

HEAVEN IS ALL AROUND US

Fourteen-year-old Reat Griffin Underwood had many dreams. But perhaps at the top of that very long list was the dream to sing the national anthem at a major sporting event. On June 7, 2014, almost two months after he was murdered, Reat's dream came true.

Almost 40,000 people packed the stadium that perfect summer night, among them the families of Reat and Bill Corporon and Terri LaManno. As the Kansas City Royals and New York Yankees players lined the field, ball caps in hand held over their hearts, the crowd in the stands came to their feet. Mindy, Len, Lukas, Melinda and the entire family all stood together looking up at the jumbotron. The screen then filled with images of Reat taken just months before the shooting, when he sang in front of 1,100 people at a community breakfast. Video of Reat singing "The Star-Spangled Banner" played on the screen. The entire stadium reverberated with the sound of his voice. He belted out that iconic last line, *"For the land of the free, and the home of the brave,"* holding that final note, and the stadium erupted in wild applause as thousands wiped tears from their eyes. It was the most bittersweet of moments for Mindy and the rest of the family. They had just witnessed Reat's dream come true. But he wasn't there to celebrate it.

Or maybe he was.

From the very first moment she heard he was gone, Mindy knew her son was in heaven with her father. She was certain of this. Since the murders, Mindy's grandparents, as well as her friend Kyle, who died when they were just teenagers, had appeared to Mindy in visions and dreams. They each told her the same thing: not to worry, that they had Reat and were watching over him.

Her faith was unwavering, but since the murders, Mindy's belief in heaven had shifted. She now realized that heaven is not some far-away place. She now knew that although Reat and her dad were gone, they were still often so close by, sometimes right there beside her. Mindy could sense it. She could feel it and she could see the signs everywhere, often in the moments when she needed that reassurance most. She saw Reat in the yellow butterflies that fluttered around her when she was thinking of her son. She saw her father in the red cardinal that flew, sat and sometimes lingered nearby as she was thinking of Bill. Sometimes it was the small animal that would stop and catch her eye, holding its stare just a moment too long. Yes, there were signs that heaven was all around, and Mindy was not the only one who saw them.

Mindy and Len are avid athletes who share a love for running. Reat . . . not so much. It was a recurring joke in the family that unlike his parents, Reat hated to run. He hated it so much that Mindy had Reat buried in his favorite T-shirt, with the words RUNNING SUCKS emblazoned across the front. Exercise has always been a release for Mindy. Some days it was an outlet; other days it was an escape. She completed a triathlon just three months after the murders and felt that her dad and Reat were right there with her at the finish line. But there were also days when she went for a run and found herself sitting on a bench and crying instead.

One morning, a few months after the shooting, Mindy went to a local park for a run. It was rainy and cold, not an ideal day to go running, but Mindy was meeting a friend, so she could not back out. As she was waiting, she struck up a conversation with a woman who was there with her family. The woman explained that they were planning a day of activities for three of her young nephews who had lost their mother recently. Mindy listened, feeling an instant connection with this family, and told the woman that she believed in signs from heaven. The woman agreed, saying she did too. And then the woman turned around. On the back of her T-shirt were printed the words I LOVE YOU TO THE MOON AND BACK. The woman explained this is what her niece would say to her kids each night before bed, and they were the last words she spoke to her children before she passed. They are also the same words that Mindy had said to Reat over and over again since he was a tiny baby. The same words Mindy had placed all over the house on various pillows, signs and trinkets—a constant reminder of a mother's love for her sons. Mindy read the words on the T-shirt and she knew Reat was with her.

That very afternoon, our dear friend Omar Lugones was home in Los Angeles shopping with his wife, Theresa. As he was browsing in the store, he glanced down at his phone to read Mindy's Facebook post recounting what happened in the park that morning. The very moment he looked up, directly in front of him was a picture frame with the words I LOVE YOU TO THE MOON AND BACK on it. Omar reached out to Mindy, sending her a picture of the frame, and immediately she knew it was a sign from Reat.

And sometimes Reat reached out to other loved ones, offering a sign of encouragement when they needed it most.

Christiana was nervous. She was trying out for JV softball and she was anxious about doing well and making the team. As she walked across the gym floor that afternoon, something caught her eye. It was shiny and small, and she asked her classmates if anyone had lost a charm or a piece of jewelry. No one claimed it, so Christiana picked it up and put it in her hand. She looked down and smiled, clenching her fist tightly around the little charm. And like Mindy, she knew.

It was a small crescent moon, etched with the words I LOVE YOU TO THE MOON AND BACK. Reat was cheering her on from heaven.

It was exactly the encouragement she needed.

Christiana made the team.

As I was writing this book, Mindy came to visit us in New York. On her last night with us we went out to dinner at our favorite sushi restaurant. We paid the check and walked out the door. As we were walking away, a waiter ran out to the street after us.

"You dropped something," he said, as he held up his hand toward us. Each of us took a quick personal inventory of bags and jackets. We had no idea what he was referring to.

"You dropped something," he said again, as he opened his fist to reveal a necklace. It was Christiana's necklace. A gold crescent moon and diamond that Lukas had given her just a few months before. I took the necklace in my hand and examined the clasp. It wasn't broken. I looked at the chain to find where it might have broken and fallen from Christiana's neck. The chain was intact. There was absolutely nothing wrong with it. Anyone else would have wondered how that necklace could have fallen off and onto the ground. But we didn't wonder, not at all.

I called, texted and emailed Mindy several times in the immediate aftermath of the shooting. She was overwhelmed with an avalanche of support and messages. I wasn't sure if she would even see my notes, but eventually, and to my surprise, she did respond, and in that gracious beautiful way of hers. I struggled with what to say and how to say it. Each time I tried to put words together, they seemed inadequate. I couldn't find the words to properly acknowledge the hell that Mindy and the entire family were living through. I don't think such words even exist, in any language. How can mere words accurately reflect the staggering and senseless loss of that beautiful boy and his grandfather?

"I'm so sorry." I could think of nothing else, nothing. "I'm so sorry," I repeated again and again. Mindy was her strong, stoic self on the phone when we finally spoke weeks after the shooting. We talked about sweet Reat. She told me of their last moments together, how excited he was to audition that day, and again Mindy told me how Reat would have loved to come visit us in New York. And then we talked about her dad. Mindy told me Bill was a voracious reader and about that novel he had always been determined to write.

"You know he was proud of you," she said. "He was reading your book. It was on the table next to his chair."

I sucked my breath in and felt the familiar tingle in my eyes. I pictured Bill, sitting in his chair, his shirt tucked in over his belly, suspenders on display. I thought of him there, reading the words I had written, a story of a Jewish family saved by Christians in Greece, only to have the unthinkable happen in a quiet Kansas town.

It was too much for me to contemplate. What did it mean? Did it mean anything? Could it be a mere coincidence? I had come too far in my own personal journey to believe that such things can be explained away by mere coincidence. As I struggled with understanding the implications of it all, Mindy was struggling with far greater questions, trying to make sense of her loss, and what exactly God's plan for her was.

Each time Mindy was interviewed, by Savannah Guthrie on the *Today* show and by Eric Shawn and Elisabeth Hasselbeck on the Fox News Channel, and by every local Kansas City broadcaster in between, she was asked the same question again and again. "You seem so strong. How are you getting through this?"

"Our faith is helping us get through this," Mindy replied. That same sentiment was echoed by each and every member of the family. Faith was the resounding common denominator. Missing Bill and Reat was excruciating, but knowing that they would see them again in heaven gave them so much comfort, solace and strength.

From those very first chaotic moments at the Jewish Community Campus the day of the shooting to the weeks and months following, the Jewish community of Kansas City embraced and cared for Mindy and our family as their own. The rabbis and members of the community stepped in and helped with every detail that they possibly could, from providing comfort, meals and a private place for the family to gather to offering spiritual guidance and prayers. Mindy and the entire family felt embraced and loved by the entire Jewish congregation and community.

In the weeks and months following the shootings, Mindy felt such gratitude toward her new Jewish friends, as well as a strong pull toward them. As she struggled to make sense of what happened to Reat and to her father, Mindy replayed every moment and nuance over and over again. Her father and son were murdered at a Jewish community center by a man who thought they were Jewish. Surely there must be some significance there, Mindy thought. She was a woman who had grown up in a small midwestern Christian community who had never even met a Jewish person until she went away to college.

And yet, Mindy felt suddenly drawn to Judaism, with an insatiable need to learn more. She began studying, immersing herself in the religion, philosophy, traditions and culture. Mindy knew that God had a plan for her, and that her journey to learn more about Judaism was part of that plan. But what that plan was exactly, she was still trying to decipher.

Maybe I'm meant to be Jewish, she thought. *Maybe God is calling me to Judaism.*

As she continued with her studies, immersing herself in centuries-old prayers and traditions, Mindy consulted with a rabbi and told him of her plans. She told him that she was considering converting, that she thought perhaps God was sending her some sort of sign. That maybe all of these factors, these horrific circumstances and details converging together, meant that God wanted her to be Jewish. The rabbi listened, and then he spoke. "You can stay on the path with Jesus," he said. "I'd be okay with that."

And so she did. While she was still drawn to learn more about Judaism, Mindy continued practicing her own faith. Along with her family, she attended church services regularly, often driving daily to the Church of the Resurrection to sit in a small chapel where she felt peace, and where she felt close to the spirit of her father.

Six months after Reat's death, Mindy was still struggling with the new reality of her life, finding solace in her Christian faith while continuing to learn more about Judaism, when her phone rang. It was Pastor Hamilton with horrible news, and a request.

Abdisamad Sheikh-Hussein, known as Adam, was 15 years old. The son of Somali immigrants and a devout Muslim, he had just finished helping with evening prayers at his mosque when he stepped off the curb into the street with a group of friends. A car sped toward the group and Abdisamad managed to push a friend out of the way before he himself was struck and killed. Like Reat, the death of this beautiful, bright young man was not an accident. It was murder, a hate crime. The man who killed Abdisamad professed to be a Christian and said he hated Muslims.

Pastor Hamilton told Mindy that a Muslim woman had called the church looking for her. There was to be a vigil at the mosque that evening and Abdisamad's friends and classmates had one request. They wanted Reat Underwood's mother to be there.

Muslim? Mindy thought. *I don't know anything about the Muslim faith. I'm just getting to know the Jewish people.*

Of course, Mindy agreed to go. Her brother Tony and mother, Melinda, joined her.

When the family arrived, a young girl approached her. "Are you Mindy Corporon?" she asked.

"Yes," Mindy replied.

"Do you know what time you speak?" she asked.

Speak? What? Mindy had no idea that she was expected to speak. She didn't know enough about the Muslim faith or Islamic traditions to feel comfortable getting up and comforting Abdisamad's friends and family. Mindy had never spent any considerable time with people of the Muslim faith. Reat did have a Muslim friend at school, a wonderful young man named Belal. Belal and Reat met in elementary school, but it was just that year, as high school freshmen, that they had grown closer and spent more time together in homeroom and on the debate team. Mindy had gotten to know Belal from attending debates, and she knew he was a bright young man. But a few conversations with a teenage boy was not enough to have given her insight into Muslim customs, faith and traditions. Mindy had never had an extended conversation with a woman wearing a head covering, nor did she know the significance of the scarf, or that the proper term was *hijab*. Mindy had never attended services at a mosque, she had no idea what the tenets of the Muslim faith were, and she didn't know anything about proper protocol or etiquette.

Standing in the mosque that evening, Mindy wanted desperately to be able to provide some sort of solace to this devastated family and community, but she didn't know where or how to begin. Mindy grabbed her phone, and right there, did a quick search of the Muslim faith to find some common ground of which she could speak. Almost immediately, she found her answer. Muslims believe in heaven. It was a shared common ground with their friends of the Christian faith.

Heaven. I can do this, Mindy thought. *I can talk about heaven.*

That night, Mindy consoled the heartbroken friends and family of Abdisamad Sheikh-Hussein and spoke to them about heaven. After that evening, after speaking in the mosque, Mindy felt like she was finally beginning to understand what God's plan for her might be. She was a Christian woman, drawn to the Jewish faith, and now Islam was calling to her as well.

Little by little, Mindy's path and purpose were becoming clearer to her. "God was saying, I need you to bring these people together, I need you to bring these faiths together. I need you to meet these people and have conversations with them. Christian, Jew, Muslim and others. We need to band together. Because there is evil. And we can't get rid of evil, but we can band together to fight it."

And in that spirit of working together to promote faith, education and awareness, Faith Always Wins was founded. Through events, speeches, media interviews, merchandise sales and donations, the foundation has raised hundreds of thousands of dollars toward its cause. But even more importantly, Faith Always Wins raised awareness and began a dialogue on the importance of faith and interfaith education.

Just don't call it interfaith tolerance. Mindy won't tolerate it.

"Think about the word *tolerate,*" she explained. "*Tolerate* means that you still don't like them and you still might not understand them. So it's really not tolerance. It's more understanding and education. It doesn't mean you need to agree with them . . . I think if you're busy tolerating someone you're not taking the time to learn who they are. So it's about educating people so that they understand more and that they aren't afraid."

Getting to know her Muslim neighbors and finding common ground with them at Abdisamad's vigil was the first eye-opening step along Mindy's journey to interfaith awareness. "Now I feel more comfortable talking to women who wear scarves." And she won't stop until she helps others feel the same.

Learning about different faiths was the initial step. But as the one-year anniversary of the shootings approached, Mindy, Melinda and the entire family wanted more. They wanted dialogue, but they also wanted action.

Melinda noted that Reat, Bill and Terri were murdered on Palm Sunday. Easter, Christ's resurrection, the light from the darkness, came seven days later. Because of this, Melinda told Mindy, she wanted the one-year anniversary of the murders to be marked by seven days of kindness, an entire week of hope and good deeds to be shared with the community and world. Light from the darkness, just like the light of Christ's resurrection came from the darkness of his crucifixion and death.

Seven days.

From that idea, the SevenDays™: Make a Ripple, Change the World movement was born. And that idea, if Mindy has her way, will indeed be the ripple that leads to changing the world.

SevenDays™ is a week's worth of events and programs aimed at promoting acts of kindness and interfaith awareness. Seven days of action, education and dialogue.

From the very first day, the day of the shootings, Mindy and the entire family had experienced firsthand the extraordinary effects of even the smallest acts of kindness. A meal delivered to the house. A kind word. The outpouring of support from friends and the community. The angel wall. They wanted those ripples to grow and to spread across the community, country and globe.

Seven days.

The plan was straightforward. Each of the

seven days was assigned a theme that would be promoted through programs and events.

Day 1, LOVE: Reach out to those you care about today.

Day 2, DISCOVER: Take time to broaden your worldview.

Day 3, OTHERS: Give of yourself to others, whether an individual or a charitable organization.

Day 4, CONNECT: Gather together with family/friends to reconnect.

Day 5, GO: Choose an activity that benefits your physical well-being and mind.

Day 6, YOU: Remind yourself that you are special. Take care of YOU so that you can take care of others.

Day 7, ONWARD: Let it begin with you. Be the change. Make a ripple to change the world.

The week would be filled with events, guest speakers and panel discussions to promote each theme. The goal would be to educate, inform and spread love in the world, so that no more families would have to experience the pain and horror of losing their loved ones because of religious intolerance or hatred.

During the week, scholarships would be awarded, honoring students whose work and initiative creates ripples of kindness. And to honor Bill and Reat's love of music, the Faith, Love and Song competition was born. The competition honors young songwriters whose songs promote faith and love.

The week's events would come to a close with a three-mile walk beginning at the Jewish Community Campus, where Reat and Bill were killed, continuing past Village Shalom, where Terri was killed, and ending at the Church of the Resurrection. Thousands of people wearing blue T-shirts would walk together, resembling a moving river of hope and change. Inside the church, the lights would be dimmed as Pastor Hamilton stepped out on the stage holding a single lit candle. The light from that one candle would then be passed on to the next. Soon the entire church would be illuminated, a beautiful glow washing over the whole community, pushing back the darkness together.

Healing. Together. Onward.

———

I had spent so many months beating myself up for not attending Bill and Reat's funeral, for not traveling to Kansas to be with the family. And so when Mindy filled me in on all the extraordinary things she had planned for SevenDays™, I knew I had to be there. Mindy explained everything that she had planned—the speakers, panels and prayer services. She also told me of her plans to travel to Reat's favorite places and sprinkle his ashes across the globe. Again, I was amazed by her faith, focus and conviction. And like millions of others, I still wondered the same thing—how did she do it?

I found out when Christiana and I made the trip to Kansas for the first SevenDays™ event. It was the first time I had seen Mindy in person since our coffee date at Starbucks a few months before Reat and Bill were killed. I hugged her tight and I looked at her, and then I looked closer. I could not put my finger on it, but something about her looked different to me somehow. She caught me staring.

"Eye makeup," she said. "I don't wear mascara or eye makeup anymore. There's no point, because it comes off and gets all over when I cry."

The world saw a stoic and strong woman, seemingly unstoppable in her mission to keep her son and father's memories alive. She seems at times superhuman in her strength. I was reminded in that moment that while she was brave and tenacious, Mindy is first, foremost and forever a mother grieving the loss of her son.

The television cameras aren't always around to capture that side of the story.

Christiana and I stayed with Mindy, Len and Lukas for the weekend. Also staying with us that weekend was a young woman named Jacqueline Murekatete. Jacqueline is a survivor of the Rwandan genocide and founder of the Genocide Survivors Foundation. After hearing Jacqueline speak in Washington, DC, Melinda and Mindy were so moved and inspired that they asked her to come to Kansas and speak at the first SevenDays™ event. Unfortunately, Christiana and I arrived in Kansas too late to attend Jacqueline's speech. But through the course of the weekend, with long talks over coffee in the morning and wine in the evening, I got to know Jacqueline and her story. She is an extraordinary and beautiful person, as inspiring as her family's story is heartbreaking. She is a woman who radiates light even as she details the darkest depths of humanity.

Jacqueline explained that she was nine years old in 1994 when the Rwandan genocide took place. For generations, the ethnic Hutu and Tutsi lived side by side in that beautiful country. But then the Hutu government propaganda campaign began. Incessant radio broadcasts began calling the Tutsi snakes and cockroaches, warning the ethnic Hutu to be wary of them. And then in April 1994 came the call over the radio for the

Hutu to pick up their machetes and rid Rwanda and the world of the Tutsi cockroaches. Again and again across the airwaves, the Hutu were told that complete and total extermination of the Tutsi was their patriotic duty to Rwanda. Mob mentality spread like contagion. Neighbor turned on neighbor, friend turned on friend. The killing spree lasted nearly 100 days, from April to July. In those three terror-filled months, approximately 800,000 ethnic Tutsi were murdered by the Hutu.

When the killing spree began, Jacqueline lived in her grandmother's village, where she attended school. At first, she hid with her grandmother in the home of a Hutu man who risked his own life to shelter them. Then one day there was a knock at the door. "We know you have cockroaches in there," the men said. Jacqueline and her grandmother were convinced that the end had come. Somehow, the Hutu man who hid them convinced the machete-wielding men to leave. But their hiding place was no longer safe.

From there, Jacqueline's grandmother brought her to an Italian orphanage where priests were hiding Tutsi children. They would take Jacqueline, the priests explained, but they could not hide adults. As much as they wanted to help, the priests were certain that everyone would be murdered if the Hutu learned adults were hiding in the orphanage among the children. Jacqueline's grandmother left her with the priests, telling Jacqueline she would be back for her.

Jacqueline never saw her grandmother again.

For nearly 100 days, nine-year-old Jacqueline experienced the almost daily horror of watching men, women and children being dragged to their deaths. She heard the screams of people being murdered, of limbs being hacked off with machetes for the crime of being born a Tutsi or for being a Hutu who helped Tutsi survive.

Despite daily threats from the Hutu who would storm the monastery, machetes in hand, threatening to kill everyone inside, the priests managed to save several children. Jacqueline was among them.

When the killing spree was over and it was safe for children to leave the orphanage, Jacqueline learned that in addition to her grandmother, the rest of her family was gone. Her mother, father and six siblings had been dragged to a river and murdered. Their bodies were tossed into the water, never to be found.

Like Mindy, Jacqueline struggled with debilitating survivor's guilt.

"I've spoken to other survivors of genocides and survivors of the Holocaust and survivors of hate crimes," Jacqueline says. "And I think all of us always ask ourselves, why me? Why did I survive when my parents and my siblings and my baby brother did not? He wasn't even a year old. He didn't even know what ethnicity was. He didn't know what his name was."

After the genocide, Jacqueline was brought to the United States and adopted by an uncle who had managed to escape Rwanda. Like so many survivors, like Rosa and Spera, for years Jacqueline remained silent about what she had suffered. But then one day when she was in high school, a Holocaust survivor came to speak to her class. Listening to his story, Jacqueline was changed and inspired. From that moment on, she knew that she was not powerless. She knew silence was not the answer. Jacqueline made the decision to use her voice as a tool for change. She would speak up and tell the world what happened, what she had witnessed, and she would do all she could to make sure it never happened again.

"Part of my work in speaking out against genocide, in speaking out to people, sharing what happened to me, is about encouraging more people to speak up. I tell people, especially young people, that if they ever find themselves in circumstances where everybody around them seems to be doing the wrong thing, there's always an opportunity to do the right thing. There's always an opportunity to stand up for your friend, like your grandmother in Greece did," she explained to me.

Today, in Rwanda, surviving Tutsi who returned to their homes after the genocide often have no other choice than to live side by side with the Hutu neighbors who murdered their families. Many Hutu defend their actions with the claim that they were just doing what their government told them to do, simply following orders.

I was just following orders. It's the same defense used by notorious Nazi war criminal Adolf Eichmann. Eichmann, responsible for the deportation and transport of millions of Jews to the death camps, was captured in Argentina in 1960. He was extradited to Israel and tried in a Jerusalem court for war crimes, crimes against the Jewish people and crimes against humanity. Eichmann pleaded for his life before the court, claiming that he was "simply following orders" when he sent millions of Jews to their deaths. He was found guilty and sentenced to death.

Jacqueline works tirelessly, traveling the world to inform, empower, educate and warn about the dangers of *just following orders*. Her dream is that people will never again blindly listen to their leaders, or follow orders to hate and to hurt. That never again will a mob mentality lead to such devastation as it did during the Holocaust and in Rwanda. And like Marcia Haddad Ikonomopoulos's tireless commitment to seeking out and honoring those who performed acts of moral courage during the Holocaust, Jacqueline takes every opportunity to put the focus on those who had the moral strength to stand up and say no.

"It's comforting," Jacqueline says, "to hear the story about your grandmother or the story of other families who were protecting Jewish people during the Holocaust. When you look at Rwanda it's comforting to know that even when neighbors were turning against neighbors, when the government had turned against a group of its citizens, there have always been people who have stood up to their own government. Who took the risk of losing their lives in order to protect their neighbors, sometimes in order to protect strangers."

He who saves a life, saves the world.

Watching Jacqueline and Mindy together that weekend, it made perfect sense to me that they had found each other. Individually they were survivors speaking out in memory of loved ones lost to hate. Together, they were a chorus of hope, change, compassion and action.

"It's unfortunate that this is the reason why we were introduced," Jacqueline explained, "but we now know that we both have a mission and it's good to know that we are now fighting this fight together."

I spent the entire weekend taking it all in, inspired by Mindy and Jacqueline, realizing how extraordinary this circle of survivors is. I was very grateful that Christiana was there with me to experience SevenDays™ and to learn from both of these amazing women. It was especially important to me that Christiana spend time with Jacqueline. It was one thing for me to tell her about the secret of Erikousa, to explain how selfless and brave her great-grandmother was in hiding a Jewish family. It was quite another thing to sit and laugh with Jacqueline, to grow to love and admire her, knowing she is alive today because someone took a chance, someone listened to his own moral barometer and risked his life to save her. In meeting and spending time with Jacqueline, the enormity of what happened on Erikousa sank in for all of us.

As the weekend came to a close, we were all exhilarated, as well as physically and mentally exhausted.

That Monday was the seventh and final day of events, and we had just completed the walk from the Jewish Community Campus to the church. I stood in the darkened Church of the Resurrection as Pastor Hamilton stepped out onto the stage with one lit candle. As the flame passed from person to person, I received the light from the person beside me. Turning to share the flame from my own candle, I stood with my family as we watched the church light up all around us. It was a beautiful ending to an incredible weekend. Christiana and I were leaving Kansas for New York the following morning. As much as I wanted more time with Mindy and the family, it was time to go home. We all needed to privately and quietly heal, to process everything we'd learned and experienced.

I sat in my seat in the church and thought about what would come next, for Dave and myself, and most importantly, for Christiana and Nico. Then, a video appeared on the screen above the altar. It told the story of Sonia Warshawski, a Holocaust survivor Mindy had befriended who spoke at a SevenDays™ event before Christiana and I arrived in Kansas.

I watched the screen and listened to Sonia tell her story. She, like Mindy and Jacqueline, is committed to using her voice for change; to educate and inform, and to warn of the dangers of hate. She is a woman committed to inspiring others to have the moral courage to stand up for what is right and what is just. I learned how her life was forever changed, her family destroyed by the Nazis, but how she refused to allow them to destroy her will to live or her humanity.

Before the video had finished playing, I knew there was something I needed to do. I could not leave Kansas without meeting Sonia.

A friend of Mindy's managed to find Sonia's number for me, and I called her right then and there, standing on the floor of the church moments after the service finished, as people filed out all around me.

"Hi, Sonia. My name is Yvette. I'm a cousin of Mindy Corporon's. I would really love to meet you. I just heard about your story and I was so moved. I would really love to speak with you. My grandmother helped save a Jewish family in Greece. They were from the Jewish community of Corfu. Most of the community was completely wiped out in Auschwitz."

"Of course I would love to meet you too," Sonia replied in that beautiful, melodic voice of hers—part Polish, part Midwest, and all personality, spirit and warmth.

"Wonderful. Can we meet tomorrow morning? I fly back to New York tomorrow."

"No, I am sorry, dear. My granddaughter, Leah, is here. Do you know Leah? She is a filmmaker. She is making a movie about my story called *Big Sonia* and we have an appointment tomorrow morning. I'm so sorry, dear—another time," Sonia said.

I was devastated. I didn't know when I would get back to Kansas and I didn't want to miss my chance to meet Sonia.

"Well, what time is Leah coming to you tomorrow?"

"She will be here at nine."

My news producer instinct kicked in. "Great. I'll see you at eight." And I hung up the phone before Sonia had a chance to say anything more.

At precisely 8:00 the following morning, Mindy, Lukas, Jacqueline, Christiana and I pulled up to

Sonia Warshawski's home just outside Kansas City.

With her pink lipstick freshly applied, hair teased and lacquered and outfit perfectly tailored, pressed and accessorized, Sonia greeted us at the door and welcomed us inside. Standing at four foot eight, Sonia Warshawski is a woman small in stature and big in personality. She wasn't just Big Sonia; she was larger-than-life Sonia.

Mindy made all the introductions. "And this is Jacqueline," she said as Jacqueline extended her arm to shake Sonia's hand. "Jacqueline is the survivor of the Rwandan genocide that I told you about."

"Yes. I wanted to meet you," Sonia replied. "You must meet my granddaughter, Leah. She is a filmmaker. Leah and her husband made a movie about Rwanda. She fell in love with the people of Rwanda, you know. She made the documentary called *Finding Hillywood*. Do you know it?"

Not only did Jacqueline know about *Finding Hillywood*, Leah's film about how the emerging film industry is helping Rwanda heal after the genocide, but she also told Sonia that she knew some of the people who were featured in her granddaughter's film.

"Then you'll have to meet Leah. She lives in Seattle but she is coming later. You will meet her," Sonia said.

"Here? Leah's coming here?" Jacqueline could not believe the coincidence. But I knew it was nothing of the sort. Standing there in the foyer of Sonia's home, the great and vast world felt so very small. From the hills of Rwanda, to the islands of Greece, to centuries-old Polish cities, and finally the plains of Kansas, it was as if something had brought us all together, like an invisible thread connecting us through the years and across the globe. It was simply meant to be. *Beshert.*

We had only an hour together before Sonia had to leave. She ushered us all to a wood-paneled den filled with sunshine, comfortable sofas, handmade knitted throws and family photos. We were ready to listen and Sonia was ready to hold court.

I had so much to ask her, with so little time. Breathless, I jumped right in.

"We saw your story yesterday in the church. I think I told you my grandmother was one of a group of islanders—we're from Corfu, and all of the Corfu Jews were sent to Auschwitz. And there was a man who was a tailor, like you . . ."

I went on to tell her about Savvas and the girls my grandmother helped save, and her response was visceral. It was as if Sonia could see them standing before here, more than 70 years later.

"They were all beautiful girls. Tall, very, very slim," Sonia said. "One was a very famous singer.

I remember because when we were together at night and it was already completely quiet, she would sing the song 'Mama.' Do you know it? It was a very famous song."

"The Jews from Corfu in the camp?" I felt the goose bumps up and down my arms. "Did you know the girls from Corfu?" I inched closer to Sonia.

"From Greece. I don't know if it was Corfu. I don't remember. It made us all cry." Sonia continued, making sure to look each and every one of us in the eyes as she described the day she watched the Greek Jews arrive at the camp.

"One day when we were working there. And suddenly we heard the cries and here are two open trucks and the girls were standing all naked, all naked. In those days they were rushing us to kill us off faster and faster because things were getting bad for them. And the transfers were coming in constantly and the crematoriums were going constantly, constantly, you know, killing the people. And so this I'll never forget in my life. When those girls—their cries—and you could—I don't know, a normal person will never understand this. Seeing them going to their deaths . . ." Sonia's voice trailed off as she shook her head and closed her eyes.

Sonia explained that she was raised in Poland and was used to the cold, harsh winters, which helped her survive. This was not the case for the Jews of Greece, born and raised in the Mediterranean sunshine or on beautiful Ionian islands, like Corfu.

"Greece had such a different climate. You didn't have winters there. It was very mild and they couldn't adjust. They were dying off right and left, maybe because of the climate and of course the other conditions. They could not handle it. They could not handle it."

Sonia detailed for us how as a young girl of 17 she worked in a brush factory in her hometown of Miedzyrzecz. When the Jews were rounded up by the Nazis, her family was forced to live in the ghetto. After two years, as the Nazis emptied the ghetto, Sonia's father and brother were shot when they tried to escape. Her 14-year-old sister managed to get away and survived the war by hiding in the woods. But there was no escape for Sonia and her mother. They were crammed into a cattle car bound for the Majdanek death camp. Sonia survived Majdanek and later Auschwitz and Bergen-Belsen. On liberation day she was accidently shot in the chest by a British soldier, the bullet barely missing her heart. Another prisoner lifted Sonia in his arms, holding her up in the air, telling her to look. He wanted her to see the liberation before she died. But Sonia didn't die. She wouldn't give the Nazis the satisfaction. She wanted to live.

Sonia was proud of the fact that despite all of

the horrors she experienced and witnessed, she refused to give up. She admitted that during her time in the camp she thought about committing suicide, but could not bring herself to do it. Sonia felt in her heart that she was a survivor, that in some way, for some reason, she was meant to live.

She told us of the daily beatings she endured, of starvation, of watching babies, the elderly and everyone in between murdered before her eyes. Discarded, as if they were trash. She told us of the sadistic female guard who threw prisoners down the latrine and then watched as they drowned in filth and human waste. She told us that dying from thirst is far worse than dying from malnutrition, explaining how in the cattle car she stood on the bodies of the dead, desperate to catch a sip of water from the one communal bucket or a hint of breeze from the one tiny window.

When she came to the next part of her story, Sonia focused her attention on Lukas and Christiana, making certain that they listened carefully to what she was about to describe: The day her mother was selected for death by the man known as the Nazi Angel of Death, Dr. Josef Mengele.

"This was the middle of the day, sunny. This was already the end of the summer. I remember we were all naked. You walked outside and he was standing—I will never forget this man; he was short. He was always wearing white gloves and a stick, you know, in his hand. He looked always perfect, and I came in front of him with my mom and he put my mom to the left and me to the right. At that moment I wanted to go with my mom, but the SS woman, she was beating me and pushing me back to the right."

Sonia would have done anything to go to the left with her mother, even though she knew what that meant. Left meant Dr. Mengele deemed you no longer fit enough to work. Left meant death. Later, back in the barracks, in her darkest moment when she didn't think she could go on, Sonia heard a voice. Like Mindy when she stumbled upon on her father's body in the parking lot, Sonia Warshawski heard a voice guiding her.

"It was like God telling me to see my mom one last time. I rushed into the big door and there was just a little peephole. And I looked out and I saw in this hole, you know, the women walking to the gas chamber. And I saw my mom with another lady from my hometown. I'll never forget them holding together. This was a night that I really fell apart."

When she smelled the smoke rising from the crematorium that night, Sonia knew her mother was gone.

Even as others all around her lost their faith, Sonia continued to pray. She asked for strength and guidance, and day after day she asked that God grant her one wish: "Turn me into a little bird so I can fly away."

But even as she prayed for a way out, escape was not an option for Sonia. She told us that as long as she lived, she would never forget two young girls who tried to escape, but were captured and executed as a warning to the other prisoners. The prisoners were all marched out into the yard and forced to watch. As the noose was tightened around their necks, the girls shouted out their final words, "Never forget." Their bodies hung like that for days, rotting in the sun, a reminder of what happens when Jews tried to escape. Each day as she passed their corpses, Sonia made a solemn vow that she would carry out their final wish: that she would never forget.

But after the war, Sonia remained silent. She never forgot, but she never discussed what she'd witnessed or the horrors she'd lived through and survived. Like Jacqueline and Mindy, Sonia was consumed with survivor's guilt, asking herself again and again how and why she survived when her loved ones did not. For 20 years, Sonia kept her memories of the Holocaust a fiercely guarded secret. Then, one day, everything changed.

Sonia was home in Kansas City watching television. She was so angry and upset about what she was seeing and hearing. It was a story about skinheads, neo-Nazis who claimed the Holocaust never happened. They declared that it was all a myth, a lie made up by the Jews. In that moment Sonia knew she could stay silent no longer. She finally understood why she had survived, what God's plan for her was. As the skinheads spewed their lies and hate, Sonia Warshawski made a vow that she would be quiet no more. She would use her voice to silence theirs. Sonia would speak out and never stop talking as long as she had air in her lungs. She would fulfill her promise to those two tragic girls and speak up in honor of her mother, father, siblings and every single victim of the Nazis. Sonia Warshawski made it her life's mission to do everything in her power to make sure the world never forgets.

Shortly after watching the skinheads on television, Sonia began speaking about the Holocaust to groups, schools and even inmates in prison. Even the most hardened of criminals were frequently reduced to tears when she told her story, and when she told them that their lives in prison were like "living in a hotel" compared to what she'd endured. To this day she shares her story with anyone who will listen, and she especially tries to make time to speak to students. Sonia knows that young students are our future, our greatest hope, as well as our most vulnerable demographic. She watches the news and reads the newspapers, heartbroken and worried about the rise of anti-Semitism again across the globe.

She was devastated the day Reat, Bill and Terri were killed. That 70 years were not enough to rid the world of Hitler's vile propaganda; that Nazi vitriol and violence had followed her across the years and miles to her new home in the United States. She sees how history is tragically repeating itself today. How propaganda is still being used even now to fuel the agenda of hate groups in Europe, the Mideast and the United States.

"How can you comprehend young people from normal countries joining things like ISIS? It's because of the young you can brainwash much faster. And this is why I speak at schools."

Christiana and Lukas sat silently and listened to each and every word. Sonia's message was for them, for all of us, every single person in that room and beyond the walls of Sonia's house.

"I am only hoping that maybe there will be a change in this world, with this, all that comes from hate and propaganda. When I talk to students, I tell them, 'Open your heart for love. Take out any hate.' And sometimes a smart student will ask me a question: 'How can you still love and talk about love after what you went through?' And I say, 'That's a wonderful question.' I tell them: 'I shall never forget. I shall never forgive, but I will never hate. If I'll hate, I destroy myself.' "

As we sat in that room taking in Sonia's words,

I looked around. Sonia. Jacqueline. Mindy. Each suffered unimaginable loss. Each struggled with similar challenges: guilt, pain and forgiveness. Each carried the overwhelming responsibility of keeping alive the memory of those who were murdered, and of struggling to find any hope amidst gut-wrenching hopelessness. All three had dedicated their lives to making sure their loved ones' deaths were not in vain, to doing all they can so no more families experience the hell they've lived through. A trinity of survivors, each at a different point in her healing process. But *healing* isn't really the right word, is it? Because you are never really healed after suffering losses like theirs. You are changed. All three women faced the same daunting challenge: how to allow themselves to live again, to feel love and happiness and to laugh, without feeling like their joy is a betrayal of the ones who were lost.

"Mindy has to stay strong," Sonia said as she looked over at Mindy again, knowing how fresh and painful her wounds still were. Mindy draped her arm around Lukas, pulling him closer and stroking his face as Sonia spoke.

"You know you are a different person when you come out from this hell," Sonia said. "I was, completely. You see life in a different way, you know . . ." Sonia's voice trailed off again.

Sonia. Jacqueline. Mindy.

The Holocaust. Rwanda. Overland Park, Kansas.

As each one of us attempted to process it all, Sonia, with her eloquence and perspective, drove home the reality that our family tragically already knew to be true. "We're going backwards; we didn't learn anything. When we came out from this hell, I felt I had more hope that people would be different."

After all she had been through, suffered and lost, Sonia Warshawski had emerged damaged, and yet unbroken and ever hopeful. And still, the world had let her down.

I made a promise that morning, seated in that sun-drenched den surrounded by Sonia, Mindy and Jacqueline. I was brought to tears and inspired by them, individually as women and survivors, and together as a chorus of hope and of action. I promised that like them, I too would somehow find a way to use my voice, to do my part and make certain we never forget.

PART FIVE

chapter nineteen

IT WAS NOTHING.
IT WAS EVERYTHING.

I returned from SevenDays™, from spending time with Mindy and meeting Sonia and Jacqueline, with a new perspective on my yia-yia's life and story. It was eye-opening and overwhelming to think about how a split-second decision in a time of crisis—whether to extend yourself and offer help or save yourself and turn your back—could mean life or death for generations to come. I was reminded again of the story I learned about Daniel Soussis's family during the Holocaust, of the Christian woman who changed the course of his family's history and signed Daniel's mother's death sentence when she leaned her head out the window and shouted to the Nazis that there was a Jewish woman hiding just across the way.

I kept replaying the different scenarios in my mind. What if Yia-yia had turned her back, kept her door locked and not welcomed Savvas's girls into her home? What if someone had extended the same kindness my yia-yia had shown and offered a safe haven to Sonia Warshawski and her mother? Would Sonia's mother have survived?

What if Jacqueline's neighbors not risked their own lives to save hers? Would she be here today as a witness to genocide, warning the world of the horrors of hate? What if Mindy had decided to mourn privately and quietly? Would she have touched, changed and inspired so many lives?

We'll never know the answers to these questions. How was it decided who was saved, who died, who survived and who went on to bear witness to the world? Was it predetermined? Was it fate? Was there some grand master plan? How and why were we all brought together from across the globe, at that very moment in time, with similar stories and the same resounding theme? I couldn't wrap my head around it. But I knew that somehow and for some reason it was all connected. That *we* were all connected, that there were lessons to be learned from each of us, and that Marcia's words rang true for all of us.

"My feeling is that we should be teaching the next generation not the names of the perpetrators, may they rot in hell, but to emulate those who had the moral courage to make a difference."

And it was with that goal of honoring the islanders of Erikousa who had shown so much courage that the plans for the Award of Moral Courage celebration and ceremony began to take shape.

While Marcia and I sorted out minutia and organized the ceremony from New York, my cousin Effie helped iron out the details on Corfu and Erikousa. While Effie and I were cousins, we were closer than sisters could ever be. It was Effie, with her deep belly laugh, sarcasm and razor-sharp wit, who had welcomed me back to Corfu each summer, prepared with a full itinerary of bars, clubs and beaches that we needed to hit. Together, we had danced on countless tabletops and watched the sun rise over the Ionian Sea as we stumbled home arm in arm. It was Effie who was the inspiration for Popi, the sassy cousin and best friend in *When the Cypress Whispers*. Effie took pride in announcing, "I'm Popi," to anyone and everyone familiar with my book.

Over and over, I asked Effie the same thing: "What is everyone on Erikousa saying about all of this?"

"They are excited," Effie would reply. "They think it's amazing."

"Are you sure? Is anyone complaining about this? About me?"

"No. You're being crazy." Effie laughed. "And so what if anyone has something to say? Who cares what they think? This is a wonderful thing for the whole island," she insisted.

But even so, even with all of Effie's assurances, an unsettled voice kept nudging at me and just would not quiet down.

As wonderful as it all was, the fact remained that I had basically dug up long-forgotten, buried memories and sprung them on the entire island. I was used to chasing down stories, hunting for answers and figuring out solutions to the seemingly unsolvable. That's what journalists and television producers do. That's what my career was based and built on. But this wasn't just some anonymous news story or celebrity interview that I was hunting down, hell-bent on securing at any cost. This time it was about family and history and legacy and real life, involving more sensitivities than I could even begin to imagine.

The facts were clear. Seventy years ago a group of people on Erikousa did something courageous and extraordinary. And then it was over, just like that. People simply went on with their lives as if it had never happened. Many of the young islanders had never even heard the story of the Jewish family. My yia-yia had always had a flair for the dramatic. She loved to hold court, to cook for a crowd and spin her tales about the past. And yet there were those who lived through every moment of the war, along with my yia-yia, and chose not to relive or revisit those awful years with their families.

I knew in my heart that I had done something good and worthwhile in finding Spera and Rosa's families. Since that first meeting with Rosa's sons over Skype, we had communicated several times, with Aaron and Gilad acting as translators. I had seen Peretz's three beautiful daughters on

Skype and also in family photos. This was not just some old story. This was a beautiful family, people who were alive today because of the courage of Erikousa. And this beautiful family seemed genuinely thrilled to at last learn their family's lost history. Rosa's sons, along with Spera's beautiful family, had confirmed to me that yes, they would be making the trip to Greece to join us for the Award of Moral Courage ceremony on Erikousa. They would come with me to walk the same paths that Spera and Rosa walked, to visit my yia-yia's home and to meet some of the islanders who had helped Spera and Rosa survive. It was an ending to our story that was indeed beyond my wildest dreams.

But what I feared, what kept me up at night with worry, was that perhaps I had overstepped some invisible boundary. Rosa and Spera chose to never share this story or their memories of the war with their families. It was their conscious decision to never speak of what happened. Who was I to do so? Who was I to rip the scab off an old wound when it wasn't even my own family? I couldn't shake the feeling that I had meddled where I did not belong.

But at this point it was done. The airline tickets were booked, the plans were made, and despite my own insecurities and second thoughts, it was all really happening. Spera and Rosa's families would be making the trip back home to Corfu and Erikousa. And Erikousa was getting ready to welcome them home.

While still remote, rustic and quite insular as a society, Erikousa has changed in a multitude of ways since my yia-yia's generation, and even from when I was a teenager. Today, Erikousa is still a beautiful and, for the most part, pristine and undeveloped escape from the stresses and complexities of the modern world, but now they had all the modern conveniences. The gravelly dirt roads are now freshly paved over; the old donkeys used to transport people and luggage have been replaced by pickup trucks and ATVs. And in several locations across the island, hotspots offering perfect Wi-Fi connections replaced the old party phone line of the past. There's a lone policeman stationed at his small home overlooking the port, and with no doctor or hospital on hand, the helipad overlooking the small harbor serves as a lifeline for emergency medical care.

Gone are the days when it was forbidden for girls to be seen in swimsuits. Today the beaches are filled with families and friends, young and old, men, women and children, together enjoying the beauty of the caramel-colored sand and splashing, diving and swimming in the calm, warm waters of the impossibly blue Ionian Sea.

There are still a small handful of old widows adorned in their black dresses and head scarves, but you'll no longer find them congregating at the port, ready to gossip about which visiting American girl was seen out unchaperoned after dark. Even the yia-yias have evolved in their thinking. They're quite modern now, by old yia-yia standards anyway. They are no longer consumed with making sure their children and grandchildren marry only Greeks. Some don't even bat an eye when a couple opts to live together or even have a child before getting married. But although the islanders and even the yia-yias themselves have evolved with the times, some island traditions remain perfectly intact. Those same yia-yias are forever smothering their grandchildren with love, pinching their cheeks, squeezing them tight and cooking for them over an open fire, slicing freshly dug potatoes and frying them in olive oil for impossibly sweet and delicious treats.

Today, Erikousa is an island where young and old celebrate life together on the beach and in the handful of outdoor restaurants. There are only a few dozen islanders who live on Erikousa year-round. Most bide their time during the winter months until summer comes again and their children and grandchildren will return to the island to fill their homes with laughter and love. Today, the island is still filled with the aunts, uncles and cousins of my youth, only now they're all older and grayer, and those of my generation have children of our own.

Just like when my yia-yia and papou first moved to New York, the epicenter of Erikoushoti life in the United States is still based in and around the Bronx and the Church of Zoodohos Peghe. Each summer, as US schools go on summer break, families with roots on Erikousa pack up and head to the island. It's a running joke that those with roots on Erikousa never travel or visit anyplace but Erikousa. "Why would we?" always comes the response. "What we have is our very own paradise. What idiot would ever want to visit anyplace else?"

On Erikousa, there is never any such thing as an adult gathering or a children's gathering. Families here do everything together. By day you can find groups of all ages laughing together on the beach. By night, parents, grandparents and children dance together on the flower-filled patio of the Hotel Erikousa under the stars. Often, as the night gets later and later, the children simply curl up together on the couch in the corner of the patio and fall asleep. When the party is over, after the last drink is finished and the last bouzouki note is strummed, parents pick up their sleeping children and carry them home as the cicadas' song and the gentle lapping of the sea fill the air with a melodic summer serenade.

Now, as back in my yia-yia's time, the Erikousa community—no matter how far across the globe they have spread—continue to support one another as if we all still lived just down the dirt road from one another. As word spread about the ceremony and homecoming, Erikoushotis both in Greece and in New York were amazed that it was all really happening. The elder islanders, my yia-yia's friends who remembered Savvas and the girls, could not believe that life had come full circle and that they would have the chance to meet Spera and Rosa's families. The ones who grew up, as I did, hearing the names Savvas, Spera, Rosa, Nina and Julia could not believe I had actually found them. And the ones whose parents and grandparents continued to keep the secret of Savvas could not believe that such an amazing thing had happened on our little island.

"How could I not know this story?"

"This is incredible."

"Bravo. Your yia-yia would be so proud, Yvette. I bet she would make a giant pan of *patatopita* and invite everyone over to celebrate."

"What an honor for our island! I only wish my yia-yia and papou were alive to see this."

The response was incredible, and the support staggering. I knew deep down that this was a wonderful thing. I knew deep in my heart, after living through what happened to Reat and Dr. Bill in Kansas, that the world needed to be reminded of stories like this. Now more than ever, as we tried to wrap our heads around the anti-Semitism that devastated our own family, and as the world wrestled with the daily headlines about the very real horrors of ISIS and the refugee crisis coming out of Syria, I knew that the gentleman in the basement of the synagogue that day was right: "We need to hear the good. We need to be reminded that good things happened too." And because of that, what was happening on Erikousa was a very good thing.

But even so, I kept coming back to the fact that so many of the islanders never told their families about the Jewish family they had saved. Why? Was it just too painful to revisit? Did they, like my own father, prefer to simply look forward and never look back?

"You really are being crazy," Effie replied each time I asked her if I was overstepping. "And by the way, it's too late now. It's done. There's no going back. I already shelled out money to print the programs. So just stop it already."

Effie was right, despite my own insecurities. It was all really happening. There was no going back.

As Marcia and I worked together to organize a plan and finalize our itinerary, we realized that simply bringing the families back to Erikousa was not enough. Spera and Rosa and their families had been a vital part of the large, thriving Jewish community of Corfu. Marcia reached out to her friends in the small but dedicated Jewish community still there, who were just as eager as the Erikousa community to welcome the families home.

In the end we decided that the ceremony would be part of a two-day homecoming and celebration, a reunion of discoveries and tears. The plan was that we would all meet first on Corfu and visit the Jewish quarter together. There we would learn the history of this once vibrant, thriving and still beautiful community. We would stop at the Holocaust memorial first, to lay flowers and say kaddish, the Jewish prayer for the dead. After touring the Jewish quarter, we would visit the last remaining synagogue on Corfu, where we would learn more about the families who had once filled the congregation. Together we would walk the same cobblestone streets, explore the same narrow lanes and shops. We would experience firsthand where the Jewish community of Corfu lived, laughed and worshiped before everything changed in June of 1944.

And then, the following day, we would travel together across Corfu's narrow mountain roads to the port towns of Agios Stefanos and Sidari. From there, we would board small ferryboats for the 45-minute trip across the sea to Erikousa. On Erikousa there would be a ceremony to welcome the families home and honor the islanders for their bravery and sacrifice. Finally, the day would end with a traditional Erikousa meal on the sun-drenched patio of the Hotel Erikousa, with everyone on the island invited to take part in the celebration.

Marcia made it very clear that as grand in scope as our event had become, she wanted this to be an intimate celebration. She wanted to hear from the families. Speeches from the heart, not pontificating from politicians.

"I want music and dancing," Marcia insisted. "This is a celebration. We will honor those who have passed, of course. But this isn't a memorial service. We are going to celebrate life. It's going to be a happy day that none of us will ever forget."

When Marcia says she wants something, it's as if the universe has no choice but to listen and to make it so. Marcia was quickly proving to be our very own Jewish-Greek oracle.

When Marcia announced she wanted dancing and singing, what Erikousa offered up in return was so much more than music. Lina Orfanos is an incredibly talented young woman and a world-renowned soprano. Lina's father, Spyros, is a PhD and NYU professor of psychology who was born on Erikousa. Like all of us with roots on the island, Lina carries with her a deep love for her father's birthplace. But it wasn't just Lina's paternal lineage that made her the perfect choice to provide the music for the ceremony. Lina's mother, Sophia, is Jewish and was one of Poland's hidden children of the Holocaust.

From the age of two until she was four years old, Sophia and her mother hid in plain sight, Jews living as Christians in Nazi-occupied Poland. Sophia's father was sent to a concentration camp but managed to escape, eventually finding his family and hiding in the attic of their apartment. To keep the secret and keep her husband hidden, Sophia's mother warned her never to go into the attic, telling her that a hungry wolf who ate children lived there. Little Sophia never learned it was her father in the attic, not a wolf, until after the war, when it was safe for him to come out of hiding. Sophia detailed the trauma of her experience in her memoir *A Wolf in the Attic*. For Lina, the Holocaust was framed by the unique perspective of being both a descendant of rescuers and a child of survivors. If anyone was meant to sing at a ceremony honoring the islanders of Erikousa for saving a Jewish family, there was no one more perfectly suited than Lina Orfanos. Lina is based in the United States, but she was to be performing in Europe around the time we would be on Erikousa. And as it turned out, her incessantly busy calendar just so happened to be free the days of the ceremony.

"Yes, of course I'll be there," Lina enthusiastically replied.

Her parents, however, were scheduled to be in Canada for a psychology conference that they were hosting and chairing. It seemed an impossible scheduling conflict, one that tore at Spyros and Sophia. Spyros had grown up as I did, listening to his mother and aunts sharing stories about their dear friends, Spera, Nina, Julia and Rosa. All of the women on Spyros's side of the family were incredibly close with the girls. His aunt Theodora was especially close with Nina, sharing a bond that went well beyond friendship.

Theodora had lost her mother at the age of seven, during the time of the German occupation when Nina, Savvas, Spera, Rosa and Julia were hiding on Erikousa. Every day Theodora was sent off to school, and every day she would escape the schoolhouse and run away to the nearby cemetery, where she would sit beside her mother's grave and cry. Every day the schoolteacher would fetch her from the cemetery and send her home, knowing the child was in no emotional condition to learn. To this day Theodora remembers that Nina would be there waiting for her, and the safety and security she felt in Nina's warm and welcoming embrace. Nina, who had herself lost so much, knew what it was to be motherless. It was Nina who stepped in to act as Theodora's surrogate mother. In Nina's embrace, Theodora felt the love and security she craved. Knowing this, and knowing how much Nina, Spera, Rosa and Julia all meant to his aunts and mother, Spyros was devastated to learn of the scheduling conflict. It tore him up to think he would not be on Erikousa to welcome the families and witness his daughter sing at the ceremony. But Spyros had organized this entire conference, and it was taking place in Canada on the exact dates that we would be on Corfu and Erikousa.

Hearing this, Marcia sprang into action. She had full faith that even the most seemingly insurmountable problems have solutions. Within moments of hearing Spyros's dilemma, Marcia moved mountains, plans and all sorts of schedules. Instead of Sunday and Monday, June 28 and 29, Marcia moved the entire production one day later, to Monday and Tuesday, June 29 and June 30. This new plan ensured that Lina's parents could race to the airport from the conference, get on the first flight out of Canada and make it to Corfu in time.

Soprano Lina Orfanos, descendant of Erikousa rescuers and the child of a Holocaust survivor, was on board to sing her heart out. And her proud parents, with their unique personal perspective on the Holocaust, would be seated front and center to savor every note.

In the final months leading up to the ceremony, Marcia received a call from the International Raoul Wallenberg Foundation. The foundation is named for the Swedish diplomat Raoul Wallenberg, who is credited with saving tens of thousands of Jews during the Holocaust. The caller explained that the foundation had launched

"House of Life," in which a plaque is affixed to a home in honor of people who risked their lives to save Jews during the Holocaust. It was a fairly new program, and they were searching for more stories of people who had sheltered Jews, particularly in Greece. Did Marcia know of any stories that might befit House of Life?

With only four months to go before the ceremony, there was not much time to submit all of the required information and go through the incredibly thorough vetting process to qualify. As we inched closer to getting it done, the investigation hit a snag. The House of Life is a singular citation, affixed outside a single home, honoring those who provided refuge and shelter in *that* home. But what happened on Erikousa was not about a singular home. It was a community effort, and there were many homes and many families involved.

My eyes instantly filled with tears when I was asked by the Raoul Wallenberg Foundation to affix the House of Life plaque to my grandmother's house. I could not believe that our humble little home was singled out for such an incredible recognition. What would Yia-yia say or think if she were here to see this, I wondered. It was a great honor, an honor neither Yia-yia nor I ever would have imagined.

It was an honor that I immediately and politely declined.

Yes, it was my yia-yia's story of welcoming Savvas's girls into her home each night that brought this long-forgotten story to light. But my yia-yia's story was no more significant than anyone else's. It just seemed that unlike some of the others who played a prominent role in the saving of Savvas, my yia-yia liked to talk—clearly a trait I had inherited. Our stories and roles were no more important than those of others. It just seemed we happened to have the biggest mouths.

It was the entire island and community that sheltered and saved Savvas's family, and every single contribution was important. Even those who made it known that they did not want the Jewish family on Erikousa, the ones who insisted that they leave the island, even those who simply stayed away—even they were heroic and deserved recognition. Because despite their feelings, despite their fears, opposition and disagreements, even they kept the secret and never told the Nazis that there was a Jewish family hiding on the island. They were all heroes, every single one of them. It would be impossible and so incredibly wrong to single anyone out.

We went round and round a few times, with everyone offering suggestions on where the plaque should be affixed, who was deserving of the House of Life recognition. As we worked to find the best solution, it was Marcia who again emerged with wise words and sage advice that put everything and everyone in perspective. In an email, Marcia wrote:

> As a dear friend of mine answered, when asked who had saved her and her family during the Occupation, "Was it the baker who gave us a piece of bread when we were starving? Was it the policeman who looked the other way when he knew our IDs were suspect? Was it the man who hid us in his home, risking his life and that of his family? For them it might have been nothing. For us it was everything."

For them it might have been nothing. For us it was everything. It was the perfect way to sum up what happened on Erikousa. In the end, we all agreed that while the entire island would be honored with the House of Life, it was Father Andronikos's name that would be etched into the plaque. As the island's spiritual leader, we decided that naming the priest was by far the best way to honor the tradition of the House of Life initiative as well as symbolically the entire spiritual community of Erikousa. The priest's home, the *keli*, where the family was originally hidden, would be the home designated by the

House of Life honor. And since the priest's home is removed from the center of town, we decided to place the House of Life plaque where more people would see it, in the tiny but perfectly beautiful Erikousa Museum.

The Erikousa Museum is an old restored windmill situated on top of a hill, overlooking the sea and the main beach and port of Erikousa. It's where, generation after generation, the island's women would come together to mill their grain and catch up on all of the island's news. For years, the dilapidated ruins of the mill remained a hollowed-out stone shell overlooking the beach below. It was a place where teens would gather to smoke cigarettes and drink. Today, the windmill has been beautifully restored. Its pale stone exterior and cream-colored sails spinning around and around in the breeze is often the very first thing visitors notice as they approach Erikousa's port. The windmill is a beautiful, lyrical welcome, the very symbol of the pristine perfection of our little island, situated atop a craggy hill above the impossibly blue sea. It now houses Erikousa's tiny cultural museum filled with photos, artifacts and memories of the island's rich history. Everyone agreed the windmill museum was the perfect and appropriate place to house both the Award of Moral Courage and the House of Life honors.

It was really happening.

Every day as we got closer to the events, it felt more and more surreal. I still could not believe this was actually all coming together. I found myself thinking it was too good to be true, that something had to give. Something was surely going to go wrong. It had to, didn't it?

But every day, things continued to fall into place. In New York, Marcia and I worked together to organize and plan. Lina and her father organized the musicians and selected pieces to honor both our Greek and Jewish heritage. In Israel, the MyHeritage team continued to dig and search for information and help to arrange travel for the families. On Corfu, my cousin, confidante and savior Effie worked tirelessly with the Erikousa and Corfu communities to secure permits, prepare the island, produce the plaques and get the word out to all of the islanders. The Association of Friends of Greek Jewry generously offered to sponsor the event, making the financial challenges and often seemingly impossible logistics possible. We hired buses, vans and two boats to ferry our ever-growing group back and forth between Corfu and Erikousa. We began to hear from educators, historians, politicians, journalists and survivors who had heard about the secret of Erikousa and wanted to be on the island for the ceremony.

"What an incredible story," we heard again and again.

"The world needs to hear more stories like this."

"God bless your grandmother and your island."

"We'd love to join you for the festivities."

"Is there room on the boat?"

Every day as we got closer to the ceremony, I waited for the proverbial other shoe to drop. I waited for something to happen, something to go wrong and blow up all of our plans. Every day I woke up bracing myself for the bad news that was sure to come. I waited for the day when it would all catch up to me, the karmic realization that the story of the Jewish family hidden on Erikousa, and especially Spera and Rosa's stories, were not mine to tell.

There were days when certain logistics seemed overwhelming, insurmountable. How could we construct a marble plaque to be affixed to the museum when the walls were curved and made of brick? And the mill is a designated historic landmark, so you can't drill holes to hang anything. Did I mention we had three languages in play—English, Greek and Hebrew? If we didn't translate into all three languages, so many people wouldn't be able to understand what promised to be incredibly moving moments and speeches. But if we actually took the time to translate everything into three languages, the ceremony would take hours upon hours, and we'd be there all day and into the night. How could we make Rosa and Spera's families truly feel at home despite the language barrier and lack of kosher food on the island? How could we ferry 150 people back and forth between Corfu and Erikousa if the seas were rough?

For every problem, we found a solution. The plaques would be displayed on a lovely table in the museum surrounded by photos and flowers. No need to drill holes. We had all of the remarks and every speech translated into Hebrew, Greek and English and placed in a booklet distributed at the ceremony. Anyone who needed translation could simply read along, without adding precious time to the ceremony. Rosa's family told us not to worry; they were seasoned travelers and used to bringing their own food when they visited countries where kosher food was not readily available. "Please, don't worry about us," they said. "We are just so happy to be here with you all. Thank you for everything."

They were gracious, kind, loving and beautiful. Even through my own doubts and uncertainties, it was clear: They wanted to be with us. They wanted to see Erikousa.

We did all we could. Every issue was sorted out, situated, addressed and resolved. Except for one. There was one very large issue that remained, and it was totally out of our control.

Despite the most meticulous planning, the fact remained that we were at the mercy of the weather. Erikousa's remoteness made travel to and from the island a constant question mark. There was never any guarantee that one could get on or off the island. If the seas were rough that day, transportation would be impossible and despite everything, the entire event would be cancelled. And, if the weather suddenly turned bad, as it often does, we faced the daunting reality of having more than 150 people stranded overnight on Erikousa with not enough hotel rooms to accommodate them all.

On paper, this homecoming, celebration and ceremony all sounded like a great idea. In reality, I wasn't so sure anymore. The reality and fragility of it all was overwhelming.

"You realize just how remote this island is?" I cautioned again and again. So often I wished someone would step in as the voice of reason and say *yes, what are we thinking, we'll never pull this off. It's too risky.* But no one ever did.

As we approached the event, my stress level grew, as did Marcia's confidence that all would work out in the end.

"Seriously, if the weather is bad, we'll be stuck. There's no way we can pull this off and get everyone there. Everything will be cancelled," I cautioned.

"Our people have always had a direct line to God about the weather," Marcia would simply smile and say. "It's the one thing we've always had on our side."

Marcia remained calm and convinced. I, on the contrary, did not.

The minutia and semantics took their toll, even as everyone around me marveled at what we were planning and, by all appearances, pulling off. Internally I was reeling. I never lost sight of the importance of what happened and that the rescuers on Erikousa deserved every recognition and honor known to man. I have never been one to back down from a challenge. I thrive on them. Adrenaline and competitiveness had been my way of life since I was in school, and had driven my entire career. But I felt like this one had gotten away from me. One challenge had led to another, and then it was out in the world and out of my control. And despite the fact that I truly felt inspired to shout Erikousa's praises from the rooftop, I was simultaneously wrestling with that all familiar, crippling self-doubt.

I imagined myself as Erikousa's very own Icarus, the mythological character who, despite warnings, flew too close to the sun with wax wings. Every day I waited for the moment that my wings would melt and that this entire plan and I, along with it, would come crashing to the ground.

But unlike Icarus, it appeared I had a Greek-Jewish oracle on my side. No matter what tremendous hurdle we came up against, even the times I thought it might be better off if the entire event was just cancelled, Marcia just repeated her mantra. "I just have a feeling everything will be fine."

Everything was confirmed, the plans were in place, and people were flying in from all corners of the globe. We had done all we could do. It was out of our hands now. If there was ever a moment we needed *beshert* on our side, this was definitely it.

chapter twenty

PIECING TOGETHER THE STORY OF SAVVAS

In Or Yehuda, Israel, the staff at MyHeritage was working at a frenetic pace. With the website growing exponentially around the world, it was all hands on deck to keep up with client demand. A lot had changed since those very first years as a garage startup in the pretty cottage behind a picket fence. The MyHeritage logo now stands several feet tall on the side of a gleaming new office building just a short drive from the quaint cottage of those early days. But even so, even with hundreds of new employees across the globe, millions of new users around the world and all the demands and work that come with success, the large staff in MyHeritage's sleek new modern offices still functioned very much like a family. And that is exactly how Gilad wanted it.

Each day, come lunchtime, the hundred or so employees in the vast, loft-like headquarters come out from behind their desks to gather in the large, open kitchen, where Gilad provides lunch for everyone. No matter how busy they are, the staff members take the time for a meal together each day, sitting out on the office's large, bright terrace that looks out across the horizon toward Tel Aviv and the Mediterranean Sea beyond. Sitting out on that deck, the staff congregate and catch up, enjoying perfect warm, sunny afternoons and the magical glow of Israeli sunsets. Out on that sun-drenched terrace you feel as if you can reach your arms up and touch the planes as they take off and land at Ben Gurion Airport just down the road.

With all he had on his plate, as the June date for the reunion and ceremony on Erikousa ticked closer, Gilad was in a race against time. For Gilad, it wasn't enough that he had solved the mystery of Erikousa, found Spera and Rosa's families and was helping with travel arrangements to ensure everyone would be able to attend the ceremony in Greece. As far as Gilad was concerned, all of that was merely the beginning.

Roi Mandel had been at his new job as senior researcher of MyHeritage for exactly one week when Gilad summoned him into his large and meticulously organized office. A seasoned journalist, Roi had spent years on the front lines, covering the biggest news stories in Israel and around the world. But even for the most dedicated of journalists, working in war zones can take its toll after a while. Married now, with two young children, Roi was looking forward to applying his skills to the challenges of his new job. Challenges that didn't involve wearing a flak jacket to work.

Roi wasn't exactly sure what to expect when he walked into Gilad's office that day. Standing across the desk, Gilad handed Roi his first assignment: to research the Jewish community of Corfu further and build Savvas Israel's family tree. Roi at once understood the significance of the task. This was not about simply filling in names, dates, births and deaths on the branches of a chart. This was about bringing Savvas Israel's family tree, and by extension, Savvas Israel himself, to life.

Gilad had already uncovered so many secrets that had been fiercely guarded over the years, and yet he knew there were still so many more to uncover. And among them all, there was one Gilad could not get out of his mind. Perhaps the most important missing piece of the puzzle that Gilad had yet to fit into place.

We knew from the residents of Erikousa that Savvas had died on the island shortly after the Germans left and that he was buried just outside the Christian cemetery. The islanders clearly remembered Savvas's daughters returning to Erikousa years later to have their father's remains removed for burial in Israel. But after scouring every cemetery across the country, Gilad had yet to find the grave of Savvas Israel. Gilad and I both understood that without finding the final resting place of Savvas Israel, the Jewish tailor of Corfu, the mystery of Erikousa would never fully be solved.

The stakes were high and Roi felt intense pressure to prove himself to his colleagues, and especially his new boss. After all, Gilad had been the one to find the proverbial needle in a haystack. Gilad had located Spera's and Rosa's families with nothing more to go on than first names and an occupation. Now it was up to Roi to uncover the secrets that Spera and Rosa had guarded so fiercely.

When they finally arrived in Israel after surviving the war, losing their entire community and countless family members, and spending close to two years in the British refugee camp on Cyprus, Rosa and Spera were told to never look back. They, like so many Holocaust survivors, were advised to simply forget the hell they had endured. The girls were told that their lives began anew the moment they set foot on Israeli soil. And as a part of their rebirth, they were encouraged to never speak of the past. It seems Spera and Rosa both took this directive literally and to heart. Neither Spera nor Rosa ever spoke of the countless losses, the pain and the evil that existed during that dark and dangerous time. But in never looking back, they also never spoke of the love and the friendships that had sustained and saved them.

Roi's assignment was daunting, but he was

eager to put his investigative skills to the test. Roi dove right in, anxious to uncover more hidden secrets of a family and community that seemed to have been forgotten by history.

As a veteran investigative journalist, Roi knew from the very first moment that this investigation would be a tricky one. He faced several challenges right off the bat. First of all, there were absolutely no records from Erikousa. Every single book, document and ledger from the war years had been destroyed. During the war, everyone on Erikousa knew that in Nazi hands, those documents and ledgers could have been used to weed out the Jews from the Christians—a death sentence for Savvas's family as well as the islanders. The Germans had made this clear, telling the islanders that they would kill anyone found helping Jews and burn down the entire island as punishment. So the people of Erikousa took initiative and burned the proof instead, setting their own history and records ablaze rather than have them fall into Nazi hands.

It was a similar situation on Corfu. The Jewish community had lived on the island for more than 800 years. Theirs was a large, thriving society, and Roi knew that detailed records had been kept throughout the generations. But so much of that history had been lost or destroyed during the war. The entire Jewish ghetto had been ransacked and looted, and Allied bombs then destroyed what little was left. Two of the three synagogues were reduced to rubble, along with so many records of births, deaths and marriages.

Even if he were to locate documents, Roi knew that this was not a straightforward investigation. It wasn't merely fitting together the pieces of a puzzle. Even all these years later, there were so many sensitivities involved, so many raw emotions, and so much bitterness, betrayal and heartbreak. As the survivors attempted to piece their lives back together, they also learned the painful truth of what happened on Corfu after the deportations, of the signs plastered across the island by Corfu's mayor at the time. Even today, it is as if fresh wounds are opened each time the words are read:

> Now that the island was cleared of the riffraff, our island can go back to its rightful owners and we, the true Corfiots, can enjoy the fruits of the island.

More than 70 years later, the pain of that betrayal and of what happened in June 1944 is still raw for the survivors, their families and friends. In the Jewish quarter and across the island, it is still felt to be an ugly stain on the history of a place that prides itself on such beauty and rich culture. To this day, so many of the island's residents still do not know or fully understand the horror of what happened to their Jewish neighbors. And often those who do know are unwilling to discuss it.

To reconstruct the family's story, not only would Roi have to uncover the community's forgotten history, he would also have to earn their trust.

It is within that daunting framework that Roi Mandel dove into the investigation. He soon learned that while records on Erikousa and in the Jewish quarter were nonexistent, the archives of other parts of Corfu proved to be a treasure trove.

But accessing them . . . well, that was another story.

The archives of Corfu, among the oldest and most meticulously kept in all of Europe, are yet another product of the island's rich and storied history. Through the centuries, Corfu has seen a multitude of rulers and invaders, from the Venetians to Napoleon to the British. But unlike other islands and parts of Greece, Corfu never fell to Turkish invaders, a fact that the islanders of Corfu attribute to protection by their beloved patron, Saint Spyridon. All across Greece, on island after island, city after city, the Turkish pillaged and decimated the communities they conquered, burning everything in their wake, including ancient and priceless archives. The fact that they failed to conquer Corfu, despite many attempts, saved not only the beautiful green island, but her exquisite archives as well.

Just a short walk from the grand arches and crowded outdoor cafés of Corfu's Liston promenade, past the ornate iron gazebo and cobblestone paths of the grand Spianada square and across the imposing footbridge to the old fort, where the Jewish community of Corfu were herded at gunpoint, sits the Historical Archives of Corfu building. Located in the shadow of the imposing old fort, this unassuming building, with its pristine stucco facade, holds no indication of the rich history and treasures within.

Inside, the beautifully restored rooms are lined with carefully bound and meticulously catalogued records and documents dating back centuries. Deep beneath the building, in a climate-controlled basement running the length of the archive, lie stacks upon stacks of additional records and documents. There are volumes of passports, travel documents, census and municipal records and maps, many dating back to Venetian times. These maps are exquisite pieces of art, beautifully hand drawn, down to a detailed rendering of each and every individual cypress and olive tree on the properties.

Today, amidst the backdrop of the Greek financial crisis, cutbacks and austerity measures, a small yet dedicated team of researchers and archivists work to preserve and record this rich history of Corfu. Corfu's chief archivist, Nella Pantazi, a lovely and soft-spoken woman, leads her team with quiet professionalism and single-minded determination. Tall, slim and always meticulously dressed, with an easy chic about her, Nella is a woman who exudes both elegance and excellence. It is no wonder that Nella has chosen to live within walking distance of her beloved archives. She has cared for and cultivated the collection with fierce pride and careful attention to detail that speaks more of passion and a life's calling than a job.

When Nella's phone rang in the Corfu archive in March 2014 the caller identified himself as Roi Mandel, a researcher with MyHeritage in Israel. Roi requested help and some information, explaining that he was researching the lost history of one of Corfu's Jewish families.

And then he called again. And again and again and again.

"They thought I was too pushy," Roi recalls. "And they were busy. I was calling every day, asking for documents and trying to explain this complicated story." Roi can laugh about it now. But he wasn't laughing then.

At first, Nella and her staff didn't quite know what to make of the persistent Israeli on the other end of the phone. But then Nella softened a bit, just enough to hear Roi out. After all, Nella was already quite familiar with MyHeritage. Just a few years before, she had used MyHeritage to map out the history and family tree of one of Corfu's oldest noble families. At the time, Nella learned that it was the only family history website to support the Greek language. By using MyHeritage, Nella was able to complete her project and her presentation. That family tree, dating back centuries, now proudly hangs in Corfu's Historical Archives building, with the MyHeritage logo on full display. Since the company had helped make her project such a success, Nella decided to give Roi a chance and at least hear what he had to say. Roi eventually earned Nella's trust and enthusiastic support.

With Nella's help, Roi's investigation quickly moved forward. She and her staff began sending him relevant archived material from Corfu, and Roi sorted through Nazi war records, Holocaust documents and Israeli government files from various other sources.

The results were staggering and heartbreaking. Roi soon learned that tragedy stalked Savvas Israel's family even before the Nazis finalized their plans on Corfu.

From Corfu birth records, Roi learned that Savvas had been married twice. His first wife, Ester Politi, died at an early age. Savvas had one child from this first marriage, a girl named Rachel, who was born in 1911. The fate of Rachel remains a mystery. Roi has been unable to locate any records about Savvas's firstborn child.

Savvas then married his second wife, Rosina. Again, Savvas was made a widower, left alone to care for his children. Rosina also died at a young age, before the Nazis occupied Corfu. Together, Savvas and Rosina had six children, including Spera, Julia and Nina. While Spera, Julia and Nina were all saved on Erikousa with their father, the fate of their siblings was quite different.

Corfu birth records show that Savvas's son Solomon, who was named after Savvas's own father, was born on Corfu in 1916. According to family stories and interviews with surviving members of the Corfu Jewish community, Solomon was a member of the navy but was falsely accused of being a Nazi collaborator. He was murdered in Thessaloniki by Greek resistance fighters.

While searching through Corfu's archives, Roi also uncovered records of another son. Zacharias was born to Savvas and Rosina on December 10, 1917. Since there is no mention of Zacharias in any documents and he is not seen in any photos, it is thought that he died in childhood.

As tragic as their entire family's history is, the story of Savvas's second youngest daughter, Vittoria, is perhaps the most devastating. From Corfu records, Roi learned that Vittoria was married to a man named Zacharia Osmo. In digging through Holocaust testimony from Yad Vashem, Roi discovered that Vittoria and

Zacharia had three children together. But Roi could find no other trace of Vittoria and Zacharia Osmo. It was as if Spera, Julia and Nina's sister, Vittoria, had simply vanished.

Weeks after our first Skype session with Rosa's sons, Avraham and Peretz, Roi reached out to the family and asked if he could pay a visit to the Rehovot apartment Avraham had shared with Rosa before her death.

"I would love to look through Rosa's papers and photos, if that would be all right with you," Roi asked.

"Of course," Avraham quickly responded. "Anything you need. Anything at all."

Always the eager host, Avraham not only opened his home to Roi, he also opened the family archives. Box after box, file after file, Avraham and Roi sorted through Rosa's papers, photos and documents together. Avraham also gave Roi his mother's phone book.

"Here. This might be helpful," Avraham said as he handed Roi the book. "You can take it with you."

That phone book proved more than helpful. The names and numbers written in Rosa's own hand proved to be a lifeline and link to a tragic family history that Rosa had tried so hard to keep buried in the past.

Roi would soon learn that not every member of Rosa's family was able to put the past behind and move on as Rosa had. Others were still searching for answers and some sort of resolution, even 70 years later.

Back in his office at MyHeritage, Roi picked up Rosa's phone book and began dialing the numbers inside. One after another, the numbers led to dead ends and disconnected phones. But then he dialed a number listed under the last name Osmo. Roi was stunned when a woman answered, identifying herself as Ruth Osmo.

"Of course I know about Rosa and her family," Ruth said. "Yes, yes. Of course. I'd he happy to tell you everything I know."

Ruth Osmo is a warm and welcoming woman with kind eyes and a smile to match. Ruth lives in a suburb of Tel Aviv with her family, where you can find her kissing and hugging her grandchildren at every opportunity, cherishing each moment with them as a gift from God. She knows how lucky she is to live in Israel, to have her family close. Not a day goes by without Ruth stopping to remember family members lost in the Holocaust, as well as those who survived yet lost a part of themselves in the death camps. She feels it's her duty and obligation to remember the ones who were murdered, even those she knows so little about.

Ruth's daughter, Matilda, never understood her mother's obsession with lighting so many memorial candles for family members she'd never met, many whose names she didn't even know. But Ruth paid no mind. She grew up listening to her father's stories about life before the war. She knew theirs was a large, vibrant family, filled with loving, good and kind people. It was her duty to remember and honor them, even if she didn't know their names.

When Ruth picked up her phone that day, Roi explained that he was looking to reconstruct a family tree and asked if she knew anything about Savvas Israel and his girls. Ruth was overcome. It was as if she had been waiting her whole life to share what her father had told her.

"So you know the story, then?" Roi asked.

"Of course I know the story," Ruth responded. "My father was married to Savvas's daughter, Vittoria. I'm Zacharia Osmo's daughter."

Ruth explained that she was born after the war, the daughter of Zacharia Osmo and his second wife. She said that during the war, her father was married to Vittoria. At that time, it was common for the Jewish community to move and frequently travel between Corfu and Trieste, Italy. In both locations, the same names were used again and again, often making it difficult to distinguish between family members. During the German occupation, Vittoria and Zacharia lived in Trieste with their three small children. When the Nazis began deporting the Jews of Trieste, Vittoria and Zacharia escaped, looking for a safe place to hide. They made their way to Rimini, Italy, and sought shelter in a monastery. The priests explained that they would hide Vittoria and the children, but they could not take Zacharia; there was not enough room. Zacharia left his wife and children at the monastery and went in search of another hiding place where they could all stay together. He found one, but when he told the other Jews who were hiding that he planned on returning with Vittoria and the children, they told him it was too risky to bring more people and refused to let them in.

As Zacharia tried desperately to secure a hiding place for his family, word reached the Nazis that children were being hidden in the Rimini monastery. One day, a knock came at the door. Nazi soldiers rounded up all the children. Some of the adults managed to escape, but not Vittoria. Vittoria refused to hide. She refused to run away or stay behind without her babies. Her twins, Sabino and Rachel, were three years old; the baby, Rosa, was not even a year old. If she could not save her children, she would not save herself. Vittoria and her children were all murdered in Auschwitz.

Zacharia survived the war, eventually moving to Israel and remarrying. But until the day he died, Zacharia never forgot or forgave, holding those who refused his wife and children shelter responsible for their deaths. Ruth remembers her father as a man who never smiled and never showed any joy. Just one time, on her wedding day, Ruth recalls seeing the tiniest glimmer of a smile. Zacharia was so traumatized by the loss of Vittoria and the children that from the moment Ruth was born, he never let her out of his sight. Zacharia smothered Ruth with all the love and attention he was never able to lavish on the son and daughters who were murdered by the Nazis.

The horrific story of Vittoria and her children is made even more tragic by the realization that Vittoria's three children were Savvas Israel's only biological grandchildren. None of his surviving children—Spera, Julia or Nina—had children of their own. Savvas Israel's family bloodline died that day in Auschwitz with Vittoria and her little ones.

Months after their initial phone call, Roi and I visited Ruth in her home just outside Tel Aviv. The three of us sat at the kitchen table, piecing together more of the family's story and looking through old photographs that Rosa and Nina had left behind. Ruth picked up several of the photos and recognized her father. And then she saw a photo of herself as a young girl from a long-forgotten family gathering.

Roi pulled out his computer to show her Savvas Israel's family tree. Every day it was getting larger and larger as he worked to fill in the generations.

"I light candles for all of them, you know," Ruth told us. "But I don't know some of the names. Like Vittoria's mother. I light candles for her all the time, but I never learned her name."

"She's right here," Roi said as he pointed to the screen. "See? Vittoria's mother is right here."

Ruth leaned in closer and looked at the family tree. There she was: her father's first wife, Vittoria Osmo. And directly above was a photo of Vittoria's father, Savvas Israel. Beside Savvas was a photo of his wife, Vittoria's mother, the woman Ruth had been lighting candles for all these years without knowing her name. She was a beautiful young woman, elegant and fine-boned, wearing a lace-collared dress, hair swept into a bun, a faraway look in her dark eyes as she stared off into the distance. Beside her photo was her name, the name Ruth had been searching for all those years as she prayed for the grandmother of her baby brother and sisters who were murdered in Auschwitz.

Ruth smiled as she read the name out loud. "Rosina."

chapter twenty-one

ROSA'S FAMILY

To the islanders of Erikousa, she was known as "the little one," Savvas the tailor's granddaughter.

To the survivors of the Jewish community on Corfu she was simply known as "the orphan child."

To her family, she was the loving mother and grandmother who gave them everything she could, except for the one thing she was incapable of giving—a glimpse of herself as a young girl.

And to those of us trying to piece together the 70-year-old secret of Erikousa, Rosa Hassid was perhaps the biggest mystery of all.

"Well, she was the granddaughter. I mean, that's what Savvas told us," my aunt Agatha insists. "Why would we question him? Of course we believed him. We believed them all."

"She was Vittoria's daughter. I know it for a fact." Theodora Musakiti is to this day adamant. It was Theodora who developed a maternal bond with Nina when her own mother passed away when Theodora was just seven. "I remember Nina crying every day, all day for her sister. She knew Vittoria was murdered by the Germans.

She was Rosa's mother. Come on, I know these things."

Everyone who remembers Savvas, Julia, Nina, Spera and Rosa on Erikousa recalls the same thing, that Savvas and his daughters identified little Rosa as his granddaughter. But in reconstructing Savvas Israel's family tree, Gilad and Roi actually found that Savvas was misrepresenting Rosa. Savvas Israel, the tailor, was not Rosa's biological grandfather.

"But I don't understand," Agatha says. "After everything we did for him and his family, why would they lie to us?"

At first the deception seems to defy reason and logic.

But there does seem to be a reason Savvas lied to even his closest friends and confidants on Erikousa about who the timid, dark-haired little girl was. At a time when families were being ripped apart, Savvas likely passed Rosa off as his own grandchild in an effort to protect her. Little Rosa had lost so much already—her mother, father and all of her siblings. By passing the child off as his own granddaughter, he was likely trying to ensure that no matter what happened, Rosa would not be separated from the only people she had left in the world.

"She never spoke to us about the Holocaust. She never told us any of this family history, or any of these stories," Peretz insists.

"She only ever came close a few times," Avraham remembers. "Every year, on Holocaust Remembrance Day. It was a day of mourning in our house. We could not turn on the radio or the television. There was no laughter or playing. We had to be very quiet and still. We knew. She made it very clear that it was a day of mourning. But our mother never told us who it was we were mourning for."

And even when it came to their three beloved aunts, Nina, Julia and Spera, the women who showered the boys with affection, attended birthdays and bar mitzvahs, Rosa still maintained her silence about them. The boys never knew how or if they were really related to the three loving women who whispered with their mother in Greek.

While she never confided in her children about the past, there was one person in whom Rosa Hassid did confide. Ninety-four-year-old Mazal Cohen was Rosa's best friend. With her short, dark hair and clear, beautiful skin, Mazal is a woman who looks much younger than her years imply. But while she appears to defy the hands of time, those years have come at a heavy cost. Mazal carries with her the weight of all those difficult years and the scars of a generation who had to rebuild their lives after the war. Originally from Turkey, Mazal immigrated to Israel. She married a Holocaust survivor from Athens who lost 70 family members in the camps. He was the only person from his own family to survive.

Mazal lives in Rehovot, in a small, tidy apartment not far from the apartment Rosa shared with Avraham. The two women raised their children together, sharing holidays, birthdays and other celebrations. Like so many survivors after the war, Mazal and Rosa did their best to form a new type of family, attempting to fill the large void left by all those who were murdered. But while some women chat, gossip and laugh with their girlfriends over coffee, it wasn't like that for Mazal and Rosa. When Mazal and Rosa got together, the two women often simply sat side by side in silence.

On one of the rare occasions that she did speak of her past, Rosa offered Mazal a small glimpse of her family's story. Rosa explained that during the war she lived on Corfu with her parents and three brothers and sisters. She also told Mazal that like her own husband, Rosa's entire family was murdered in Auschwitz.

It was during one of those rare conversations about her past that Rosa finally broke her silence and explained how she was able to escape Corfu and the Nazi roundup. Mazal shared her memories of that conversation with me as we sat side by side one afternoon in her Rehovot home. She explained that Rosa's family was close with Savvas's and that young Rosa loved nothing more than to visit with Nina, Spera and Julia in the tailor's shop.

"Rosa told me that Savvas was a gifted tailor whose specialty was clerical garments," Mazal recalled. "She said he had finished some robes for the priest and Savvas asked Nina to deliver the package for him. Rosa asked if she could go along with Nina, and of course Nina said yes. When they arrived, the priest told the girls that things were getting dangerous on Corfu and that it was not safe for them to return. The priest insisted the girls stay. Rosa said the priest brought her food and that they hid in a basement."

"Did she ever tell you anything about Savvas himself?" I tried to make sense of this. So Nina and Rosa had come first, and Savvas, Spera and Julia joined them later.

"How did he and the other girls make it to Erikousa also?" I asked.

Mazal looked at me with heavy eyes. She simply shook her head from side to side. No.

It was the same with the Erikousa community. While no one could remember the details of when Savvas and the other girls arrived on the tiny island, several did recall one detail that helped piece together what happened back in the early days of June 1944.

"Of course I know where they lived," Theodora insists, in that *well, why didn't you just ask me* way. "They were my friends. I knew the apartment well. Savvas didn't live in the Jewish area of Corfu. He lived a few blocks away, near the Municipal Theater. On Mantzarou Street."

Piecing together the memories of Rosa's friends in Israel and Greece, a clearer picture emerged. With Savvas's apartment located away from the chaos of the Jewish quarter, it's likely that Savvas, Spera and Julia were able to slip away to meet Nina and Rosa unnoticed, buying the valuable extra time they needed before the Nazis realized they were missing.

"Rosa told me that she knew," Mazal recalled. "She told me that she knew the Germans were looking for her. They knew that when they came and took her family away, Rosa was missing. She was always so afraid that the soldiers would find her."

And Rosa also knew that because of the Nazis, life would never be the same. As we sat together, Mazal explained how after the German surrender, Savvas pulled the girls close and broke down the stark reality of their situation.

" 'That's it,' he said to them. 'They're all dead. We have to start from the beginning,' " Mazal recalled. Rosa was just ten years old when Savvas delivered the crushing news.

Spera was a young woman, 23 years old, when the war ended. At a time when Jewish women her age would traditionally be busy tending to their parents, husbands and children, Spera had no one left. Perhaps it was the cold reality of her father's statement, that she needed to "start from the beginning," that contributed to her decision to leave Greece. Or perhaps it was the taint of anti-Semitism that still permeated life in the Jewish quarter. Whatever the reason, once Spera made up her mind to leave Greece, she simply refused to leave Rosa behind. As I learned from Gili's original email from Yad Vashem, and from piecing together the rare stories that Spera did share with her family, we know that on July 30, 1946, Rosa and Spera boarded the illegal refugee ship the *Henrietta Szold*, bound for Mandatory Palestine. They spent two weeks on rough seas. Conditions on board were crowded and difficult, and things did not improve once they reached land. Once the ship pulled into the dock at Haifa, British soldiers immediately seized the refugees. The refugees had survived the war, survived the Nazis and survived a torturous journey, only to be herded at gunpoint behind barbed wire once again. Some fell to the floor, kissing the ground of the Holy Land, even as the British soldiers pushed them along. Instead of a new life in the Promised Land, they were sent to a British refugee camp on Cyprus, where they spent the next two years. Not only were Rosa and Spera alone in the world, they were two unchaperoned girls in a refugee camp under incredibly difficult conditions.

On Erikousa, the entire island had worked together to help feed and protect them. On Cyprus, all they had in the world was each other.

"Rosa said that life in the camp was very, very hard for them." Mazal shook her head as she spoke. "Finally, when they began to allow people to leave the camp and enter Israel, they only allowed married couples entry. They did not let single people pass. So Spera did what she had to do, for herself, and for Rosa. That's why Spera married Vittorio Moustaki. So they would be allowed to come to Israel."

I knew from one of my first conversations with Michelle that Spera's marriage to Vittorio was a difficult and contentious one, eventually ending in divorce. It seemed that Spera was willing to sacrifice anything, perhaps even her own happiness, to ensure that she and little Rosa were finally allowed entry to Israel.

As they settled into their new lives in Israel, Spera began using her Hebrew name, Tikva, and did her best to provide Rosa with a stable and happy life.

"At one point Spera sent Rosa to live in a kibbutz," Rosa's son Peretz recalled. "She thought it would be good for Rosa to be around other children. But a few days later, Spera was shocked when she came home to find Rosa waiting for her at the door. She left the kibbutz, got on a bus and went all the way back home all by herself. She was just a little girl. 'What happened, what are you doing here?' Spera asked her. Rosa turned to her and said, 'I don't want to live with anyone but you.' " Peretz laughs each time he remembers his mother telling him the story. And then gets quiet again, now that he knows what Rosa lived through, understanding finally what it all implies.

From that day on, Rosa lived with Spera and was never far from her side. Rosa craved stability, family and a sense of security, the very things the Nazis had ripped away from her. The very things Spera did her best to lovingly provide.

"Rosa always felt like she was born on a black day," Mazal explained. "That everyone she ever loved left her or died. First her family, then her husband, in a work accident when her children were still so small. She loved Spera like a mother. She loved her children. But there was always a sadness about Rosa, like she never found real happiness."

"But now you know how loved she was on Erikousa," I said to Mazal, telling her how my yia-yia would put food aside for young Rosa, and how my aunt Agatha and Rosa would play together and fall asleep side by side. "So many people loved her. So many people risked everything to try and help her. We tried so hard to find her."

Mazal looked at me but did not speak. She stayed like that for a few moments, quiet, simply shaking her head. There was a heaviness in the room. It was so easy for me to picture Rosa, seated in the very spot where I sat. I could see and feel the two friends there, together, enveloped by the silence and the weight of their memories. I reached out to touch Mazal's arm as she wiped tears from her eyes. Finally, she spoke.

"Sorry," she said. "It's hard for me."

We sat in silence a little longer, just like she and Rosa used to do.

While Mazal offered a rare glimpse into Rosa's family and history, there were still so many unanswered questions.

Roi continued searching through Rosa's papers, as well as government documents and Holocaust records, for any mention of Erikousa. He found none. But a file among Rosa's papers led Roi to a document at the Israeli Ministry of Finance that he obtained with power of attorney given to him by Rosa's sons. In her application for a pension, Rosa testified about her experience during the Holocaust. In it, she wrote:

> In '43, the Germans came to Corfu and immediately began to round up all the Jews, but the Germans could not capture those who fled. I ran into the mountains and villages with the help of other people. After the Germans occupied the city, I wandered from place to place with no

clothes and no food. I feared that the Germans would capture me.

In the same file was a doctor's report:

> The Germans took her parents, her brothers and sisters and since then she has never seen them. The Germans didn't take her because she wasn't at home at the time. A Greek family temporarily took her under their custody and moved her to a remote village outside the city. She suffered from cold and hunger.

In that same report was also the doctor's notation on Rosa's emotional and mental health. For the duration of her life, Rosa Hassid lived with the fear and anxiety that the Nazis were still hunting her and were coming to take her away. Even though she had managed to build a loving home for her two sons, and was surrounded by friends and family, in many ways Rosa forever remained the broken and scared little girl who had lost everything and everyone.

Since 1955, Yad Vashem has worked toward documenting the names and records of the six million Jews who were murdered in the Holocaust. The museum has also documented and recorded the testimonies of hundreds of thousands of survivors.

Roi discovered that among them was Rosa Hassid.

In her 1999 statement to Yad Vashem, Rosa provided the one vital bit of information that had been missing from our search. She stated her name before marriage as Shoshanna Belleli. Shoshanna is the Hebrew version of the name Rosa. In the statement, Rosa listed her father's name as Peretz Belleli and her mother's name as Rina Mizan, both murdered in the Holocaust.

Armed now with the names of Rosa's parents, Gilad, Roi and their team of MyHeritage researchers once again combed through the vast Corfu archives as well as German and Israeli Holocaust records. With this new information, gradually, the tragic story of Rosa's parents and her siblings became clearer.

After the deportation from Corfu, German documents placed Rosa's father, Peretz Belleli, at the Flossenbürg concentration camp in Germany and also at the Buna-Monowitz labor camp, located six miles from Auschwitz. German records show that Rosa's father was murdered on March 9, 1945, just two months before the Nazis surrendered to the Allies on May 7, 1945.

There are no records about the fate of Rosa's mother, Rina.

A search of the Corfu archives resulted in locating the birth records of Rosa's siblings.

Menacham was born in 1928, Gabriel was born in 1930 and Elpis was born in 1932. Rosa, the baby of the family, was born in 1934. The name of Rosa's sister, Elpis, means "hope" in Greek.

Hope. It was Gilad's examination of the name Spera—also known as Esperanza and Tikva—that solved the original search for Savvas's girls and led us to Spera's family in Los Angeles. Hope had unlocked family secrets in Israel, in Greece and in the United States. How ironic that hope is the very thing that this tragic family had so little of. But as Roi was searching through every document, ledger and testimony that he could uncover, he discovered something that no one expected, the one thing that could perhaps bring hope back into their lives.

In her 1999 statement to Yad Vashem, Rosa testified about her brother Gabriel's death at the hands of the Nazis.

"My brother Gabriel Belleli, age 15, was killed in Auschwitz."

But it turns out Rosa may have been wrong.

In a stunning discovery, MyHeritage uncovered German documents listing Gabriel Belleli, who was born on Corfu in 1930, as a survivor of the Bergen-Belsen concentration camp. Gabriel Belleli's name is also listed on a document from September 1945, four months after the war ended. Gabriel's name shows up in one more document, this one from the Corfu Municipal Records in

1955, where he is removed from the population registry and listed as "not in existence."

This discovery opens up a heartbreaking possibility. Could it be that siblings Rosa and Gabriel survived the war without either knowing that the other had as well? In a family history filled with such tragedy, this irony is almost too painful for Rosa's sons to process. We continue searching for any information about Gabriel, with the hope that Rosa's family may one day be reunited with relatives they feared were lost forever.

Contrary to what the islanders of Erikousa believed, we know that Rosa was not Savvas's granddaughter. Instead, by painstakingly re-creating Savvas Israel and Rosa Hassid's family trees, Gilad discovered that she was related to the family through Savvas's second wife, Rosina. Rosina Israel, the mother of Spera, Julia and Nina, was first cousins with Rosa's mother, Rina Belleli. In other words, Rosa's mother was the aunt of Spera, Julia and Nina, and not their sister. Through this new information, Avraham and Peretz finally learned how they were related to "the aunts." In Greece it is customary to refer to elder relatives, regardless of the familial relationship, as aunt, or *thea*. Even in her new life in Israel, Rosa adhered to Greek tradition, always referring to the three sisters as the aunts.

Despite what the branches on their newly formed family tree said, the Hassid brothers knew that the relationship between Rosa and the aunts went deeper than they knew or could understand. Spera's granddaughter Michelle described Spera's love for Rosa as a maternal love, even wondering at one point if Rosa could have been her illegitimate child. But since we now know that Spera and Rosa were born almost 12 years apart and have a clearer picture of what they lived through together, it makes perfect sense that they would form such a deep, unbreakable and maternal bond.

It began with nothing more than a list of first names, an occupation and a long-forgotten secret. From those small fragments of memories, with meticulous research and tenacity, we'd been able to reconstruct an entire family's tragic story and give Rosa's family their history. But despite all the progress, all the digging and discoveries, one vital element to this story was still missing.

None of the documents, testimonies, statements or stories that Rosa, Spera, Julia and Nini shared mentions Erikousa. On Erikousa, everyone kept a secret that helped save the girls' lives. It seems that even after the Nazis were long gone, even when they no longer had anything to hide, even then, Savvas's girls never spoke of their rescuers, fiercely guarding the story of their survival and taking the secret of Erikousa to their graves.

When the Nazis surrendered, it was Savvas himself who told the girls, "That's it. They're all dead. We have to start from the beginning."

Soon after this, Savvas Israel died and was buried on Erikousa. His grave was placed in the shadow of the church, just outside the Christian cemetery gate, on the other side of the wall from where many of his rescuers are now buried. The girls were now more alone than they could have imagined. It was up to Nina, Spera and Julia to make their way in the world, and to take care of young Rosa as well. They were four young girls alone with no family and with nothing to their names.

The paths that the girls chose for their new beginning were decidedly different. But even so, there was one resoundingly important similarity. In their early years, their lives were marked by so much heartbreak and tragedy, but by the end of their lives, Savvas's girls all left this world having found love and happiness at last.

Sitting with Mazal in her tidy apartment, I got more than a cup of coffee and a glimpse into her friend Rosa's life. Mazal was also able to share some insight into the lives of Savvas's daughters, the women who Rosa knew as the aunts and who had cared for and loved little Rosa like their own. Between Mazal's memories, snippets of childhood celebrations gleaned from Avraham and

Peretz and interviews with the survivors of the Jewish community of Corfu, we were finally able to piece together a clearer picture of what life was like for Julia, Spera and Nina after they left my yia-yia and their friends on the tiny island of Erikousa.

JULIA

After living for several years on Corfu, Julia eventually settled in Athens and was quite successful as a seamstress. While in Athens, she fell in love with a Christian man named Jehoshua Baluli. While her sisters were happy that Julia finally found love, the marriage was initially a source of friction, because Julia made the decision to convert to Christianity for her husband. In the end, the bond between the sisters proved stronger than any rift. The sisters stayed close until Julia's death in Athens in 1994. Despite having converted to Christianity during her marriage, Julia was ultimately buried in a Jewish cemetery in Athens.

NINA

After Julia's marriage, Nina moved from Athens to Israel to be closer to Spera and Rosa. Despite having many suitors, Nina never had any desire to be married, according to everyone who knew her. But finally, at the age of 50, she met a man named Rahamin Levy and they fell deeply and madly in love. Nina and Rahamin married and lived together in what everyone who knew them describes as pure wedded bliss. When Rahamin suffered a stroke a few years after their wedding, his devoted wife Nina took meticulous care of him until his death in 1980. Nina once again stepped in as caregiver when Julia was diagnosed with cancer in 1994. She moved to Athens and nursed Julia until her death. Nina then returned to Israel, where she spent her final years surrounded by Rosa and her sons. Nina died in Israel in 2000 at the age of 85.

SPERA

For her entire life, Spera continued doing what she loved best, taking care of her loved ones. After raising Rosa and divorcing Vittorio Moustaki, Spera went on to work as a nanny for Meir Levy, the father of three young girls. Eventually she married him. Spera relished her role in Meir's life and lavished all of her love and attention on his three daughters. Eventually, Spera and Meir moved to the Los Angeles area with their youngest daughter, Rachel. When Rachel's daughter Michelle came along, the beautiful dark-haired little girl filled Spera's life with joy. Once again, just as she had with little Rosa, Spera found her purpose and greatest joy in life, showering her granddaughter with love and attention. She made her honey-drizzled almond cakes and savored each and every tea party together. Spera died in Los Angeles in 1997. Honoring her final wish, her family buried her in Israel.

ROSA

Life was certainly not easy for any of Savvas's girls after the war. But having lost her entire family and lived through the trauma of hiding at such a young age seems to have affected Rosa in ways different than it did Spera, Nini and Julia.

From the day the Nazis came and took her family away, Rosa insisted that her life was in some way cursed, that everyone she ever loved died. Rosa found happiness as a young wife and mother with her husband and small children, but that joy was short-lived when her husband, Yaakov, was killed in a work accident when her younger son, Peretz, was just two years old. Even as she devoted herself to her children, doing all she could to ensure they had good lives, happiness seemed to elude Rosa. She was devastated when the aunts died one by one— first Julia, then Spera. When Nina too passed away, Rosa turned to her friend Mazal and said, "There is nothing left for me. I want to die too."

But then Rosa's three beautiful granddaughters were born.

In perhaps the most meaningful birthday gift of all, Inbar, the first of Rosa's granddaughters, was born on Rosa's sixtieth birthday. Beautiful Inbar shared more than just a birthday with her grandmother. It was as if the birth of this beautiful baby girl had breathed new life into Rosa. After Inbar, the family was blessed with two more little girls, first Sapir, and then the baby, Maayan. While the deep wounds and scars of the Holocaust never left Rosa, she at last found true happiness as she cradled, danced and sang with her precious granddaughters. They were her life, her joy. They were her everything.

In the final years of her life, Rosa Hassid no longer sat in silence. The laughter, songs and giggles of her three granddaughters filled the air with their sweet voices and banished that dark cloud once and for all.

chapter twenty-two

MODERN MIRACLES

Corfu is one of the most beautiful and magical islands on the planet. I feel about Corfu the way I feel about Israel—there is an indelible spirituality that permeates the very land, the sea and even the air. It's in the island's churches, perfuming the air with the scent of burning candles and deep, earthy incense wafting on the breeze. It's in the old cobblestone streets, which generations have walked and buffed to smooth perfection with their footsteps and where Saint Spyridon is said to walk each night, protecting his beloved island and her people. But Corfu's otherworldliness is not confined to her churches, patron saint and protector. There is spirituality in the island's natural beauty, in the deep shades of green in her centuries-old olive and cypress trees, in the cliffs and coves carved out by the patient and persistent sea and in the rich spectrum of blues and turquoise, a kaleidoscope of color so stunning that the scenery can be described as nothing less than a gift from God.

As we prepared to welcome Spera and Rosa's families to Corfu for the ceremony, it was important to me that all of our guests had an unforgettable first impression of Corfu that would speak to the island's rich history of both spirituality and natural beauty. To welcome everyone, for them to witness and experience the full magic of Corfu, only the most enchanting and beautiful locations would do for our first dinner together. For this reason, Flisvos Café was the perfect choice to host our welcome meal.

Flisvos Café is located in Kanoni, one of the most picturesque, postcard-perfect spots on Corfu. It is a small seaside restaurant, a cluster of tables situated directly on the sand, where the sea laps at the shore just a few feet away. It overlooks the iconic tiny green island of Pontikonisi. Translated into English, Pontikonisi literally means "Mouse Island." The tiny island, located just about a half mile from shore, gets its name from the narrow, winding trail of steps leading to the church that's visible through the thick brush of ancient cypress and olive trees. When viewed from a distance, the trail resembles a mouse's tail. The trail leads to the twelfth-century church of Pantochrator, which is opened to the public only once a year, on August 6, the feast day of the Transfiguration of Jesus. According to legend, Pontikonisi was created when Poseidon changed Odysseus's boat into earth and stone. Just beside Pontikonisi, steps from the shore of Flisvos Café, is the stunning whitewashed church of Panagia Vlacherna. Built in the seventeenth century, the church is one of the most iconic and photographed spots on Corfu. Once used as a monastery, it sits on a tiny island in the shade of a single towering cypress tree. The island, consisting of the church, attached cemetery and that solitary tree, juts out into the sea, attached to the shore by a long concrete walkway. The walkway is dotted with small traditional fishing boats moored along the pathway, bobbing in the sea with the tide. The ethereal beauty and calming otherworldliness of Flisvos Café is matched by its exquisite cuisine and the charm and warmth of its owner, Spiros Catechis.

The day before everyone was scheduled to arrive and we were to have our dinner at Flisvos, Spiros and I met with my cousin Effie at the patio bar of the Corfu Palace hotel to go over the details and menu of our dinner. This wasn't just another catered event for Spiros and his perfectly magical restaurant. The celebration was personal for him, as it was for Effie and myself. With roots on Erikousa, Spiros also grew up hearing about the Jewish family that survived the Holocaust because of the bravery and generosity of our island community.

Family, survival, second chances. These are all themes Spiros knows about quite well. Spiros wasn't always the owner of this magical café. Just a few years before this, he had been working in New York City, living the hectic life of a Wall

Street trader. But then Spiros's health began to fail and he learned he needed a kidney transplant to survive. Spiros's salvation came with the gift of a kidney, donated by his brother.

After the surgery, Spiros left behind the chaos of New York City and settled back home in Corfu, trading the frenetic pace of Wall Street for the serene beauty of a seaside café overlooking the Church of Panagia Vlacherna. If anyone understands the importance of second chances and the spiritual healing powers of Corfu, it's Spiros.

As Spiros, Effie and I sat on the terrace of the Corfu Palace that afternoon, going over every detail of the welcome dinner, my phone rang. I looked down to see Mindy's name on my screen. I excused myself from the table and walked a few feet away where I could answer the call in relative quiet. Only when I answered, it wasn't Mindy on the other end of the phone; it was her husband.

"Yvette, it's Len."

"Len. Hey, how are you? What's going on? I'm in Greece."

"I know. I'm here with Mindy. She wanted me to call you. She's really sick. She's too weak to get on the phone. She's in the hospital. We're not sure what's going on. The doctors think it might be cancer."

At once I felt the blood drain from my face.

I stood there shaking, doing my best to stay focused and to stay on my feet. I wanted to cry and scream. How? Why? What? This could not be happening. This could not happen. What about Lukas? That little boy had lost so much already. He could not lose his mother too.

All around me life went on. Everything was picture perfect on that bright, beautiful patio overlooking the bay, with potted palm trees and flowers all around. There was sun and swimming and sunbathers and cocktails and laughter. It was as if nothing had changed. But everything changed in that split second. Len went on to tell me that Mindy had fallen ill suddenly and that she was incredibly weak. The doctors had done all sorts of blood tests and they were not sure what was wrong. The tests showed it might be some sort of aggressive cancer, maybe leukemia, but they still were not certain. Everyone was scared.

And then it came to me. A feeling of pure calm overtook me and steadied me. I looked out across the patio, past the bar and the pool and the sunbathing tourists, and I remembered where I was. In front of me was the turquoise perfection of Garitsa Bay, to the left was the hulking craggy mountain of the old fort, and behind were the labyrinthine streets of Corfu Town. And there, tucked away behind the ancient alleyways, courtyards and cobblestone, was the Church of Saint Spyridon.

"Len. I'm on Corfu. It's going to be okay."

"Okay," Len said. He had absolutely no idea what I was talking about.

"Len, I'm telling you. It's going to be okay. I'm here on Corfu and I'm going to go to the Church of Saint Spyridon and say a prayer for Mindy. He's performed many miracles for my family. And he's going to help Mindy too. I'm telling you, I know it. Don't worry," I repeated, calmed and confident. "I'm on Corfu and everything is going to be okay."

As much as Len wanted to believe me, he still had no idea what I was talking about. But I did. I had every faith that Mindy would be fine. I knew it. I walked back to the table where I had left Spiros and Effie planning our dinner. I told them about Mindy and they, like I, understood exactly what I needed to do.

Like my yia-yia before me when she prayed for her own family and for Savvas's family to stay safe and hidden, and like my father 25 years before when he prayed for my brother to recover, I would go to the Church of Saint Spyridon and ask him for a miracle. I would ask Saint Spyridon to make Mindy well.

We had lost too much already. We couldn't lose Mindy too.

Two days later, when I was still on Corfu, Len called me again.

Mindy's blood work showed significant

improvement. It wasn't cancer. It was a virus.

"She's going to be fine," he said, sounding so very relieved.

"I know," I replied. "See? I told you. I knew she would be okay. I'm on Corfu."

chapter twenty-three

REUNION

Corfu, Greece
June 2015

On Monday, June 29, 2015, it finally happened.

It was a gloriously sunny day. Unusually heavy winds had plagued Corfu that week and stirred up the typically calm seas. But the breeze coming in from the bay that morning provided a lovely relief from the midday heat. I stood on the patio of the Corfu Palace, wearing a red cotton sundress, my hair long and loose and my olive skin glowing with just the slightest hint of a suntan. At first glance I might have looked like any other tourist out on the patio that afternoon. But the way I paced frenetically across the flagstones, incessantly checked the time and continually asked, "Are they here yet?" should have surely given it away. I wasn't just some carefree tourist on the deck that day.

Not even close.

All across the palm-tree-and-flower-filled patio, tourists were enjoying a perfect Corfu afternoon. The gentle waves of Garitsa Bay glistened in the distance. Just below me, sunbathers lounged in their chairs and sipped iced drinks while small children splashed and swam, filling the air with their squeals and laughter.

And there, on the patio, I paced back and forth, never taking my eyes off the entrance to the hotel. Any moment now, I would finally come face-to-face with the families of Rosa and Spera, to finish the story our grandmothers began more than 70 years before.

Spera's granddaughter, Michelle, was the first to walk through the door and out onto that beautiful sunlit patio.

"Oh my gosh!" I ran toward her and threw my arms around her, and we hugged and hugged.

"Nice to meet you," Michelle said as we stood there together, savoring that glorious hug and that surreal moment.

"How are you?" I asked. It was the most rhetorical of all rhetorical questions.

"I'm good." Michelle laughed as we stood there holding hands, taking it all in.

With her striped sundress, sunglasses and long dark hair, it was striking how alike Michelle and I looked. It was the strangest thing. Michelle and I had only spoken on the phone and emailed a few times, but it was as if we had known each other for a long, long time. We were so similar, Michelle and I. Close in age, each married with two children, careers in the entertainment industry. We even had friends in common. We understood each other. We hugged again and looked at each other and all around us and laughed, marveling at the fact that this was really happening. We were actually here, together.

As we hugged and held hands on that patio, meeting face-to-face for the first time, I imagined our grandmothers watching, maybe huddled together again, marveling that we had found each other. Or maybe that had been the plan all along?

"Can you believe this?" I asked.

"I know. I know," Michelle replied as we both looked around. "This is crazy."

It was completely and totally crazy. But crazy in the most wonderful of ways.

Next, Rosa's sons, Avraham and Peretz, walked through the door and onto the patio. Avraham stepped up first. He is the elder of the two brothers, olive-skinned and hulking, with a face that looks both stern and intimidating until he breaks out in a wide, mischievous grin, which is often. It was Avraham who would later be interviewed on an Israeli news program about our shared journey. At the end of that interview, after running through the timeline of what happened and how Avraham was shocked to learn about his mother's salvation on Erikousa, the host asked him how he felt about me. Avraham paused for the briefest moment and then answered:

"She is my sister. Yvette, she is my sister."

As he walked out of the hotel and into the Corfu sunshine that morning, Rosa's son, Avraham Hassid, stepped forward and folded me in his arms. He hugged me tight and repeated my name over and over again: "Yvette. Yvette. Yvette." I tried to be strong and keep it together, but it was no use. I drenched his shirt with my tears. I had learned a thing or two from Mindy by then and had kept the eye makeup to a minimum.

We lingered in that hug as emotion overcame us both. I was full-on ugly sobbing now, but I didn't care. We might have just met, but we had a long history together, Avraham and I. It was his mother, Rosa, that my father and aunt Agatha had played with in the dark, falling asleep side by side in Yia-yia's bed as the adults whispered and sewed together in the next room. It was his mother, Rosa, that my own yia-yia would set aside precious food for each night, often going hungry herself to make sure Rosa did not. These were the bonds that cemented our families, then and now.

When we pulled away from that long hug, as I dried my eyes Avraham pointed to his arm, running his finger up and down the length of it to show me that he was covered in goose bumps.

Rosa's younger son, Peretz, stepped up next. He is smaller and fairer than olive-skinned Avraham. Peretz wore a yarmulke and a stunned expression on his face. "Yvette," he said, "no words."

He shook his head and repeated, "No words."

We hugged and we cried in a jumble of English, Greek and Hebrew, but we understood each other perfectly. Peretz was right; no words were needed.

For me, it felt like I was in a dream. I feared I would be woken and returned to reality at any moment. I couldn't even begin to imagine how it must have felt to Michelle, Avraham, Peretz and their families. It was overwhelming, and comparatively speaking, I had the easy part. While I was simply claiming new members of our family, Avraham, Peretz and Michelle had come to Corfu to claim their heritage and their family's secret history.

Peretz then introduced me to his warm and wonderful wife, Sigalit, and three beautiful daughters, Inbar, Sapir and Maayan, the girls who had brought so much light and joy to Rosa's life. These were the same three girls whose giggles, laughter and singing had drowned out the silence in Rosa's life once and for all.

Rosa's granddaughters were very quiet that morning, barely saying two or three words at first. But the silence was short-lived. As the day wore on, as we got to know each other better and they spent time with Christiana and Nico, it was replaced with girlish banter and bonding over shared obsessions like Sephora and all things Kardashian.

"You know Kim Kardashian?" Sapir, the middle granddaughter, asked.

"Well, I've interviewed her many times. She's actually very nice." I laughed at how absurd this all seemed.

Sapir tugged at her mother's arm. "Mom, she's met Kim Kardashian."

It seemed we had more in common than just our histories.

Michelle stepped forward and introduced me to her cousins, Spera's other grandchildren. And then I met Hedva, the middle child of Spera's stepdaughters. Lovely and elegant, Hedva shook her head as we all did, still processing the fact that she knew so little about her beloved stepmother's life. Hedva was just nine years old when Spera stepped into her life to love and care for her and her sisters. Rosa was also only nine when Spera's love saved her as well.

After the introductions and tears and hugs, we sat in the shade together at a long table and looked through photo albums that they'd brought from home to share. There, before us, in black and white, the pieces of our puzzle fit so neatly together. We flipped through the yellowed pages as Hedva, Peretz and Avraham pointed out each other and themselves at weddings, bar mitzvahs and family dinners. I pointed and called out the names of the faces that were so familiar to me now, the people whose names and stories had been mysteries for so many years. Now they too had come home at last.

Soon it was time to leave that perfect patio. As wonderful as it was to get to know everyone, it was time for the families to get to know their history and our magical island of Corfu.

We met Marcia and her group of about 20 from the Association of Friends of Greek Jewry in the Jewish quarter. Marcia hugged and kissed everyone before leading the way to Corfu's Holocaust memorial statue. Erected in 2001, the bronze sculpture is a haunting reminder. There are four sculptures, each individually heart-breaking, but as a group, the result is devastating. All four figures are nude. A young boy hides his face in the thigh of a man whose arms are outstretched, palms open to the sky, as if asking *why?* Beside them are the sculptures of a woman cradling a baby, the child pressed against her body as the woman's arm is placed in front of her, hand up, palm facing out, as if protecting the child, as if gesturing *stop.*

Beneath the memorial is the inscription *Never Again for Any Nation.*

I had passed this memorial countless times, at first not even stopping to take notice. Later, as I had begun to search for answers, I returned to the memorial hand in hand with Dave, finally taking the time to read the inscription and look closely at the images and what they symbolized.

I remember standing in front of the sculpture and from there walking to the synagogue. We knocked on nearby doors and entered shops, asking if anyone remembered the story of Savvas and his girls, and how they were saved on Erikousa. Each and every time we were told no, my hopes dimmed as Dave's grip on my hand tightened.

And now, just three years later, Dave and I were here again, hand in hand, only this time we were together with our family, with our children, and the children and grandchildren of Spera and Rosa.

Marcia stepped forward, first to greet the families, and then to explain what would come next. She shook her head again and again, taking it all in, not believing we were all really here, together. She wrestled with the tissue she held in her hand, knotting and twirling it this way and that, struggling to get the words out as the wave of emotion overtook her.

"We will be going to Erikousa tomorrow to celebrate the fact that a Jewish family was saved in light of the fact eighteen hundred of the Jews of Corfu perished in the Holocaust. So today, before we celebrate, we must remember. We are going to say the kaddish here at the memorial to remember those who perished here in Corfu."

Peretz stepped forward and led the group in kaddish, the Jewish prayer for remembering the dead. As soft-spoken as Peretz had seemed earlier on the patio of the Corfu Palace, his voice now resonated and rose as he led us in prayer.

"May there be abundant peace from heaven, and life, for us and for all Israel; and say, Amen."

"Amen," the group responded together, loud, unified and bursting with meaning and emotion.

When the prayer was finished, the final "Amen" proclaimed, Marcia then handed Avraham and Peretz a beautiful bouquet of locally handpicked wildflowers and asked them if they would do the honors.

Together, Rosa's sons walked up to the sculpture, placing the flowers at the feet of the haunting figures of a family.

Never Again for Any Nation.

I held tight to Dave's hand. I looked up at him and again wiped the tears from my cheeks. He and I both knew that despite what was etched into that stone, it had happened again, and to our own family.

Never Again. I wondered if there would ever come a day when the world would truly take those words to heart.

From the Holocaust memorial, our group wound its way through the narrow alleys of the Jewish quarter to the Scuola Greca synagogue. Built in the seventeenth century, the Scuola Greca was crafted in the Venetian style and is the only synagogue that survived the Allied bombing of the island. Today, the building has been beautifully restored and is maintained by the small and dedicated Jewish community left on Corfu.

We made our way inside. Row after row, our group filled nearly each seat in the synagogue that day. I wondered when the last time was that the synagogue was filled with so many eager faces.

Marcia stood before us in front of the room and told our story to everyone who was gathered there. She related the story of Savvas on Erikousa and how together with MyHeritage, we had defied the odds and laws of reason and logic to find Spera and Rosa's families. She explained how we all came to be reunited on Corfu. Marcia then turned and pointed to a marble plaque on the wall that the Association of Friends of Greek Jewry commissioned and dedicated in 2002. The plaque reads, *In memory of the Jews of Corfu who perished in the Nazi Concentration Camps of Auschwitz and Birkenau in June 1944.*

"Avraham, Peretz, come here." Marcia gestured to the brothers to join her as she pointed to a name etched into the marble.

"I want you to see something. This your family. Belleli. This is in memory of your family that did not survive. And Michelle." Marcia beckoned for Michelle to come closer, to join her beside Avraham and Peretz, beside the plaque on the wall. "Michelle, this is your family, your family that also perished."

There it was, etched in black and white, the name we had searched for, for so long. *Israel.*

Everyone in the room wiped tears from their eyes. It was quiet in the synagogue at that moment, save for the sound of dozens of people sniffling and opening and closing their purses to find tissues. Marcia was overcome. There was no sniffling to contain her own tears; they flowed freely down her face at this point. Clutching a tissue in her hand, Marcia leaned in to hug Avraham and Peretz and then Michelle, repeating over and over again the words, "Thank God you're here. Thank God you're here."

From where I was standing, also in front of the room, I inched closer to the plaque. Three columns of names, 74 family names in all. There, listed among them, were all the names I had come to know. Osmo. Nachschon. Israel. Belleli. Aaron. Moustaki. The names of everyone who had helped me on this journey, who made it possible for us to be there together that afternoon. But they were not just names. They were not just marble and ink. They were mothers, fathers, sisters, brothers, grandparents. They were families. And now they were my family too.

I did my best to compose myself, to keep my emotions in check as we prepared to file out of the synagogue. But then I saw him. I didn't know who he was or anything about him, but just that one glance told me everything I needed to know. His name, I soon learned, was Moshe Velleli, a local shopkeeper and member of the Jewish community of Corfu. When Moshe heard about us, and that our group would be visiting the synagogue that afternoon, he knew what he needed to do. Moshe ran to his shop. There was something in it he wanted us to see, something that had belonged to his father, Rino.

Rino, his two brothers and two sisters had all lived with their family in the Jewish quarter. And in June 1944, Rino and his family were all herded into the old fort at gunpoint and then transported to Auschwitz. Only Rino, one brother and one sister survived.

Moshe returned to the synagogue with an old striped shirt that had belonged to his father. This was the shirt Rino wore as a prisoner in Auschwitz, the shirt he wore the day he was liberated by the Allies, the shirt Rino carried with him when he returned home to Corfu. That shirt now hangs in Moshe's shop as a reminder of what his father lived through and endured. Moshe stood there in the synagogue that day as we filed past him, his father's striped shirt on a hanger beside him.

Moshe wanted us to see it, for us to remember Rino and every single member of the Jewish community of Corfu.

They were not just names etched into a plaque.

chapter twenty-four
ERIKOUSA'S ICARUS

Erikousa
June 2015

L ook, Yvette," the driver said to me the following morning.

He pointed to the front of the bus, through the windshield. The front right wheel of the bus was literally off the mountain road as he maneuvered around the sharp turn. I didn't think it was funny. Not at all.

I had spent so much time worrying about the wind and sea conditions, it seemed I had forgotten to worry about how the hulking bus would manage to maneuver through the narrow roads with their hairpin turns. Having driven this route countless times, the driver expertly navigated us around what seemed to us impossibly sharp turns and at one point, through a maze of narrow village streets where the top of the bus was just inches from the terraces above us and the buildings on either side. For him it was just another day on the road. For the rest of us, it was an often terrifying and carsickness-inducing road trip.

An hour later, the bus made it down the mountain to the tiny port of Agios Stefanos. Our small ferry was tied to the dock, among a cluster of small weather-beaten fishing boats, ready to take us on the seven-mile journey to Erikousa.

"See, I wasn't joking about how remote the island is." I forced a smile as everyone stepped off the bus, shaking their heads at what they had just experienced. I motioned across the sea, where the green hills of Erikousa were visible in the distance. "Just think about it. The Nazis traveled all this way, just so they wouldn't miss a single Jewish person. All this, so they wouldn't leave even one Jew alive. It really puts it in perspective, doesn't it?"

As if anyone needed reminding of how bloodthirsty the Nazis were. But physically experiencing the difficult journey from Corfu brought the point home.

Yet that was just the first portion of our journey. We still had the seas to contend with. Fortunately, in the past 24 hours, the windstorm that plagued Corfu earlier that week had died down considerably. It was as if our prayers had been answered. Together, Avraham, Peretz, Michelle, Hedva and our families boarded the small ferryboat for the trip across the water to the tiny green island in the distance. Finally, together, we were all going home to Erikousa.

We filed onto the boat, along with several of

my cousins from Erikousa, including my cousin Effie and Lina, Spyros and Sophia Orfanos. Overcome with emotion, Spyros hugged and kissed everyone and greeted the families like long-lost relatives, which they were. With Michelle interpreting, Spyros shared with Avraham and Peretz all of the stories about Rosa and Spera that he had grown up hearing. He then held up an old cherished black-and-white photo of his aunt Theodora and another aunt named Netso, with two young cousins standing alongside Spera and Nina.

"That's me," cousin Nick Manessis chimed in, pointing to himself in the photo, the young schoolboy wearing knickers and a stern expression. He smiled now, beaming, as he was able to share his memories of Spera and Nina with their families.

As we set out from the dock, the air was filled with the sounds of excited chatter and laughter. But as we sailed farther out, away from the protected cove of Agios Stefanos and into the open sea between Corfu and Erikousa, the boat got quieter as the seas grew choppier. Yes, the winds and seas had calmed considerably since the windstorm of the previous days, enough for us to make the trip. But those winds had whipped the waters into a frenzy from which they had yet to fully recover. I looked around me and suddenly the reality of the situation became incredibly and painfully clear. All around the boat, people were reacting to the rough seas. The situation quickly escalated from quiet, uncomfortable nausea to full-on seasickness.

This was supposed to be the most wonderful and rewarding time. It was the culmination of all those years of searching, the brilliant detective work by the team from MyHeritage, the generous sponsorship from the Association of Friends of Greek Jewry and the incredible amount of work done to be granted the House of Life honor by the International Raoul Wallenberg Foundation. This was it. What we had been waiting for. And this was not what I was expecting. Not at all.

As we approached the port of Erikousa, many of our guests, most of whom had traveled from Israel, suffered the effects of full-blown seasickness. All around me, people were getting sick. We scoured the boat for bags and towels and napkins to help everyone, but there weren't nearly enough to go around.

It was messy and it was horrible.

I looked at Michelle and all I could say was, "I'm so sorry. I'm so so sorry."

Michelle managed a smile and shook her head. "We're desert people," she replied.

As we prepared to disembark, everyone pulled themselves together as best they could. I looked around at the families of Rosa and Spera, who were at last about to be welcomed home to

Erikousa, to finally see for themselves the island where their mothers and grandmothers were saved. But I wasn't overcome with euphoria or pride. I kept thinking and feeling the same thing, again and again: *What have I done? Dear Lord, what have I done?*

As we pulled into the dock, I kept repeating the same words over and over again. "I'm so sorry. I'm so, so sorry." In that moment, I felt like I had made the biggest mistake of my life. My worst fears had come to fruition. This was not *beshert*, not at all. I had tempted fate, meddled where I didn't belong, and now everyone around me who was so sick was dealing with the repercussions of my actions. This was indeed my Icarus moment, only I wasn't the only one crashing to the sea. It seemed I was taking others out with me.

I turned to one of our guests, a friend who'd traveled from New York to witness the reunion and one of the most violently ill. "Don't worry," I tried reassuring her. "The ride back is usually smoother."

"I'm not going back," she replied. Deadpan and serious.

The guilt and doubt crept back in. What right did I have to revisit the past that they'd kept buried and hidden from their families? I couldn't hide the tears that rolled down my cheeks as the boat docked and the gangway was lowered. Everyone who saw me there in that moment, everyone who reached out to me to offer a hug and a smile, assumed I was overcome with emotion at our homecoming. At the success of our search and of honoring my grandmother's memories.

But that wasn't the case at all. As our ferry pulled into port, as the islanders of Erikousa waited on the dock to welcome us home with open arms, my tears were about guilt and frustration.

"I am so sorry," I repeated over and over again. "I'm so, so sorry."

———

After the boat was secured and docked, everyone did their best to clean up and get themselves together.

Avraham, Peretz, Michelle, Hedva and the extended family stood on the boat and looked out across the island and to the dock. Savoring the moment and inhaling the fresh sea breeze, each of the family members scanned the island scenery and the faces of the crowd before disembarking into a mob of handshakes, greetings, hugs and kisses.

Young girls in traditional island dress, some wearing colorful head scarves, others with wreaths of red flowers, all stood side by side to welcome the families home.

Maybe it was the power of sheer will, of wanting to be well enough to enjoy the day.

Maybe it was the healing powers of the Erikousa island air. Or maybe it was Saint Spyridon saving us once again. Whatever it was, I thanked God it was happening all around me. From the moment they walked off the boat and stepped foot on Erikousa, everyone, even the most ill of the passengers, immediately began to feel better.

And the islanders, in that wonderful traditional Erikousa way, stepped in to do what they do best—take care of those in need. Several came forward, offering to bring any of the ill visitors home, offering a clean change of clothes, a shower or a place to simply rest.

Together, our entire group walked through Erikousa's tiny but picturesque town area, past the Hotel Erikousa and pristine salmon-colored homes with white trim accented by large, colorful pots of beautiful flowers and fragrant basil plants the size of bushes. We passed the homes of islanders who came out to welcome the families, kissing them on both cheeks and in many cases, sharing their memories of Savvas, Julia, Nina, Rosa and Spera. Dozens more Erikoushotis lined the path through the port area, offering hugs and hellos. One of my favorite uncles on the island, George Orfanos, hugged and kissed Avraham, Peretz, Michelle and Hedva, showing them grainy black-and-white photos of himself as a young man with a group of islanders, pointing to young Spera among the friends.

We walked to the *keli*, the home of the island's priest, where Savvas and his girls first found refuge. A Greek Orthodox priest dressed in black robes who'd made a special trip to Erikousa from Corfu that day waited at the door to greet the families. He personally escorted Avraham, Peretz and their family inside to show Rosa's sons where the island's priest had given up his bed so that Rosa and the others would have a place to hide and sleep.

We walked up a rocky hill and across an overgrown path to my yia-yia's home, which has sat empty since she died 25 years ago. My brother and I unlocked the door and welcomed the children and grandchildren of Spera and Rosa's families inside, just as our yia-yia did so many years before when our father was just a small boy living in fear of the sound of German boots outside his window. Everyone crowded inside the small living room where this entire journey began. Our families stood together, in the very space where Avgerini, Spera, Nina and Julia sewed and talked together in the darkness, and where my father, aunt Agatha and Rosa curled up and slept together side by side in Yia-yia's bed.

We climbed farther up the hill to my aunt Magdaline's house. Just a few days before, my beloved aunt had pulled me aside.

"When our guests come, you must bring them to my house," she insisted.

"*Thea.* I love you and you are an amazing cook. But I really don't think we'll be able to bring everyone over. Thank you for offering, but it's going to be such a busy day."

My aunt laughed. "That's not what I mean. I have something to show you, something they will want to see."

And as always seemed to be the case with my relatives on Erikousa, Aunt Magdaline was right. I should have known better than to question her. Together, the day of the reunion on Erikousa, we all hiked up yet another hill to Aunt Magdaline's home.

As we made our way up the steep slope under the hot sun, Avraham motioned to Michelle and said he had a message for me, something he needed her to translate. As we trudged farther, Michelle parlayed Avraham's message for me.

"He says he's mad at you. That you're always making him walk everywhere."

Everyone burst out laughing as we slogged up that hill.

"This is what it is to be from Erikousa," I replied. Hiking up steep, rocky trails like a goat was second nature to anyone who spent considerable time on the island. "Congratulations, you're one of us now," I announced. And they were.

Finally, we arrived at the house.

"We have something to show you," I said,

before ushering everyone inside. There, just inside the door, tucked in a corner of the old house, was an old sewing machine. The heavy machine was still intact, in working condition, with decades of old, faded spools of thread, needles and scissors still held in its drawers.

"This was Savvas's machine," I announced as everyone inched forward. One by one, they placed their hands on the sewing machine, touching it in reverence.

This was the machine Savvas used while he was hidden on Erikousa. This was the machine he and the girls taught their friends to sew on, where the Jewish tailor and his girls continued to craft beautiful clothes, often out of old bedsheets, to be given as gifts to the friends and families who did so much to keep them safe.

Amalia Katehi was one of those friends. A young woman when the family was hidden on Erikousa, Amalia is 94 years old today. She is one of the few elderly widows still keeping alive the tradition of dressing head to toe in black, including a black head scarf. We visited Amalia in her home, where she held court in her lush garden as her chickens pecked and clucked just behind us.

"They were good people and we loved them. They were like us. Greek, Jew, it didn't matter. They were beautiful people," Amalia recalled after embracing and kissing everyone one by one.

"Rosa was a sweet girl. She was the youngest," Amalia remembered before sending her granddaughter back into the house to get something for Avraham and Peretz. There was something she wanted them to have.

"Nini made this for me," Amalia said as she held a black pleated skirt in her hands, wiping away tears with fingers gnarled and bent by severe arthritis. "I want you to have this. I want you to take it home with you. To remember us the way we remember them."

It was a day of memories long forgotten and memories newly made. Rosa's family joined me at the Erikousa cemetery, where I showed them the area where Savvas was originally buried, just outside the cemetery wall. We walked to the other side of the wall, within the cemetery, to my family's grave, where my beloved papou and yia-yia Avgerini are buried. Avraham and Peretz stood at the grave of my yia-yia, honoring her and thanking her for the kindness she showed their mother. I knew Yia-yia was looking down on us and wondered what she must be thinking. She was no doubt wondering why on earth we were all making such a fuss and why I had not fed our guests yet.

Everyone on the island came together in the Erikousa town square, located just below the *keli* and steps from the cemetery and church. More than two hundred people gathered under the hot sun that afternoon for the ceremony to officially recognize what happened on Erikousa during the Holocaust and to remember those who had risked their lives to save a Jewish family.

Marcia asked all of the islanders who were alive on Erikousa at the time to come forward and stand beside her. About a half dozen people stood, including Uncle George and Aunt Magdaline.

"Thank you." Marcia could barely get the words out as she hugged and personally thanked each of them, while the crowd stood and applauded wildly.

Together we listened as Marcia reminded everyone why we had traveled such a long way to come together, to celebrate the brave islanders of Erikousa and welcome Savvas's family home. "The Association of Friends of Greek Jewry are humbled to be in the presence of the islanders of Erikousa," she said. "We will never forget your act of moral courage. May the world know of your courage and sing your praises."

We all watched and listened as wonderful and warm Danny Ranier from the Raoul Wallenberg Foundation next explained the work of the foundation and the significance of the House of Life honor. "The people of Erikousa have displayed a joint spirit of civic solidarity very much in line with the legacy of Raoul Wallenberg," he said. "On behalf of the International Raoul Wallenberg

Foundation, I would like to congratulate the people of Erikousa, whose island is about to be declared as a House of Life."

Soon it was my turn to speak. I left the history, the symbolism and the significance to the scholars, historians and educators. We had several there with us that day. I wasn't the one best suited to speak to the magnitude of what had happened 70 years ago, or even today. That was never my intention and it wasn't my place. I stood there that afternoon, just down the hill from my ancestral home, on the island where my father was born and raised, steps from the cemetery where generations of my family had been buried. I stood there that day and spoke not as a journalist, producer, author or researcher. I spoke from the heart, as the granddaughter of Avgerini Manessis and as a child of Erikousa. "I spent summer after summer on this beautiful island, with Effie and our big, fat beautiful and crazy family . . . There is no place like this in the world—no place more magical, no people more beautiful, warm and loving," I said. "I have been fortunate enough to travel around the world and see and experience the most wonderful things, but nothing can compare to our Erikousa— nothing in the world.

"I grew up listening to my yia-yia's story of Savvas and his girls—it's a story of friendship, sacrifice and bravery. But until today, the story had no ending. We now know how the story of Savvas and his girls ends. Just look around you. It is a beautiful ending, the most beautiful ending I could imagine, and for that I am so overwhelmed and grateful."

"Michelle, Avraham, Peretz, Sigalit, Hedva, Maayan and every member of your beautiful family . . . I hope this is the first of many trips to Erikousa for you. I hope your time here is as beautiful and magical as mine always was and is . . . and I have one more thing to say to you . . . Welcome home."

In a ceremony filled with emotion and so many tears, one unforgettable moment stood out from the rest. Of Rosa's three granddaughters, only 13-year-old Maayan spoke. Maayan was the youngest, but in many ways, also the oldest. Olive-skinned and slim, she had rimless glasses perched on her nose, with straight black hair hanging well to her waist. Soft-spoken Maayan took the microphone and stood at the podium that afternoon as the entire island fell into silence and then dissolved into tears.

Maayan spoke through tears of her beloved grandmother and of the difficult life she led. She reminded everyone of what happened when the Nazis gathered the Jews of Corfu in June 1944, and how Rosa was the only one in her family to survive.

Maayan continued, her voice soft, her words

powerful. Our hearts broke collectively as her tears turned to sobs. "I have been telling you a few bits and pieces of my grandmother's life, as it had been told to my oldest sister, Inbar, by my grandma during homework assignments in family history. It was the only time Rosa spoke about this subject and it was only a few months before she passed away. She never spoke about it with any other member of the family except that time with Inbar. By one action of compassion and kindness, which involved risking herself and her personal safety, Yia-yia Avgerini Manessis, with a group of her fellow islanders, actually saved generations to come. We, the offspring of Grandmother Rosa, feel it is a special privilege to be here."

As the afternoon sun beat down on us and the Ionian Sea glistened in the distance, the ceremony came to a close with a powerful message from Sigalit, Peretz's wife and Rosa's daughter-in-law. Sigalit handed me a large frame, filled with photos of her family and mine. She thanked me again for not stopping our search until we found Rosa. Sigalit, Peretz and Maayan hugged and kissed me and then Avraham, big, hulking, beer-loving, chain-smoking Avraham, folded me into his arms and cried as he repeated again the few English words in his vocabulary. "Thank you, thank you. You are my sister." And Avraham was right; I am indeed his sister.

But Avraham and Peretz gained so much more than just a sister that day. We were able to give Rosa's sons the one thing they had prayed for all those years, growing up with just each other for comfort and company. As their families and the entire island watched, Gilad, Aaron and Roi stepped up and said they had one last surprise for the family. Everyone watched in stunned silence as they unfurled a banner and presented it to Rosa's sons. On it was their family tree.

The two boys who had grown up wondering about their history now had a glorious and large family tree, filled branch after branch with the names and faces of more than 300 relatives. Grainy black-and-white ancestral images of stern expressions salvaged from old, forgotten photos and the Corfu archives gave way to modern vibrant color photos filled with smiling faces. By looking at the tree, that big, beautiful, glorious tree, Rosa's family was truly brought to life.

Avraham and Peretz, the young boys who knew nothing of their mother's family or history are now part of a big, beautiful family—a family with an unforgettable story of sacrifice and survival.

In the end, we all stood together, hugging and kissing and examining the family tree while the ceremony came to a close and Lina's beautiful voice filled the air with a gorgeous and meaningful serenade.

And then, after an incredibly emotional day, it was time for us to celebrate. Together, the Erikousa family and the family of Savvas Israel did what our grandmothers could only dream of doing together during the German occupation. We all gathered on the beautiful terrace of the Erikousa Hotel, where we ate, drank, talked and laughed out loud in the sunshine and Greek danced around and around again, together as a family.

As we were savoring all of it—the food, the music, the scenery and the company—my friend George Katehis, the owner of the Hotel Erikousa, told me there was someone he wanted me to meet. George brought me over and introduced me to a man, an Israeli sailor named Danny.

"I wasn't even supposed to be here," Danny said to me. "I was out sailing yesterday and I took a wrong turn and ended up here on Erikousa. I came to the hotel and George told me, 'You're Israeli, you can't leave. There's going to be a Jewish celebration here tomorrow.' I thought to myself, a Jewish celebration on a small Greek island? I had to stay. Can you believe the coincidence?"

I clinked glasses and welcomed Danny to Erikousa, explaining, "There's no such thing as a wrong turn, Danny."

The following week, when I returned home from Greece, I received a Facebook message from Manuel Osmo in Israel.

Hello Yvette. The father of my neighbor, Danny, was a few days a go in erikcosia At your event and meet you. Very very small world. Big hug from Israel

Immediately, I responded to Manuel's email.

Hello Manuel, Shalom! !!! What?!! Are you kidding me? Was this the Israeli man who was sailing and took a wrong turn?

Just like the very first time he hit send, a message from Manuel Osmo in Israel had me at a loss for words.

He just yesterday told me about the trip and the erikosia island And about you and your book And I say to him: of course I know here we are family . . . Big family he was immidiatly white on him face.

And once again with an email, in his perfectly imperfect English, Manuel made me turn white on my face too, and he confirmed to me what I already knew to be true. In life, and in this story, there is no such thing as coincidence.

There is only *beshert.*

chapter twenty-five

FINDING SAVVAS

Corfu
June 2015

As wonderful as the celebration on Erikousa was, I knew that the story of Savvas Israel and his girls would not be complete unless we also found Savvas himself.

No one knew what had become of the tailor's remains once they were removed from outside the Erikousa cemetery wall. Yia-yia and the other islanders had remembered quite clearly that the family had returned to Erikousa to have Savvas's bones removed for burial in Israel. Consumed with uncovering one final element of this mystery, Gilad personally searched all the cemeteries in Israel. But despite his exacting and exhaustive search, the location of Savvas Israel's grave remained a mystery. Although we had managed to find Spera, Nina, Julia and Rosa, it was as if Savvas Israel himself had simply vanished.

Once again, perhaps fueled by the fact that some called the search to find Savvas's grave hopeless, Gilad pressed on, refusing to give up hope.

And then, just days before our families were all scheduled to meet on Corfu, Gilad at last found him. After he located the grave, Rosa's best friend, Mazal, helped us piece together the story of Savvas the tailor's final resting place.

Mazal explained that Nina had indeed returned to Erikousa with the intention of removing Savvas's bones for burial in Israel. But it seemed that tragedy once again stalked the tailor's family. While Nina was in Greece, making the final preparations to remove her father's body, Julia was diagnosed with cancer. Upon hearing of her sister's diagnosis, Nina abandoned her plans to leave for Israel, instead remaining in Greece to care for Julia until her death seven months later. Those months spent nursing Julia in her final days took their toll on Nina, physically, emotionally and financially. In the end, there was not enough money to have Savvas's remains interred in Israel. Nina had her father laid to rest on the island they had all called home, the beautiful green island of Corfu.

It was there, in a Jewish cemetery just a couple of miles outside of the Jewish quarter, that we finally found him.

Across a busy two-lane road overlooking the cobalt-blue sea, behind a tall iron gate, is the rarely visited Jewish cemetery of Corfu. There at the far end of the cemetery, down a dirt and gravel-strewn path surrounded by majestic cypress trees, lies the final resting place of Savvas Israel, the Jewish tailor of Corfu.

It was midafternoon when we walked through the cemetery gates with Avraham, Peretz, Michelle and their families. As the sun baked the cracked earth beneath our feet, we made our way down the center path toward the graves. We didn't tell the families why we had come to the cemetery, only that we had something special to share with them. One final surprise to make our time together on Corfu truly unforgettable.

We gathered everyone around. And then Gilad spoke.

"So we have a surprise for you," Gilad said as the entire group looked up at him, squinting against the afternoon sun. "We've discovered that Savvas is buried here."

"Wow. Wow. Wow," Avraham repeated as he clutched his chest. "Who's buried here?" he asked, to be certain he heard correctly.

"Savvas himself," Gilad replied.

Peretz silently shook his head again and again.

Gilad explained. "Savvas died on Erikousa sometime after he was hidden and saved. And they brought his bones to be interred here in the Corfu cemetery, where the other Jews from Corfu are buried."

Together we continued down the gravel path, walking to the farthest end of the cemetery. There, set slightly apart from the other graves, nearest to the cemetery wall and beneath the towering cypress trees standing sentinel all around, we at last laid eyes on the grave of Savvas Israel.

Nothing could prepare us for the swell of emotion that overcame each of us as we stood side by side and looked down upon the marble slab etched with the name Shabtai Shlomo Israel The Hebrew name for Savvas Israel, son of Solomon.

Michelle and I stood next to each other. My dark sunglasses failed to hide the tears that slid one after another, down my cheeks. I shook my head and took a deep breath.

"Can you believe this?" I asked.

"No," Michelle replied. "I can't. I really can't."

Our group gathered around. I looked up to see that like me, our friends and family were overcome by what we were witnessing. Members of Marcia's group from the Association of Greek Jewry dabbed at their eyes with tissues and even clung to one another, holding onto each other for support. It didn't matter that this was not the grave of their own family member. Everyone gathered in the cemetery with us that day knew that finding Savvas was not about bloodline. We all felt a connection to the mustached gentleman with the piercing eyes. This time it was about so much more. For all of us.

Kneeling in the dirt, Avraham wiped away tears and then covered his face with his hand.

Weeping silently, he placed his other hand on the grave of the man who had cared for his mother and protected her so fiercely. Savvas had loved Rosa as his own, helping to save her life even as Savvas's own grandchildren were denied refuge, turned away, hunted down and murdered.

Peretz came and stood beside his brother even as Avraham stayed there, on his knees, weeping silently and staring at the name etched into the stone. Peretz remained there, looking down at the grave, and then silently looking away.

Marcia approached the grave, tears streaming down her face. She didn't even attempt to hide them or wipe them away. "This is the grave of Savvas Israel," she said for all to hear. Her voice cracked and broke as she spoke.

"Come, let's find stones and place them on the grave," Marcia announced, her voice quivering with emotion.

One by one, we did so that afternoon, many kissing the grave as they placed their stones on the marble slab. We left dozens of stones on the grave of Savvas Israel that day. Each stone was proof that we had been there to remember and to honor him. That his memory would indeed be eternal.

And just as he had at the Holocaust memorial, soft-spoken Peretz once again led everyone in the Kaddish, the Jewish prayer for the dead. Standing beside his brother, Avraham lent his voice as well, reciting a centuries-old prayer as he continued to wipe tears from his eyes.

"May his great name be blessed forever and to all eternity," the brothers exclaimed.

"Amen," shouted the voices all around them.

"Amen." Again and again.

We stood there together that day, young and old, Greek, American, Israeli, Jewish and Christian, in a rarely visited cemetery on the beautiful island of Corfu. The sounds of an ancient prayer filled the air as we gathered under the cypress trees surrounding the grave of Savvas Israel. And after decades of lying there, alone and forgotten in the shade of those ancient trees, Savvas Israel was alone in silence no more.

History had come so dangerously close to forgetting the name and the story of Savvas Israel, those who loved him most refusing to utter his name, first in order to protect and keep him safe, and later, because those memories were too painful to be spoken out loud. But each one of us there in the old cemetery that day, each tear that was shed, each stone left behind, each "Amen" that was recited and that reverberated across the cemetery—each of those was proof and a promise that Savvas Israel, Shabtai Shlomo Israel, son of Solomon and friend to the islanders of Erikousa, will never be forgotten again.

That night, after such an incredibly emotional day, we all came together for what was no less than a perfect evening. As the sun set beyond the hills and cypress trees of Corfu, it cast a magical glow across the water and the whitewashed church of Panagia Vlacherna, with Pontikonisi in the distance.

Together with Rosa and Spera's families, we dined at the magical Flisvos Café. Long tables were placed on the sand as the sea lapped at the shore just inches from where we sat. It had been an extraordinary and emotional day. Not a single member of our group would ever forget what we had seen and experienced. Not a single one of us would ever forget Savvas Israel or the Jewish community of Corfu. As Marcia reminded us, it was our duty and obligation to never forget those who were lost, and also to celebrate those who had survived.

With just enough of a breeze coming in from the sea, we did what Marcia asked us to do and what our families on Erikousa during the war could only dream of doing. Together, the families of Avgerini Manessis, Savvas Israel and little Rosa Belleli talked and laughed out loud as the festive, melodic sounds of Greek music filled the air. Together, we ate, talked, cried, laughed and danced around and around in circles under the stars on a perfect Corfiot night.

chapter twenty-six

FULL CIRCLE

New York and Kansas
July 2015

"Can you believe we actually pulled that off?" I must have asked that question dozens and dozens of times to anyone who was there to witness the events on Corfu and Erikousa, and to those who hadn't. Basically, to anyone who would listen.

The truth was that I could not believe we'd pulled it off. It was magical and beautiful, and now it was over. But I knew we weren't done. On our last day in Corfu, Avraham, Peretz and our families met once again on the terrace of the Corfu Palace. We sat and talked and cried some more. And then Avraham leaned in toward me. Placing both hands on the table, he leaned in closer and looked me straight in the eye and spoke in half Hebrew and half English that somehow we all understood perfectly.

"Yvette, you are family now. So there is something I must tell you."

I braced myself for what was next. "Yes, Avraham, of course. You can tell me anything."

"I'm dying. I can't sit here any longer. I'm sorry. I must have a cigarette." Everyone burst out laughing. That moment, perhaps more than anything, cemented our bond. No more niceties or airs, no need to be on our best behavior anymore. We were family now, vices, quirks, warts and all.

"And I know what else you need." I jumped up from the table and promptly fetched him a beer. Well, after all, that's what family does for one another.

And in that moment we all realized that it wasn't blood ties, DNA or the branches of a tree that define the word *family*. We were connected by a long-ago act of kindness, brought together by detective work and modern technology. But it was laughter, putting away any airs, and the simple everyday act of giving in to a cigarette craving that finally and truly made us a family.

Back in New York, Christiana and Nico settled back into their routines: softball, hockey, baseball, friends and summer fun. But they were different now too. We all came back from Greece changed in some way. Everything now was more meaningful. We had witnessed together the power of family and history and kindness.

I called Mindy to check in, to ask how she was feeling and give her a full report on my trip. Ultimately she was diagnosed with dengue fever, the result of a mosquito bite from a recent trip to Belize. She was feeling better, she said, not quite 100 percent, but well on the road to recovery.

Every day she was getting stronger. She had been following my posts on Facebook, but as we spoke I finally had a chance to tell her all about our visit to the synagogue and Savvas's grave, the ceremony on Erikousa and, most importantly, how much I grew to love Spera and Rosa's families in the short time we had together.

I told her that everyone asked about her, that they had seen her on television in Israel and their hearts broke for her, and they all said they would pray for her. I told her that Rosa and Spera's families consider her a sister now too.

I settled back into a routine and tried to process everything that had happened. It was overwhelming. While the trip and ceremony had provided so many answers, I still had so many questions. What happens next? What does this all mean—for the families, for Erikousa, for all of us? I knew we were all connected in some way, that we were like a giant circle spanning the globe: my family, Rosa and Spera's family, Mindy's family and even Sonia and Jacqueline. They too were a part of this journey. Yet even with all we had learned, set out to do and accomplished, I felt in my heart that we were not finished yet, that our circle was not fully formed. But I didn't know what to do next.

Feeling completely overwhelmed, and maybe slightly insane, I did what I normally do when I feel myself spiraling. I went for a long run.

It was a beautiful Sunday afternoon as I set out along my favorite running route, miles and miles of shaded paths, ponds and waterfalls. It was just me and my thoughts and my music. I had been running for a few miles already and my mind was blissfully wandering when my music suddenly stopped. I looked down at my phone and the songs seemed to be in shuffle mode, only I had not pressed shuffle. I hadn't pressed anything. It was the oddest thing. The phone had not been giving me any trouble. I hadn't dropped it. It was fully charged, yet it wasn't responding to my touch. The screen images changed rapidly, shuffling past the names of songs and photos of the album covers. Dozens and dozens of songs flashed by. I tried pressing stop but nothing happened. The phone would not respond to any of my commands. Finally, as I was about to try and shut it off, the shuffling stopped. I looked down at the album cover and title on the screen as the song began playing in my ear.

"Wow," I said out loud. I remember just standing there, shaking my head as I continued to stare at the screen while the song played. I felt the goose bumps work their way across my body. It was a song I knew very well. Miranda Lambert's "Over You," a song that had been written about a young man who was killed. That young man was the brother of Miranda's ex-husband, Blake Shelton. It was also the song that Christiana played incessantly when she was thinking about Reat.

I was still looking down at my phone, not even really processing what had just happened, when the image on the screen changed. The picture went from Miranda Lambert's album cover to one word. *Mindy*.

Mindy was calling me.

She was calling me in the very moment my phone flipped out and landed on Reat's song. I felt out of my body. This was no mere coincidence. I answered immediately and started talking before she had the chance to say a word.

"Oh my goodness, Mindy. I can't believe you are calling me. You have no idea what just happened. You seriously won't believe it. I was out here running and my phone flipped out. It literally flipped out and landed on Miranda Lambert's song 'Over You.' It's the song that Christiana plays when she's thinking of Reat, Mindy, and then I look down and you call me in that very moment."

I finished my breathless rant and Mindy spoke, in her calm, cool, pragmatic way, as if none of this was any surprise to her.

"Well, I'm sitting here in my office, and I have to tell you. I've been sitting here crying and all of a sudden I was just overcome with this feeling. It's like it just came over me. I know what I have to do. I have to go to Israel. Reat's telling me he wants me to go to Israel."

"This just happened right now, right before you called me?"

"Yes, just now."

"So you're telling me Reat was giving you a message exactly as my phone was flipping out and landed on his song."

"Yes," Mindy said. Matter-of-fact. As if this were the most obvious thing in the world.

"I guess I'm going to Israel."

But before Mindy could go to Israel, there was something she needed to do—stand up in court and face the man who murdered her son and father.

Mindy's older brother, Will, was the first to speak at the sentencing. For the past year, Will had thought about what he would say when he faced the man who killed his father and nephew on his sentencing day. As he stepped up to the microphone, Will had nothing written down, nothing prepared. All he knew was that he would begin his victim impact statement with a Bible verse. His voice strong and unwavering, Will Corporon's powerful words filled the courtroom:

"If your enemy is hungry, feed him; if he is

thirsty, give him something to drink: for by doing so you will heap burning coals on his head. Do not be overcome by evil, but overcome evil with good."

As Will stood in the courtroom that day, not five feet from where the murderer sat, he felt something he'd never expected. Instead of rage, Will felt pity. Just a few days before, in the presentencing report, the family had learned about the defendant's abusive childhood, of life at the hands of his violent father. They had learned that the first book he ever received was Nazi propaganda. As he glared at the man responsible for murdering Bill, Reat and Terri, Will Corporon's words, powerful and eloquent, came to him, spontaneous and spoken from his heart.

"I pity you. I feel sorry for you because you never experienced a day of love in your life. And that is sad and I feel sorry for that. But your evil, your insensitiveness, your intolerance, your bigotry, your selfishness, you are a coward . . . It is not for me to judge you in the afterlife but make no mistake, you will be judged, as we all will. You know you may think you accomplished something, but you didn't. You brought Christians and nonbelievers and Muslims and Jews together, not only in the country, in the city, but around the world. You launched a movement that will continue long after your sorry carcass is gone."

After he spoke, as he sat down, Will turned to his wife, Heather.

"How'd I do?" he asked. Will could not recall a single thing he had said.

"You did great," Heather answered as she leaned in and kissed him.

Twelve more family members spoke in court that day, each getting a chance to address the man convicted of murdering Reat, Bill and Terri, before learning if the judge would uphold the jury's decision to invoke the death penalty.

After Will, it was Lukas's turn. He had been working for weeks on his statement and he was ready. As he stepped up to the microphone, Lukas wore his Faith Wins T-shirt under his dress shirt. In a soft voice, he began to read the statement he had worked so hard to prepare. Lukas's voice cracked and he wiped the tears from his eyes. He was just 13 years old, but his words held a lifetime of loss.

"On the afternoon of April thirteenth, 2014, I lost my childhood in a split second. Any sense of normalcy was erased by a senseless act of violence that will haunt me for the rest of my life. Now I have to watch as my grandma tries to exist with a broken heart and live in the house alone. Some of my earliest memories after the tragedy include waking to the sound of my mother sobbing each morning, feeling a sense of denial and depression and desperately wanting my old life back. I spent my thirteenth birthday in a psychiatric center, trying to determine a reason to continue my new life because of what you did to my family. Killing people because of their faith is wrong. Killing people is wrong. I want to thank the Jewish community for embracing us even though we are not of their faith. I am now going to continue to live my life without my brother and Popeye, but with the great community surrounding me I'll continue to find that faith wins."

When asked by a reporter how he felt after he spoke, Lukas replied, "Fantastic. I got out what I needed to say."

There was so much Lukas's grandmother, Melinda, wanted to say too. But how can you sum up in a few words what it feels like when the love of your life and your cherished grandson are murdered, ripped away from life in the blink of an eye? Melinda stood before the court that day and recalled some of her favorite memories with Bill and with Reat. But perhaps it was the memory of her final moments with Bill, as they stood together on Palm Sunday morning looking out at the birds and the squirrels and discussing the schedule for the day, that resonated most.

"The last words I said to Bill were, 'You have the most important job.' He said, 'I know.' And he did have the most important job. He took our precious Reat to heaven with him."

And then it was Mindy's turn. Mindy, the grieving mother and daughter who had shown the world such strength and grace, stepped up to face the man who murdered her father and son. She tried so many times to make eye contact, but he sat there in his wheelchair, never lifting his face, never looking her way. As she stood there, Mindy felt like she was standing next to the devil.

She began by reciting the Apostles' Creed, declaring her faith out loud, sharing how her faith in God had helped her survive the darkest moments. Showing more composure than anyone could imagine, Mindy Corporon stood and shared her thoughts with the court, and with the man she described as pure evil.

"In response to evil, we will show grace, kindness and understanding. To all those of the Jewish faith, thank you for your love, prayers and deep support of our family. We stand stronger because of you.

"Dad, Reat and Terri did not die in vain. Their deaths are *not* for the benefit of evil, but have, from the day they were taken, been making good things happen. Do I want them back? Yes, more than my own life itself. I didn't get to choose this path and instead of hate, I choose faith."

Somehow, Mindy maintained her composure as she kept to the speech she had so meticulously prepared.

But Mindy wasn't done yet. There was something she had not planned on, yet realized she needed to do. The judge, the families, those present in the court that day had all heard from the victims' families as they shared stories about Reat, Bill and Terri. What Mindy realized is that there was still one more person who needed to address the room. One last person whose voice needed to be heard.

"I'm Mindy Corporon, and I am Reat's mother. We won't ever hear him sing live again, but we can hear this."

Mindy stood at the podium, phone in hand, as she held it to the microphone.

She smiled as she pressed play and the entire room was filled with the beautiful sounds of Reat Griffin Underwood singing the national anthem. Lukas got up from his seat and came to stand by his mother's side. Len came and stood on the other side of Mindy. One by one, the family, friends, attorneys—everyone in the courtroom stood. With tears filling their eyes, they placed their hands on their hearts as they listened to Reat's sweet voice sing our national anthem.

Everyone stood but one.

When Reat's song was over, the man convicted of his murder, still seated, attempted to address the room. As he began to speak, one by one every family member and friend stood and filed out of the room. They refused to hear what he had to say.

That same evening, just a short time later, the judge handed down his sentence. He would uphold the jury's decision, imposing the death penalty.

Upon hearing the verdict, the murderer raised his arm and shouted, *"Heil Hitler!"* several times, just as he had when he was arrested.

When it was over, Lukas went outside. He cried and hugged his friends and family.

"I'm glad it's over," he said.

Nothing would bring his brother and grandfather back, but Lukas has stayed strong. He stood up to face evil in the courtroom that day and he knew that his grandpa and brother would be so proud. And then he said what were perhaps the most important words to describe that day: "And then I was free."

Mindy did in fact make it to Israel, like she knew Reat wanted her to.

As she prepared for her flight and packed up her travel pillow, passport and favorite Bible, there were two final items Mindy tucked away in her bag. They were the most important things she would be bringing with her. Two tiny packages she couldn't leave behind.

Together with her church group, led by Pastor Hamilton, Mindy visited the holiest sites throughout Israel. But it wasn't until she reached the banks of the River Jordan that Mindy finally removed the two precious packages she had brought from home and packed so carefully. She dressed in a white robe and prepared to be re-baptized in the river by Pastor Hamilton, but then she stepped up to speak to him. There was something she needed to tell him before she entered the water. Mindy pulled the two small packages from her pocket and explained that they contained Reat and Bill's ashes. She wanted to place the ashes of her son and father in the river where John the Baptist had baptized Jesus. She intended for it to be a private moment, but felt she needed to let Pastor Hamilton know her intention.

"What a wonderful idea," he said, immediately seizing upon the significance of the moment and the power of sharing it with the faithful. Pastor Hamilton then explained to those who didn't know her who Mindy was and what they were about to witness. Mindy turned to face the group on the shore as Pastor Hamilton spoke. At once, she was struck by what she saw. To Mindy, the 150 of the faithful, dressed in white baptismal robes, gathered on the banks of the River Jordan, offering love and spiritual support. They looked like a choir of angels.

"It took my breath away," Mindy explained. "Because we'd been having this private moment, and there was this whole group of people and they were all leaning forward and they were all intimately involved and I felt like I wasn't alone. I just said, 'I'm so not alone,' and God gave me all of these people to do this with me."

As Mindy stepped into the frigid and murky water, she was the farthest thing from alone. Pastor Hamilton stood in the water with her and said a prayer. Mindy's hands trembled as she opened the bag containing Reat's ashes and sprinkled some of them into the flowing water. Shaking now from emotion and cold, she handed the second package to Pastor Hamilton. He opened the bag containing Bill's ashes and sprinkled them in the water as well. They, and the entire chorus of angels on the shore, prayed and watched Reat and Bill's ashes float together on the River Jordan as the current pulled them farther and farther away, and then finally out of sight.

A few days later, when she arrived at the Sea of Galilee, Mindy once again removed the two small packages, opened them, and sprinkled Reat and Bill's ashes in the water. This time she did it quietly and privately. She didn't want to draw any more attention to herself or what she had planned.

"I knew that they would want to be there where Jesus had been," she explained. "And so we went there. There was just a small group of us and we went to the back of the boat and we put them in the Sea of Galilee. To know that they are with

God and with Jesus and to know they are really in Israel now where Jesus was also . . ." Her voice trailed off.

She isn't Jewish. She has no relatives or roots in Israel. And even so, by sprinkling their ashes in the Holy Land, Mindy knew she had brought her son and father home.

"It just gave me comfort," she explained. "It just kind of sealed the circle of knowledge for me."

Circles.

It's as if our lives are an ever-growing chain of circles, interlocking and rippling, fanning out, spreading and touching people in ways we never imagined. And on her final day in Israel, with an email to me, Mindy began to close a circle that had first formed more than 70 years before, by my yia-yia Avgerini, on the tiny island of Erikousa.

I have a few hours before I leave Jerusalem. Do you think Rosa's family can meet tomorrow?

They met the following afternoon at the airport, before Mindy boarded her flight. The meeting lasted only a few minutes. But sometimes that's all it takes to write the ending of a long and complicated story that took decades to unfold.

Peretz and his wife, Sigalit, hugged Mindy as they greeted each other, making introductions, although they felt they knew one another already. Everyone agreed how wonderful it was and how happy they were to finally meet, but all the while they were so very cognizant of the pain in which our connection is rooted.

"Your children. You have three girls?" Mindy asked.

"Yes," Sigalit replied. "Twenty-one, twenty and almost fourteen."

"Fourteen. Oh, okay." Mindy paused.

Fourteen. The age Reat was when he was murdered.

Mindy went on, explaining the changes she was trying to effect through her work with Faith Wins and SevenDays™.

"So it's to help people have kindness for seven days and then to learn about other faiths. To learn about Judaism, to learn about Islam and to learn about Christianity so that there's less fear. Just so that there's less fear so that there's no more killing."

Sigalit and Peretz listened intently, understanding that tragedy was not all we had in common. Our common bonds were also steeped in love and in kindness, then and now.

"This shows what you believe in," Sigalit said. "There are still good people here and all over the world, whether they're Jewish or not Jewish.

Good people with their kindness, and they saved generations to come. My husband and children would not have stood here unless some good people in Erikousa saved them."

Good people.

It was those two words, the common denominator that tied us all together.

Good people, connecting our story across the globe and across generations.

Good people, who proved that light can filter in, even in the darkest moment, if only you allow it to.

Good people, who stand up for one another, and for what's right, even when everything and everyone around them is so sadly and terrifyingly wrong.

"Yvette said you are a soul sister," Mindy said to Sigalit. "And you really are." She then looked at her watch. As much as she would have liked to linger, to visit a bit longer, it was time to catch her flight home.

"We are family and y'all are a blessing."

It was time to say good-bye. Mindy hugged them again before turning and walking toward the gate. As she boarded the plane and headed home to Kansas, Mindy took with her the blessings of Rosa's family, now her family too, and left behind a little piece of herself in Israel, along with the ashes of her son and father.

"Y'all are a blessing," Mindy repeated.

And with that blessing, with a hug in an airport terminal between Rosa's family and my dearest Mindy, our circle was at last closed.

epilogue

Sometimes I think back to all that's happened, all we have lived through, witnessed and experienced, and I am filled with such overwhelming joy and gratitude. And sometimes I think back on what's happened, remembering the staggering loss and pain, and I feel as if my legs can't sustain my weight as I wrestle with the devastating reality of it all.

And all the while, Nico's question repeats in my mind again and again.

"But you told me the Nazis were gone and that the people were saved. How could this happen?"

After all this time, I still don't know what the answer is. I've tried to articulate one, but no words seem adequate. As a mother, I want to answer each question from my children thoughtfully and eloquently, helping them understand life and our world to the best of my ability. I'm their mother. That's my job. But sometimes there are limits to even the best-intentioned mother's abilities. How can rational minds make sense of the irrational? It is beyond me.

"We're going backwards; we didn't learn anything. When we came out from this hell, I felt I had more hope that people would be different."

Sonia Warshawski's words: so profound, so

true and so utterly devastating. Every day we see the news and read the heartbreaking headlines.

Things are not different. People are not different. The world is not different. History is tragically repeating itself. And in Greece, a familiar story continues to play out again and again and again.

From the shores of Syria, desperate mothers and fathers continue piling their children and families into overcrowded rafts, to make the treacherous journey across the sea to the safety of Greek island shores. Think of what these parents must be leaving behind, what they must be fleeing from, if the safer option is to risk their children's lives in overcrowded rafts of questionable seaworthiness. Nino and Rebecca had no choice when they found themselves on such a raft. While the circumstances are no doubt different, upon closer examination, there are also similarities that cannot be ignored. Do these men, women and children fleeing the terror in Syria really have a choice?

And once again, just like Savvas's family on Erikousa, for so many of these refugees, salvation comes on the shores of small Greek islands at the hands of poor islanders, many of them yia-yias. In the midst of the worst economic crisis to hit Greece since World War II, these poor yia-yias, who have so desperately little themselves, are sharing what they can, often going hungry themselves, to help feed, clothe and provide shelter to the desperate refugees.

Eighty-five-year-old Emilia Kamvisi is one of these yia-yias. A daughter of refugees from Asia Minor herself, Emilia knows and understands full well the pain and trauma of what it is to be a displaced person. When asked about the humanitarian refugee crisis on her home island of Lesbos, Emilia told a reporter that the scenes of despair and desperation were strikingly familiar to her. Every day she witnessed heartbreaking moments she remembered quite well from the German occupation during World War II. "We saw people crying in the boats, people leaving their homes, people sleeping in the streets," she told one reporter.

But Emilia didn't merely stand by as she watched the suffering all around her. Emilia is one of the three "Lesvos grandmothers" whose photo went viral and tugged at hearts around the world. The photo captured a poignant moment, as Emilia cradled and fed a newborn Syrian infant while sitting on a bench beside two more yia-yias, while the infant's mother stood nearby. Emilia spotted the mother, cold and wet, having just made the treacherous journey from Syria to Lesbos on a raft. As the mother struggled to feed the crying child, Emilia motioned for her to hand her the baby. When the young mother did as she asked, Emilia sang to the infant, cuddled and soothed him. And finally, the baby took his bottle. That iconic photo, which made headlines around the world, is testament to the power in a simple act of kindness—and also the healing powers in the embrace of a yia-yia.

Emilia, her fellow yia-yias, islanders and Greeks across the country who rallied to help the desperate refugees are the personification of the Greek word *philotimo*. Often called the word that has no meaning, *philotimo* is more a philosophy than a word with an easy definition. It is a word vitally important to the Greek psyche and culture that embodies the Greek mentality of helping and providing for others, of putting friendship, hospitality and honor before all. *Philotimo*. It is the word my yia-yia and the islanders of Erikousa embodied during World War II, and that Emilia, her fellow islanders and Greeks across the country embody today.

But even so, Emilia never expected *philotimo*, that act of kindness, to resonate across the world as it did. When Emilia learned she was nominated for the Nobel Peace Prize for her role in helping the refugees of Lesbos, she simply replied, "What did I do? I didn't do anything."

It was nothing. It was everything.

And it defies all reason and logic that it is still happening today.

And so when my children ask me now about the hate and the evil that led to so much devastation, that killed six million Jews during the Holocaust and three Christians in Overland Park, Kansas, I do my best to answer. And then admit that I don't have all the answers.

Instead, I focus on what I know to be true. I know that even in the darkest, most difficult moments, light and goodness can and do exist. And that even when it seems the world has been overcome with evil, beautiful things can happen too. I speak to my children about the lessons I've learned on this journey, and the ones I hope they've learned by experiencing all that's happened while standing right there beside me.

I hope that like my yia-yia, they will be strong enough to stand up for what's right and what's good in the world. And when they do, I want them to know they did it for the right reasons. Not for recognition or accolades, but simply because they are good people who follow their minds and hearts and not the baying of the crowd.

I hope that like Mindy, they will always find solace in faith and in prayer. Our family is living proof that miracles do indeed happen and that there is infinite power in prayer. I want my children to know this and to remember this every day of their lives, not only when they need a miracle.

I hope that like their cousin Reat was fond of saying, my children live life to the fullest and that they never give up. Reat had only 14 years on this earth. He should have had longer. He had so much more life to live, so many more dreams to chase. Reat packed a lifetime of love, laughter and accomplishments in those 14 years alone. I want my children to learn from their cousin, to live every day to the fullest and chase their dreams with unbridled passion.

I hope that like Sonia, my children always stand strong and never stop speaking the truth, no matter what fire they must walk through to get to the other side. It breaks Sonia's heart that the world learned nothing after the Holocaust, that history continues to repeat itself. I want my children to be catalysts for change. Because it is enough now. Something has to change.

I hope my children share my tenacity and passion for knowledge. That despite any obstacles and roadblocks, they never stop digging and searching for whatever answers they seek. And I hope they see the many mistakes I have made along the way and learn from those as well.

When I was younger, I always thought history was something that was learned in school. Written down in musty textbooks, interspersed with black-and-white photos of people who seemingly never smiled that lived a long, long time ago. I now know that's not always the case. History is something all around us; it's in our homes and in our families. History is in the very stories shared around the dinner table, or in a quiet moment shared with a grandparent, a friend or a loved one.

I want my children to learn from our family's history, understanding and seeing firsthand the seismic effects of paying attention to a story from the past. The ripple begun by my yia-yia Avgerini on Erikousa during World War II continues to expand and grow and change lives, even today. What started out as a family tree presented to Rosa's sons during the ceremony on Erikousa has now expanded to a full history of the Jewish community of Corfu, complete with 2,250 names. It is because of this meticulously researched family tree and their dedication to rebuilding the history of the Jewish community of Corfu that Gilad and the MyHeritage team were recently able to reunite a widowed and childless Holocaust survivor in Israel named Nata Gattegno with family she never knew existed. To know Nata will never be alone again, to know she will live out the rest of her days surrounded by family—there is nothing more rewarding. No better example of the power in a simple act of kindness.

And now, more than ever, I understand the power of sharing stories, speaking out loud the names of those who have passed on, making sure they are honored, remembered and never forgotten. The story once known to us as the secret of Erikousa is a secret no more. In addition to the Award of Moral Courage and the House of Life honor, Erikousa now has the honor of being featured on an Israeli stamp, commissioned by the International Raoul Wallenberg Foundation. Our tiny island, not even found on most maps, is now pictured on a stamp in Israel. What an amazing testament to the power of memories, the power of words passed from one generation to the next. I wish I'd understood that when I was younger. I understand that now.

And because I also understand that the weight of words is often heavier in black and white, I've written our story down. I want my children to know it, to remember it and to share it. One day their own children will ask questions that they will struggle to answer. And when that day comes, they can tell their children that while they may not have all the answers, what they do have is a story to share.

Because every family has a story—and this is ours.

afterword

LESSONS FROM NEW AND CHERISHED FRIENDS

When I first began this journey, I set out to learn more about Savvas Israel and my yia-yia's friends Nina, Rosa, Julia and Spera. In writing this book and researching the story of Savvas, I was fortunate enough to spend some time with three Holocaust survivors of the Jewish community of Corfu. They were all so very generous and gracious with their time and memories.

Each one did so much more than help me piece together a vivid picture of Savvas's family and the Jewish community of Corfu. Each o the survivors I met, Rebecca, Nino and Daniel left indelible impressions and imparted valuable lessons to me that I will never forget.

NINO NACHSHON

Relatives and friends filed in and out of Nino' Tel Aviv apartment all afternoon as Nino and sat and talked. His is a home filled with photos Framed pictures of candid, smiling faces ar placed next to old black-and-white photos of time when no one ever smiled. Photos of Nino'

429

family cover every inch of the apartment—both the loved ones who still fill Nino's daily life with joy and those who are long gone now, who never made it out of the death camps like Nino did.

And there, framed on the far wall in the living room, hanging above a desk stacked neatly with letters and papers and a figurine of an old fiddler, is the hand-drawn diagram of Nino's family tree that began it all.

I knew Nino's story very well by this point. I had read and studied and devoured anything I could find about the Jewish community of Corfu. Nino's story had stayed with me since I'd first learned about his family, and how his mother pleaded with him to leave her and save himself.

"How well did you know Rosa?" I asked.

Nino said he remembered Rosa and Nina quite well. He would see them once a year, when the survivors from Corfu would meet on Holocaust Remembrance Day.

"Rosa never talked," he said. "But Nina did. She talked about the island and of being hidden. They did on that island what they didn't do for us in Corfu."

I told Nino about my yia-yia, how she loved the girls, helped to hide them and shared what little she had with them. I told him her name was Avgerini.

"Panagia," Nino called out, raising his voice.

"Panagia," he said again. And again, I felt my eyes fill. I felt the tears, giant and hot, stream down my face as Nino called my grandmother Panagia, the name of highest reverence for a person of Greek Orthodox faith. Panagia. It is the name Greeks reserve for the woman for whom they hold the utmost love and respect, the Virgin Mary, the mother of Christ.

I asked Nino if he knew about my family's other story, about what happened in America. Nino looked at me, staring in disbelief as I told him about Reat and Bill, explaining how they were murdered, in the United States, because a neo-Nazi mistook them for being Jews.

"Because he thought they were Jewish?" he asked.

"Yes."

Nino looked at me in silence for a moment, shaking his head and absorbing my words. He placed his hands together and shook them as he spoke. "And what of us who were born Jews?"

Nino told me how he and his family had returned to Corfu just the summer before. They'd rented a large and beautiful villa with a swimming pool, and Nino was able to watch his family enjoy the beautiful and magical island of his youth. Together, with his loved ones beside him, Nino retraced his steps from that dark day in June 1944. He walked through the narrow streets of the Jewish quarter, where he once lived with his mother and siblings. He walked to the lower *platia*, where he waited for hours under the hot sun with no food or water as German soldiers pointed guns at him, herding him and his family like livestock. And finally, Nino walked once again across the footbridge and into the old fort. Now, as a free man surrounded by the love and support of his family, Nino needed to see where he had been held in a dungeon before being transported with his mother and siblings on a rotting death boat.

As long as I live, I will never forget my afternoon with Nino. Yes, he helped me uncover and understand more about Savvas's family and the Jewish community of Corfu. Yes, he had confirmed that Rosa and Spera were in fact hidden on Erikousa. But those details merely scratched the surface of the lessons Nino Nachshon imparted to me.

Because despite all they had done to him, all he suffered through and had lost, hate had not triumphed over Nino. He refused to let it, then and now. And, Nino refuses to stop speaking about his mother and the friends and family who lived with him long ago on the beautiful island of Corfu.

I could have stayed in that living room, listening to Nino and looking at old photos with him, all day. Sometimes, it is only by standing beside someone who came so close to death and fought so hard to live that you can truly learn to appreciate life.

DANIEL SOUSSIS

I sat at my kitchen table and smiled into my computer's camera. Smiling back at me, from his home in Athens, was Daniel Soussis, the Holocaust survivor from Corfu.

"Did you know the girls? Do you remember Nini, Julia or Spera? Or maybe Rosa? She was little, like you," I asked Daniel in our first conversation over Skype.

"No. I didn't know them. I'm sorry. I don't remember them."

"Did you ever hear anything about a Jewish family that was hidden on Erikousa? I still can't believe that such an incredible thing happened and no one ever talked about it."

"No. I'm sorry. I never heard this story," he replied. "I was a small child, only three years old. But I remember every detail of what happened to me. Like I can see it clearly, as if it was a movie playing in my head."

I was disappointed, of course. But as I sat there Skyping with Daniel, my disappointment seemed so trivial in the moment. I pushed it away, not wanting even a hint of my own frustration to taint this conversation. I realized what mattered was this wonderful man. What mattered was his incredible story of survival. And that he wanted to share it with me.

By now I was well versed in Daniel's own story of survival, how a Christian friend hid him and his sister in his villa and how Daniel's mother was so close to salvation herself, but betrayed by a neighbor as the Nazis passed her door. In my mind, I kept going back to that moment of his mother's betrayal. I couldn't get the image out of my head. That poor woman, having sent her children away to keep them safe, cowering in her home with her baby, knowing the day had finally come and that she would be reunited with her children. What hell it must have been for her to hear the Nazi soldiers below on the street, that momentary wave of relief as they passed her door. And then the utter devastation of knowing it was finished as they dragged her to the street.

"I tried, you know," Daniel continued. "I tried many times to have Yad Vashem acknowledge my rescuer. I want to do this for him. To have the world recognize him, to honor him for what he did. But they said that since I was a child, my testimony is not enough. That I was too young to understand and to know all the details of what happened when I was saved. But I can tell you, that's not the case. I remember everything."

In my career, I have interviewed thousands

of people, from the biggest celebrities in the world to presidents, first ladies and everyday citizens. But as soon as I turned on my computer and saw Daniel Soussis's smiling face staring back at me—that bright white hair, those bushy eyebrows and that dapper mustache above that ever-present broad, bright smile—I knew this would not be just another interview. This was a conversation with a new friend. And it was very clear, from that very first chat, that my new friend Daniel loved to talk. He really, really loved to talk.

"We owe them everything," he continued. "Not just us, the ones who were saved, but the entire State of Israel. The ones who were saved were the ones who went to Israel, who built the country. Think about it: in that darkest time, people like Errikos, who saved me, and your yia-yia, who saved those girls, they helped create hope and strength out of the darkest time. They should be recognized. The State of Israel owes that to them. It is important that they are recognized."

I told Daniel my own story and how I had been working with Yad Vashem. He shook his head as I explained that like the story of his own rescuers it did not seem likely that we would have enough proof to have Righteous Among the Nations designation granted.

"They all deserve to be recognized and honored

for what they did. They brought hope," Daniel insisted.

Daniel went on to tell me how life changed after the Nazis left Corfu. He finished school, lived in Italy for a while and became an electrical engineer and a journalist. He fell deeply in love and got married. But even Daniel's happy marriage had its complications. Daniel, a Jewish survivor of the Holocaust, fell in love with and married a German woman. While his home life was a happy one, again and again Daniel was inundated with the same question: "How can a Jewish survivor of the Holocaust marry a German woman?"

Daniel's answer was the same time after time. "We must not forget what happened, but we must not transmit hate. The children should not carry the weight of the sins of the fathers. I believe that all children are the same, regardless of their race, religion or color. And we all need to live in peace with one another. I would marry my wife again if given the chance."

We must have chatted for about an hour that very first day, probably a good 30 minutes longer than I intended to talk. But my new friend Daniel had so much to say. I was more than happy to sit and listen to his stories.

Often, after that initial conversation, I would glance down at my computer to find a new message or good-morning greeting from Daniel.

We realized we would both be on Corfu that summer and made a plan to meet on our beloved island. I looked forward to meeting Daniel, to linger with him over coffee and hear more of his stories in person.

As time passed, eventually I realized something was missing. It had been weeks since I had logged on to Facebook to see Daniel's face smiling back at me in an instant message with a request to chat.

I logged in one day and clicked on his profile. And there, on his Facebook page, in a message posted beneath that beautiful photo of him smiling back at me as he swam in the crystal-blue sea, I finally got my answer.

Daniel had suffered a devastating stroke. We would never have the chance to meet over coffee on Corfu. I would never again have the chance to sit and listen to his stories.

But although Daniel and I would never speak again, my friend with the bright smile and shock of white hair would in fact impart one important final lesson to me. I now realize the urgency of it all. The clock was ticking ever so fast as those who had lived through the Nazi occupation advanced in age. Every day we come closer to losing this generation and all of their memories. will never make the same mistake again. I would never again take time, or precious memories, fo granted.

REBECCA AARON

Rebecca Aaron is the last Holocaust survivor living on Corfu.

She is petite, with curly hair and a cane that she wields more to help punctuate her words than to walk. At 89 years old, Rebecca's eyes and health have begun to show the signs of age, but her memory and her mind have not. Rebecca Aaron still remembers every detail of life during the German occupation, and what came after.

Rebecca still lives in the Jewish quarter of Corfu, in an apartment tucked away behind the narrow alleyways and above the neighborhood's many cafés and shops. So much has changed in the old Jewish quarter over the past several decades. There are new neighbors now, both Jewish and Christian, and new and lively bars and restaurants line the streets. But what's important about the Jewish quarter never changes. Rebecca's apartment is located just down the road from the synagogue where her family has worshiped for generations.

Widowed now, Rebecca rarely leaves her home or ventures out to the island's picturesque squares and cobblestone streets anymore. Most of her friends and family are gone, but Rebecca remembers each and every one of them as if she saw them yesterday.

Eva Matathia lives on Corfu as well. Eva's husband, Zacharia, is president of the Jewish community of Corfu. Together, Eva and Zacharia are tirelessly committed to preserving the history and heritage of the Corfiot Jews. It is a small community, with only 65 members left living on the island. But what the Jewish community of Corfu lacks in numbers, it makes up for in the people's commitment to their culture and to one another.

It was Eva who reached out to Rebecca on my behalf and asked if she would meet with me while I was visiting.

"Yes," Rebecca told Eva. She'd heard about the Greek-American girl whose grandmother hid a Jewish family and who had searched for and found the family of Savvas Israel. Rebecca was familiar with what happened on Erikousa and had known Savvas's girls and little Rosa quite well. Rebecca would meet with me, she said, but under one condition. She wanted this to be a pleasant visit, a chat about old times and old friends. Rebecca did not want to speak about the Nazis or her time in the camps. Each time she did, each time she spoke about and relived those horrific years and events, Rebecca had nightmares that lasted for days. Rebecca was tired now. She wanted to sleep peacefully without reliving her family's nightmare anymore.

"I don't want to bring back any of those horrible memories," I assured Eva. "I want to talk about the girls. I want to know more about their lives their community and what life was like for them. I want to know if she knew about what happened on Erikousa."

Together with Roi and Eva, I went to visit Rebecca at her home. With all we had learned about Savvas and his girls, I still had so many unanswered questions. Among them, why didn't the girls ever speak of their friends and rescuers on Erikousa? I knew Rebecca was hesitant to speak of those dark times and difficult years. And as I climbed the narrow stairs to her home, I made a conscious effort to keep my expectations in check. After all, Rebecca was 89 now. I couldn't imagine that she would recall many details from more than 70 years ago.

But from the moment she opened the door and ushered us inside with the wave of her cane, I quickly realized that Rebecca Aaron is still a spitfire, full of Corfiot sass and sharp as a tack.

"How can they come visit me and not have anything to eat or drink? Nothing?" Rebecca insisted as she welcomed us inside. "We must get them a drink."

Time, age, circumstances—there is nothing that can stand in the way of Corfiot hospitality.

"You know, Miss Becca," Eva said. "These guys have conducted a very big investigation."

"Yes, for the girls," Rebecca replied.

"To find out the history of this family," Eva continued. But news travels fast in the old cobblestone streets of the Jewish quarter.

"I know, I've heard about it," Rebecca jumped in. She was all over it. Eva had nothing on her.

"They were all beautiful," Rebecca continued as she sat with us and looked through old black-and-white photos of Nina, Julia, Spera and Rosa.

"This is Rosa." Rebecca instantly pointed out little Rosa in a photo with her family. "The little one, yes."

"This is the mother," Roi said as he pointed to Rosa's mother in the picture.

"They took Rosa when she was very young," Rebecca said. "She was the only one from her family who was saved."

My eyes lit up, everything about me lit up, as Rebecca touched upon what happened on Erikousa.

"Yes. She was very young, yes, yes, yes," I replied.

She shook her head as she continued looking at the photos, images of the friends, family and neighbors who never made it home, recognizing more faces from her youth.

"And they loved Rosa very much." I knew Rebecca knew this as well, but I felt better saying it out loud.

"And who didn't love those girls?" she replied, correcting what was clearly an understatement on my part. "Everyone loved them."

Rebecca went on sorting through the photos

identifying people, families and relations, making sure to correct us when our pronunciation was even the slightest bit off.

Sorting through more photos, Rebecca looked at an image of an unidentified bride in her wedding dress.

"When my mother's sister got married, Nina made her the most beautiful dress. Whatever words I try to use to describe this dress to you, they would never be enough. It was all embroidered. I can't even begin to explain to you how gorgeous that dress was. Now everything that is made today is garbage."

Rebecca continued, telling us that Nina had "golden hands," and she was happy when she heard the news that Nina had gotten married to a good man in Israel. And while Nina was truly gifted with a needle and thread, Rebecca recalled that Spera had her own unique talents as well.

"Well, Spera would go out and about, from here to there all the time."

"She liked to be out and about, did she?" Eva smiled as she asked.

"Oh yes, yes, yes," Rebecca replied, leaning into her cane as she sat and waving her hand around for emphasis. "First of all, she left with a man from Corfu and went to Israel. Then she went to Athens with another man. She liked to be out and about for sure on these kinds of trips." Rebecca filled us in on her old friend Spera's fondness for male companionship as we all shared a laugh. That moment, that shared giggle, a fun chat among the ladies—it was nothing less than magical.

I must admit, at first I was disappointed when I learned that Rebecca did not want to speak in more detail about the Holocaust. But in the end, after meeting and spending time with Rebecca, I realized that request was actually a gift. There is no questioning the importance of revisiting and recording even the most difficult moments in our history. There is no question of the need to dig and ask questions, even the ones that dredge up the most difficult of memories. There is a time and a place for it. But there is also a time and a place, and a necessity, for nothing more than a friendly chat, a visit among friends and fond memories shared over a laugh. That afternoon spent with Rebecca, those moments spent chatting, giggling, remembering and even gossiping a bit, were every bit as important as learning more about the history and the hardships. Maybe more so.

Because as my yia-yia taught me years ago, and as beautiful Rebecca Aaron reminded me as we sat reminiscing together in her home above the cobblestones of the Jewish quarter, sometimes it is only by first experiencing the tears that we can truly learn to appreciate the laughter.

acknowledgments

Infinite thank-yous are not sufficient enough for my brilliant and kind editor, Beth Adams. Your insight, as well as gentle and wise guidance, made all the difference in the world. And thank you for cleaning up my gutter mouth. That might just have been the biggest job of all.

To the entire team at Howard and Atria Books, a million thanks for bringing this book to life in such beautiful fashion. Special thanks to my amazing publicists, Yona Deshommes and Paul Olsewski, and to marketing genius Suzanne Donahue.

To my beautiful friend and agent, Nena Madonia. You are simply the best, and I adore you. Thank you also to everyone at Dupree Miller, especially Jan Miller and Lacy Lynch.

To the ladies who keep me someone sane and the friends who have cheered me on: Bonnie Bernstein, Jen Cohn, Lauren Petterson, Adrianna Nionakis, Olga Makrias, Karen Kelly, Hilaria Baldwin, Jillian Taratunio and Albert Lewitinn.

To my brilliant friend Claire Wachtel. Thank you for guiding me and inspiring me to get this story down on the page.

To my *Extra* TV family, especially Lisa Gregorisch, Theresa Coffino and Jeremy Spiegel.

Special thanks to my cherished friend Marie Hickey: Always my go-to for sage advice, guidance and spot-on first draft notes, as well as endless laughs.

For my Erikousa family: Thank you for showing me the power of kindness, family and *philotimo* generation after generation.

To my Kansas family, Mindy, Melinda, Lukas, Tony, Dana, Will and the entire Corporon clan. There will never be adequate words to describe the staggering loss of Reat and Bill. I hope that in some way I have even merely scratched the surface. Thank you for trusting me with your stories and most precious memories.

To my Jewish family, the families of Spera and Rosa (Michelle, Rachel, Hedva, Sigalit, Avraham, Peretz, Inbar, Maayan and Sapir). Thank you for allowing me to tell your stories, for sharing this journey with me and for opening up your hearts and homes to me.

To the entire MyHeritage team, especially Gilad, Aaron and Roi. I am forever indebted to you and in awe of the incredible work you do, and the generosity of heart that you bring to each story. You are miracle workers, each and every one of you .

To Marcia Ikonomopoulos, my Greek-Jewish fairy godmother and constant reminder to never forget, and to never stop dancing.

To my Anaconda Street Production family, as

well as the Turtle Bunny Creations team—Ryan, Katie and Kouki Carrasco, Theresa Lugones, Patrick Record and Chris and Chrissy Callahan. To Omar Lugones and Tony Carrasco, aka my brothers and partners in crime: Around the world and back again, I'd do it all over again with no one but you two by my side.

Now to my blood family, my parents, brother, Aunt Agatha, Dorothy, Effie and the assorted aunts, uncles and cousins: I love you all—thank you for putting up with me and my madness all these years. To the ladies who keep me somewhat sane, the friends who have cheered me on: Bonnie Bernstein, Jen Cohn, Lauren Petterson, Adrianna Nionakis, Olga Makrias and Karen Kelly. To Dave—for taking care of our lives while I chased this story down and struggled to get it on paper. We are in this together, today and always.

To Christiana and Nico: Mama loves you more than you can imagine. You are my driving force and inspiration. I am amazed by your strength of character and how from the earliest age, you both have always stood up for what is just and right. Your great-grandmother would be so proud. You are my everythings, and I am so incredibly proud of you both.

And to my sweet, curly-haired Lukas. Thank you for showing us all what courage, grace and strength look like.